Recollections of Gustav Mahler

Recollections of
Gustav Mahler

by Natalie Bauer-Lechner

TRANSLATED BY
DIKA NEWLIN

EDITED AND
ANNOTATED BY
PETER FRANKLIN

Cambridge University Press

CAMBRIDGE

LONDON   NEW YORK   NEW ROCHELLE

MELBOURNE   SYDNEY

This edition first published in 1980

Published in the USA and Canada by
the Press Syndicate of the University of Cambridge
32 East 57th Street, New York, NY 10022 USA

English translation and annotations © 1980
by Faber Music Ltd

Original German edition *Erinnerungen an Gustav Mahler*
First published in 1923 by E. P. Tal and Co. Verlag,
Leipzig, Vienna, Zürich
Copyright 1923 by E. P. Tal & Co. Verlag

Printed in Great Britain by
Latimer Trend & Company Ltd

Library of Congress Cataloging in Publication Data

Bauer-Lechner, Natalie.
Recollections of Gustav Mahler.
1. Mahler, Gustav.
2. Composers—Austria—Biography.
I. Title II. Franklin, Peter.
780/.92/4   ML410.M23   80–834

ISBN 0 521 23572 3

Contents

Foreword   9

Introduction to the first edition   19

Early history of my friendship with Gustav Mahler   23

Part 1   Mahler abroad

Visit to Budapest   27

Steinbach am Attersee *(July and August 1893)*   29
*The Andante of the Second Symphony – The significance of Beethoven
– The symphony and life – The mystical aspect of creation – 'Das
irdische Leben' and the 'Fischpredigt' – The 'Rheinlegendchen' – The
work and its effect – A conductor's tribulations – The brutality of
noise – Brahms and Bruckner – Evaluation of Liszt – The greatness of
Wagner – Spiritual and physical birth*

Steinbach am Attersee *(summer 1895)*   40

Visit to Hamburg *(January 1896)*   42
*The performance of the Second Symphony in Berlin – The meaning
of the Second Symphony – Orchestral technique and notation*

In Hamburg again *(mid-February 1896)*   47

Mahler concert in Berlin *(16 March 1896)*   49
The rehearsals – The concert – Concern for the future

Easter visit to Hamburg *(April 1896)*   52
'What the flowers tell me' – Uncanny visions – Martyrdom

5

CONTENTS

Steinbach am Attersee *(summer 1896)*   55
In the 'Schnützelputz-Häusel' – War on the disturbers of the peace
– Early works – Truth and simplicity – Conversations about the Third
Symphony – On instrumentation – Home and childhood – Trials of
strength – Lipiner and Mahler

Reunion in Hamburg *(September/October 1896)*   73
Mahler's way of life – Clarity of line – The first movement of the
Third Symphony – The printing of the Second Symphony

Trial concert in Munich *(24 March 1897)*   78

The call to Vienna   80

Mahler's personality and appearance   81

Part II   Mahler in Vienna

The opera season *(May to summer 1897)*   89
Début – An anonymous letter – Size of the orchestra – Der Freischütz
– Musical involvement – Uneven tempo

Summer 1897   96
Deputy Director – Natural sounds as the source of music

The 1897–1898 season   98
The Ring *Cycle –* Dalibor *– Appointment as Director – The Magic*
Flute *– The claque – 'Master in his own house' – The Flying*
Dutchman *– Beating time – 'To him that hath shall be given' – In*
the Director's box – Wrong tempi: the 'Eroica' – On tempi and a
feeling for Nature – Dissatisfaction – Dealings with one's superiors –
Das klagende Lied *– Homophony and polyphony*

CONTENTS

The 1898–1899 season   117

The stage hands – Mahler becomes conductor of the Philharmonic – Das klagende Lied – Performing the Beethoven quartets with orchestra – The Norns' rope – The first Philharmonic concert – The fifth Philharmonic concert – Wagner and Schumann – Plan to perform the St Matthew Passion – Beethoven's Seventh Symphony – Mahler's Second Symphony in Vienna – Johann Strauss

Summer 1899 *(8 June to 29 July)*   129

Mahler on his Third Symphony – On Löwe – On the mountain top – Change – Composing – The Fourth Symphony – Changing one's mind – An amusing anecdote – Mahler's house on the Wörther See – Schwarzenfels

The 1899–1900 season   135

Torments of creation – On the 'Pastoral' – On invention – The living Beethoven – Die Meistersinger – Invention and form – Isolation – The problem of Beethoven's symphonies – On tradition – Mahler on his Second Symphony – On Brahms and Beethoven – The 'Pastoral' Symphony: tempo of the second movement – Marie Gutheil-Schoder

Summer 1900 *(Mayernigg, Villa Antonia, 21 June to 15 August)*   145

Hans Rott – On Schubert – Environmental barbarity – From a letter of 26 July – The mystery of art – The incomprehensibility of Nature – The second self – A bet – Conversations about the Fourth Symphony – Polyphony

The 1900–1901 season   157

Mildenburg – Mahler's First Symphony – Beethoven's First Symphony – Mahler's Fourth Symphony – On mime – Ballet – On Bach – Tchaikovsky's Pathétique – Immortal

Summer 1901 *(the Mahler villa on the Wörther See, June to August)*   167

In the new home – On birdsong – Beginning to create – Learning and intuition – On Schumann – The genius of Bach – Collecting ideas – Plan for an opera – Youth and maturity – Mahler on his Fifth Symphony – Seven songs – 'Ich bin der Welt abhanden gekommen' – Rubinstein's performance of the Beethoven sonatas

The 1901–1902 season   175

'*All dynamic markings exaggerated*' – *Bruno Walter* – Die drei Pintos – *Mahler's Fourth Symphony* – *Hidden octaves* – *Humour* – Der Trompeter von Säckingen – Dalibor *and the three greatest German opera composers* – The Tales of Hoffmann – *Liszt's* Heilige Elisabeth – *Mahler's Fourth Symphony in Munich* – *Performance in Frankfurt* – *Performance in Berlin* – *Performance in Vienna*

Editor's Afterword to the first edition   186

Bibliography and list of abbreviations used in the Notes   189

Notes   191

Appendix I: *additional material from early published extracts from Natalie Bauer-Lechner's journal*   231

Appendix II: *letter from Natalie Bauer-Lechner to Ludwig Karpath, 16 November 1900*   236

Index   243

Illustrations

MAPS

Map of the Attersee p. 15   *Map of the Wörther See* p. 16

PLATES

BETWEEN PAGES 32–3

1. Natalie Bauer-Lechner

2. Mahler with his sister Justine

BETWEEN PAGES 64–5

3. Mahler's dedicatory inscription on the cover of sketches of his Third Symphony

4. Two pages of Natalie Bauer-Lechner's letter of 16 November 1900 to Ludwig Karpath

5. Mahler's villa on the Wörther See (photo by Dr K. Sherlock)

Foreword

Natalie Bauer-Lechner's *Erinnerungen an Gustav Mahler* were published in 1923, having been selected and edited after her death from a bulky collection of notes entitled *Mahleriana*. Truncated and fragmented as it was – often necessarily so, since the manuscript was a personal journal, unprepared for publication – the volume, which is here presented in translation for the first time, rapidly established itself as one of the most important of the early memoirs of the composer. While complemented by those of Ferdinand Pfohl, Bruno Walter and, of course, Alma Mahler, it remains indispensable.

The reason is that its author had an uncanny, if sometimes overzealous, instinct for history. She is consequently a godsend to the historian: the eye-witness who knew what she was witnessing and who had a rare knack for probing into Mahler's creative, and recreative, notions – the record of which interests us now quite as much as the more anecdotal evocation of his life and times. Her accounts of his ideas about the performance of other people's music, and of conversations about his Third and Fourth Symphonies while he was working on them, occupy some of the most extraordinary and absorbing pages of these *Recollections*.

Their author is an elusive figure, whose name will rarely be found in other contemporary accounts of this period of Mahler's life. From the rather curious volume of *Fragments* (*Fragmente*, Vienna, 1907) that Natalie Bauer-Lechner devoted herself to after the end of her adoring friendship with Mahler, we discover a certain amount about her intellectual and spiritual preoccupations, many of which clearly owed much to the man she describes there as one of the 'lords' of her life. Of the details of that life we learn less. Born in 1858, the eldest child (of three) of a Viennese bookshop owner, she was educated by private tutors and much influenced by the cultured and genial atmosphere of her parents' home. An inevitable attraction to books and reading was, from the start, supplemented by a strong love of music, that was inspired by her father's piano-playing and her mother's singing. Having studied at the Vienna Conservatory (where she subsequently met Mahler for the first time), she was to become the viola-player of the

Soldat-Röger string quartet. In an English music-lexicon of the 1920s, Marie Soldat-Röger, a pupil of Joachim's, is still recalled as the founder and leader of an 'excellent ladies' string quartette'.

For further details about Natalie Bauer-Lechner, we must turn to the work of Mahler's biographer, M. Henry-Louis de La Grange. From him we learn that the crucial period of her relationship with Mahler began in 1890, when, after the break up of her marriage, she wrote to him, as an acquaintance of some years' standing, wishing to take up an earlier, general invitation and escape from Vienna and her recent experience in a trip to Budapest, where he was at that time Director of the Royal Opera. The letter, and Mahler's reply, are mentioned in the early pages of the *Recollections*, which then take up the story in their own way; or part of the story, that is.

For the rest, particularly in as much as it concerns Natalie Bauer-Lechner herself, we must turn back to M. de La Grange, who has been fortunate to discover the original manuscript of the *Mahleriana* and thus to have been able to make use of some of the more intimate passages omitted by J. Killian (almost certainly the husband of Natalie Bauer-Lechner's niece, Friedericke Killian, née Drechsler), who was the editor of the *Recollections*. He has, moreover, been able to describe the curious condition of this manuscript. At the very end of the first volume of his biography of Mahler, M. de La Grange observes: 'Most regrettably, various unknown hands have torn up numerous pages of her original manuscript, which doubtless contained a wealth of further information about the psychological atmosphere that prevailed in the Mahler family.'

I am myself indebted to some information supplied to the eminent Mahler scholar, Dr Donald Mitchell, by Professor E. H. Gombrich (whose mother, Professor Leonie Gombrich-Hock, had been a member of the Mahler circle in Vienna), for a measure of elucidation here. During the ten years or so of her close association with Mahler, Natalie Bauer-Lechner frequented the same circle of Viennese artists and intellectuals as he, but she could not always hold her own in this highly sophisticated atmosphere. Her rather too ingenuous, with Mahler too obviously worshipful, attitude was no doubt responsible for some general antipathy towards her, which expressed itself most clearly in disapproval of the *Mahleriana* manuscript, which she seems to have been quite ready to lend to friends and acquaintances. Professor Gombrich notes that his parents had it in their possession for some time, but found it too embarrassing to read in its entirety. Others who saw it seem generally to have felt that it touched rather too closely upon matters that often concerned themselves.

The flavour of such embarrassment can hardly now be recalled, while the value of what has remained, of the vivid picture painted in the following pages of one of the last great artists of a great tradition, adds a touch of the heroic to the tragic pathos that seems to shade the author's features in the few photographs by which she is known to us. If things had been otherwise, if the world were not as it is, she might have become a devoted wife and assistant to Mahler and gained a quite different place in history. As it was, the rising of the star of the brilliant young Alma Schindler in Mahler's universe inevitably entailed the final sinking of Natalie Bauer-Lechner's below his horizon. She was to die in poverty in 1921.

*　　*　　*

It is, nevertheless, Mahler himself who dominates these pages, and on whose account they will be valued. In preparing the text of Dika Newlin's translation for publication, my aim has been to still the desire to comment – a whole supplementary volume might have been written – and restrict myself largely to acting as a medium through which recent research into Mahler's life and works might throw light onto its otherwise obscure or enigmatic corners. Wherever possible, I have, in the footnotes, directed the reader to the relevant sections of books referred to – M. de La Grange's remarkable biography and Dr Donald Mitchell's *Gustav Mahler: the Wunderhorn Years* inevitably being cited frequently. The most notable omission from the bibliography will be found to be Mahler's *Selected Letters*. While constant reference to these will be essential for the serious student of Mahler's life and works, I have allowed their recent availability in translation to absolve me from the space-consuming activity of providing systematic cross-reference here.

In conclusion, two points must be raised concerning the authenticity of the text here translated, and the general veracity and reliability of its subject-matter (touched upon both in Paul Stefan's Introduction and J. Killian's Afterword). With respect to the first, only when the original manuscript, now in M. de La Grange's possession, becomes available for study will the extent of J. Killian's editorial activities become clear. The only alternative readings of certain portions of the text otherwise accessible are in the form of extracts which appeared during Natalie Bauer-Lechner's lifetime in the pages of two periodicals:

Der Merker (April 1913) and the *Musikblätter des Anbruch* (April 1920). The latter offers a small amount of material that was not included in J. Killian's published edition, although, in the main, the text of the selected passages is exactly as found there. They were in fact published as 'Mahler-Ausspruche' ('sayings' or 'remarks') 'collected by Natalie Bauer-Lechner, Salzburg', a footnote adding that they had been taken 'from a work on Mahler currently in preparation'. Still more interesting, however, is the anonymous, five-page collection of extracts 'From a Diary about Mahler' printed in the March 1913 edition of *Der Merker*. While this material can mostly be located in the published *Recollections*, there are many textual variations, even on the level of word-choice and sentence-structure, and a good deal of additional matter is to be found in it. Natalie Bauer-Lechner may well have selected and re-written these passages for publication at this time, and was herself possibly responsible for the curious, and surely mistaken, attribution of the section dealing with the Andante of the Second Symphony (see below, p. 29) to 'June 1894'. Alternatively, we might imagine that they represent most truthfully her own, original text, before she handed the *Mahleriana* over to J. Killian, sometime before the appearance of the *Anbruch* extracts in 1920, for him to edit and possibly re-phrase in places after his own fashion.

Material to be found in both the *Der Merker* and *Anbruch* collections of extracts, which appears to have been omitted by J. Killian, is included in translation in a list of addenda in Appendix 1 at the end of the present volume. The reader is alerted to the presence of such additional material by asterisks at the relevant points in the main text. As I have been unable to consult the original in order to check their authenticity, minor variations and omissions have not been indicated.

Concerning the general reliability of the subject-matter of the *Recollections*, one of its most striking, if at the same time slightly disturbing features is, of course, Natalie Bauer-Lechner's faith in her own ability to recall long stretches of conversation apparently verbatim. Nevertheless, the accuracy of the many details which can be verified from other sources can only lead one to consider the faithfulness of the rest as at least of the highest degree possible in such reporting, without the use of tape-recorder or on-the-spot shorthand notes. The volume of *Fragmente*, to which I have already referred, reveals Natalie Bauer-Lechner's life-long penchant for writing in the open air and in such unlikely places as trains and buses. Recognising her privileged position as the unwittingly adopted 'observer' on Mahler's working summer holidays with his sisters – his letters also picture 'dear, merry old Natalie' as a valued companion and the high-spirited instigator of long walks – she may well have devoted as much care and effort to the accuracy of her journal as Mahler to the creative work he had in hand.

It seems certain that her obvious attentions became irksome to him. She was specifically not invited to join the family party in the summer of 1894, and in a letter of 1897 (KBD p. 212) he was to describe her as 'excessively worked up' over the question of whether or not he should bring Anna von Mildenburg to Vienna. The complete sentence is interesting, however: 'On this question [Frau Bauer] seems to be excessively worked up, *which is quite unlike her.*' The final words (my italics) are as relevant as any that we have from Mahler's own pen to the question of Natalie Bauer-Lechner's reliability as a witness and chronicler. They must stand in the place of any more explicit testimonial.

P. R. F.

Acknowledgements

I should like to express grateful thanks to E. H. Gombrich and Donald Mitchell for permission to make use of information supplied to the latter by Professor Gombrich in 1954. I must also acknowledge a debt to the work of Dr Edward R. Reilly (Vassar), who unearthed the *Der Merker* and *Anbruch* extracts from Natalie Bauer-Lechner's journal made use of in Appendix I. For the material included in Appendix II I am indebted to Mr Knud Martner, (Copenhagen). His comments on and amendments to my transcription of the letter, which he kindly made available to me, were invaluable. I would also like to express gratitude to Dr Dika Newlin, whose contribution to this volume by no means ceased when the task of translation was completed. Her encouragement and experienced advice greatly facilitated my own editorial work. The final acknowledgement is due to Olivia Kilmartin, whose work on the minutiae of the preparation of the manuscript for printing was a model of care and patience.

P. R. F.

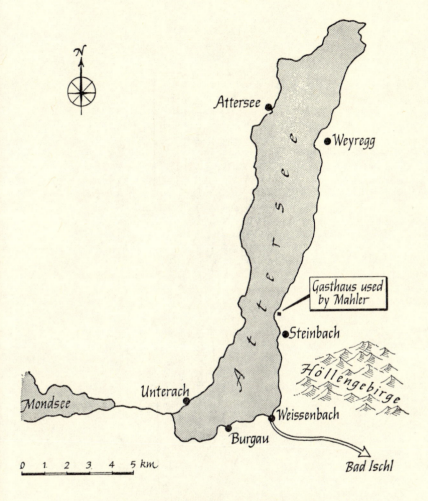

The Attersee, showing the Gasthaus used by Mahler in
the summers of 1893 to 1898

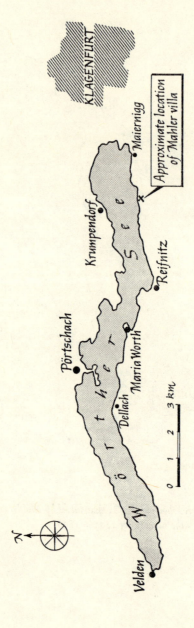

KLAGENFURT

Maiernigg

Approximate location
of Mahler villa

Krumpendorf

S e e

Reifnitz

Pörtschach

Maria Worth

W ö r t h e r

Dellach

0 1 2 3 km

N

Velden

The Wörther See, showing the position of the villa built by Mahler in 1899

Recollections of
Gustav Mahler

by

Natalie Bauer-Lechner

Introduction to the first edition

This book is one of the rare documents of Mahler's youth; the testimony of one who experienced the sustained ardour of his nature at first hand.

The *Recollections*, which I briefly introduce here, have been well known to me for many years. Thirteen years ago, Natalie Bauer-Lechner gave them to me in their first draft as material for my biography of Mahler. There was often discussion of my helping the author to prepare her work for publication, but this did not come about during her lifetime.

I would first express my thanks to Natalie Bauer-Lechner for her friendship. But I feel that the ever-growing number of those who honour Mahler, the artist and the man, will be grateful to her for her *Recollections*. A precious past is mirrored in them.

Every word that this woman said and wrote betrayed her boundless 'hero-worship' [in English in the original]. While not concerned with biographical minutiae, she always managed to sense something of his true spirit.

True, Mahler – elemental as every genius – defies description. He is at once just as portrayed and yet quite different. Even the fidelity of an Eckermann obscures the features of a demonic Goethe behind the one we meet in the *Conversations*. Then, too, men and women evaluate differently. And – last but not least – Mahler was unusually impulsive, unusually shy.

In his Afterword, the editor warns against seeking exact dates and quotations in these memoirs. For example, the negative comments on Johann Strauss are inconsistent with Mahler's often-expressed admiration for this composer. Quotations and dates – these do not constitute the true content and value of these *Recollections*. They give us perhaps less, certainly more.

The ground covered by the *Recollections* is quickly sketched. They accompany Mahler to the creative crisis which is expressed in the change of direction between the *Wunderhorn* Symphonies and the Fifth Symphony. The son of simple people, who yet recognize and carefully cherish his great gifts, is brought to the Vienna Conservatory. Fortunately, he comes into contact with Bruckner; German culture at its best influences him. The musician fights his way through; even working in a provincial theatre cannot drag him down. And so we follow the conductor's triumphal progress from Budapest, via Hamburg to Vienna. At the same time, we catch a glimpse of the simple and peaceful domestic life of a quiet man, faithfully cared for by his sister Justi (subsequently Justine Rosé).[1] We see the conquest of the great Court Opera by a man of thirty-seven; the hostile forces are not yet at work.

The *Recollections* follow the fate of Mahler the composer with equally lively sympathy. They accompany the Second and Third Symphonies from the little house on the Attersee, where they were written, to the hostile concert halls of Berlin. The songs lead to the Fourth Symphony, and the problems of the Fifth are already hinted at. Mahler would probably have expressed himself differently to a composer or a conductor. Yet he spoke to a woman who was herself a practising musician, to whom music was a calling, not merely a living.

The period immediately following these *Recollections* was to see a profound transformation in the man and his fortunes. In Alma Maria Schindler, Mahler won both a wife and the partner in a lofty spiritual relationship. His Viennese theatre, which he led towards a new 'Golden Age' [klassischer Zeit], brought him into contact with Alfred Roller. His mode of expression grew purer, more spiritual. He became the creator of the later orchestral symphonies; of the triumphant Eighth, and the eternal 'Farewell'.[2]

Roller's words of reminiscence, in his introduction to *Die Bildnisse von Gustav Mahler*,[3] picture the man and artist of those last ten years. His letters, selected and edited by Frau Alma, will provide additional documentation.[4]

And all such evidence will make still more vivid our im-

---

[1] The Notes are situated at the end of the book (pp. 190–225).

pression of that δεινότης ['intensity' or 'forcefulness'] which was the essence of Mahler. To be sure, he lived among us men in a particular time, a certain city – yet today he is already the stuff of legend. No words do him justice; no picture, not even his own creative work, gives quite the measure of him.

Paul Stefan[5]
Whit Sunday, 1923.

Early history of my friendship with Gustav Mahler

My first recollection of Gustav Mahler dates back to his Conservatory years,[1] when my sister Ellen and I, having completed our violin studies early, would go and sit in on Hellmesberger's[2] orchestral rehearsals.

It was just before the composition contest; a symphony of Mahler's was to be played. Since he could not pay a copyist, he had worked for days and nights copying the parts for all the instruments and, here and there, some mistakes had crept in. Hellmesberger became furious, flung down the score at Mahler's feet, and cried out in his peevish way: 'Your parts are full of mistakes; do you think that I'll conduct something like that?' Even after the parts were corrected, he could not be persuaded to perform Mahler's work. So, at the last moment Mahler had to compose a Piano Suite instead. As he told me later: 'Since it was a much weaker and more superficial work, it won a prize, while my good things were all rejected by the worthy judges.'[3]

This scene made an indelible impression on me. Even today, I can see the young man – so far above his so-called 'superior' – forced to tolerate such shameful treatment. In a flash I realized into what hands the genius of this young man had been placed, and what he would have to suffer in the course of his life.

At the Pichlers', the family of a Conservatory class-mate, where we were all received cordially and spent such happy, carefree hours as are known only in early youth, I later briefly met Mahler again. Once I spent more time with him in a gathering at Kralik's.[4] Asked to play the *Meistersinger* Prelude, he did so in such a grandiose style that a whole orchestra seemed to resound under his hands. Otherwise, as always in 'elegant' company, he behaved rather like an 'unlicked bear-cub', and seemed to feel ill at ease. But when we sat together at supper, he relaxed completely, and we became absorbed in a fascinating conversation about *Wilhelm Meister*.

When I met Mahler again, years later, his Leipzig period was behind him. He looked miserable, was physically very run-down and – as always when he had no position – was oppressed by the darkest misgivings, as if he would never find employment again.

A few more years passed and, at the age of twenty-eight, Mahler had become Director of the Opera in Budapest.[5] One day, he came to Vienna to visit his sister and brother: Poldi,[6] who died not long afterwards, and Otto,[7] whom Mahler had liberated from his father's business a year before and – since he showed a profound, characteristically Mahlerian gift for music – had sent to the Conservatory in Vienna at his own expense. These two, and myself, were invited one evening to the Löhrs', whose son Fritz,[8] a splendid man and scholar, was Mahler's dearest friend for many years. Mahler, who had always had a strong need for home ties, felt at his best there, among family and friends. He was in the liveliest of moods, and singled me out for special attention – as he always threw himself vehemently into a friendship whenever he felt especially attracted to a person. He invited us all to visit him in Budapest.

PART I

Mahler abroad

Visit to Budapest

A year or a year-and-a-half after Mahler's visit to Vienna I
wrote to him, explaining that I planned to visit him in Budapest.
He answered immediately and cordially, saying that the prospect
of seeing me there put him in the pleasantest of moods, and that
I should keep my promise as soon as possible. 'I'm almost
curious' he added 'to see whether we'll talk to each other or
be silent.'

Mahler led a very lonely life in Budapest. 'Except in my
distasteful profession, I've practically forgotten how to talk' he
said. 'I don't get around to composing either, or even to playing
the piano; for what I'm doing here is mere drudgery, and that's
incompatible with things closer to my heart.'

He had turned his little apartment over to me for the duration
of my stay, having moved into a hotel on my behalf.

Along with the general problems of living in a foreign
country, his artistic position in Budapest was irritating and
unbearable. He was limited first of all by the foreign language,
which had no outstanding musical literature of its own and into
which by no means all operas had been translated. Mahler
himself was the first to have a translation of the *Ring* Cycle
made; this caused him a great deal of trouble, as he did not know
Hungarian. He had difficulty finding singers, too, since only a
very few of the good ones knew Hungarian, and these were the
only ones he would consider. In order to get rid of the dreadful
abuse of having a single opera sung, during the course of one
evening, in Hungarian, Italian and often French or German as
well, he had established the artistic principle that a work must be
sung throughout in *one* language, namely Hungarian. This
'Magyarization' of art, however, was a personal torture for him.
'Oh, to hear a single word sung in German once more! You
wouldn't believe how unbearably I long for that!' he exclaimed
when we were in the theatre together.

Mahler performed miracles for the people of Budapest. Not only did he present model performances for them, but he dragged the hopelessly swamped operatic cart out of the mire, and turned its considerable deficit into a large surplus. For all this, they were anything but grateful to him; in fact, they attacked him from all sides. This was especially true of the operatic personnel, whom he had forced to unaccustomed and increased labours. Under the pretext of affronted patriotism, a few of the chorus members even went so far as to challenge him to a duel. However, Mahler published in the principal Budapest paper[1] an open letter which gave his precise reasons for opposing duels in general and this one in particular. This simply redoubled the rage of his opponents, so that he went in fear of his life.

On the street you could hardly walk five steps with him without everyone stopping and craning their necks to get a look – so well known was he. This made him so furious that he would stamp his foot and yell: 'Am I a wild animal then, that everyone can stop and stare at me as in a menagerie?'

Mahler used to recover from these ordeals on the excursions which he made alone (or, at this time, with me) into the surrounding countryside.

Steinbach am Attersee

July and August 1893

The Andante of the Second Symphony

'Here are two marvellous themes' said Mahler 'that I picked up today from the sketch for the Andante of my Second Symphony. With God's help, I hope to finish both it and the Scherzo while I'm here.' When he has just been composing, he often seems, for a while, as if he were still in another world; and he confronts his own works as if they were completely foreign to him. 'I was always disturbed by those two little pieces of paper on which I had noted the themes – it was in Leipzig, when I conducted the *Pintos*[1] there.* I see now that they might well have bothered me. For the melody pours forth here in a full, broad stream;* one idea is interwoven with the other, constantly branching out in an inexhaustible wealth of variations. And how choice and delicate the end-product of this process of self-generation – if you could follow its course right through, what a joy it would be to you!

'And that's the only way to create: in one grand sweep. It's no use playing around with some poor little scrap of a theme, varying it and writing fugues on it – anything to make it last out a movement! I can't stand the economical way of going about things [das Sparsystem]; everything must be overflowing, gushing forth continually, if the work is to amount to anything.'*

Mahler finished his Andante in seven days; and says himself that he has good reason to be pleased with it.

The significance of Beethoven

During a conversation about Beethoven, Mahler said:
'In order to understand and appreciate Beethoven fully, we

* Asterisks refer to Appendix 1, see Foreword p. 9.

29

should not only accept him for what he means to us today, but must realize what a tremendous revolutionary advance he represents in comparison with his forerunners. Only when we understand what a difference there is between Mozart's G minor Symphony and the Ninth can we properly evaluate Beethoven's achievement. Of geniuses like Beethoven, of such a most sublime and most universal kind, there are only two or three among millions. Among poets and composers of more recent times we can, perhaps, name but three: Shakespeare, Beethoven and Wagner.'

The symphony and life

'I have already thought a great deal,' said Mahler, 'about what I ought to call my symphony, so as to give some hint of its subject in its title, and, in a word at least, to comment on my purpose. But let it be called just a 'Symphony' and nothing more! For titles like 'Symphonic Poem' are already hackneyed and say nothing in particular; they make one think of Liszt's compositions, in which, without any deeper underlying connection, each movement paints its own picture. My two symphonies contain the inner aspect of my whole life; I have written into them* everything that I have experienced and endured – Truth and Poetry[2] in music. To understand these works properly would be to see my life transparently revealed in them. Creativity and experience are so intimately linked for me that, if my existence were simply to run on as peacefully as a meadow brook, I don't think that I would ever again be able to write anything worth while.'

The mystical aspect of creation

'Today' Mahler told me 'I went through the Scherzo of my Second Symphony, which I hadn't looked at again since I wrote it, and was quite surprised by it. What a remarkable, awesomely great piece! I had not thought so while composing it.

'The inception and creation of a work are mystical from beginning to end; unconsciously, as if in the grip of a command from outside oneself, one is compelled to create something

30

whose origin one can scarcely comprehend afterwards. I often feel like the blind hen who managed to find a grain of corn!

'But, even more strangely than in a whole movement or work, this unconscious, mysterious power manifests itself in individual passages, and precisely in the most difficult and significant ones. Usually, they are the ones which I don't want to come to grips with, which I would like to get around, yet which continue to hold me up and finally force their way to expression.

'This has just happened to me in the Scherzo, with a passage which I had already given up on and omitted, but which I then inserted on an additional page after all. And now I see that it is the most indispensable, most powerful part of the whole movement.

'This experience was, perhaps, even more striking in the case of a transition in my First Symphony – one that gave me a lot of trouble.[3] Again and again, the music had fallen from brief glimpses of light into the darkest depths of despair. Now, an enduring, triumphal victory had to be won. As I discovered after considerable vain groping, this could be achieved by modulating from one key to the key a whole tone above (from C major to D major, the principal key of the movement). Now, this could have been managed very easily by using the intervening semitone and rising from C to C sharp, then to D. But everyone would have known that D would be the next step. My D chord, however, had to sound as though it had fallen from heaven, as though it had come from another world. Then I found my transition – the most unconventional and daring of modulations, which I hesitated to accept for a long time and to which I finally surrendered much against my will. And if there is anything great in the whole symphony, it is this very passage, which – I can safely say it – has yet to meet its match.

'Something similar occurs in works for orchestra, when the idiosyncracies and inadequacies of the various instruments force you to resort to padding and patching. Those very patches which conceal a flaw become an additional beauty and adornment when skilfully applied, while a bungler will simply stick them on wretchedly for the sake of expediency.

'Das irdische Leben' and the 'Fischpredigt'

I asked Mahler how the 'Fischpredigt'[4] came to grow into the mighty Scherzo of the Second, without his having intended it or wanted it to. He replied: 'It's a strange process! Without knowing at first where it's leading, you find yourself pushed further and further beyond the bounds of the original form, whose potentialities lay hidden within it like the plant within the seed. In connection with this, it seems to me that only with difficulty could I conform to the limitations imposed by an opera libretto (unless I had written it myself), or even by composing an overture to somebody else's work.

'It is rather different with songs, but only because you can express so much more in the music than the words directly say. The text is actually a mere indication of the deeper significance to be extracted from it, of hidden treasure within.

'In this way, I feel that human life (in the poem to which I give the interpretative title "Das irdische Leben" ["Earthly Life"])[5] is symbolized by the child's crying for bread and the answer of the mother, consoling it with promises again and again. In life, everything that one most needs for the growth of spirit and body is withheld – as with the dead child – until it is too late. And I believe that this is characteristically and frighteningly expressed in the uncanny notes of the accompaniment, which bluster past as in a storm; in the child's anguished cry of fear, and the slow, monotonous responses of the mother – of Fate, which is in no particular hurry to satisfy our cries for bread. In the "Fischpredigt", on the other hand, the prevailing mood – as in "Das himmlische Leben"[6] – is one of rather bittersweet humour. St Anthony preaches to the fishes; his words are immediately translated into their thoroughly tipsy-sounding language (in the clarinet), and they all come swimming up to him – a glittering shoal of them: eels and carp, and the pike with their pointed heads. I swear, while I was composing I really kept imagining that I saw them sticking their stiff immovable necks out from the water, and gazing up at St Anthony with their stupid faces – I had to laugh out loud! And look at the

32

1. *Natalie Bauer-Lechner*

2. *Mahler with his sister, Justine (1899)*

congregation swimming away as soon as the sermon's over:

> Die Predigt hat g'fallen,
> Sie bleiben wie alle.
> [They liked the sermon,
> But remain unchanged]

'Not one of them is one iota the wiser for it, even though the Saint has performed for them! But only a few people will understand my satire on mankind.'

In connection with this, Mahler said: 'The Bohemian music of my childhood home[7] has found its way into many of my compositions. I've noticed it especially in the "Fischpredigt". The underlying national element there can be heard, in its most crude and basic form, in the tootling of the Bohemian pipers [aus dem Gedudel der böhmischen Musikanten].'

The Rheinlegendchen

To Mahler's exasperation, I wanted to know nothing less than how music is composed. 'My God, Natalie, how can anybody ask such a thing? Do you know how to make a trumpet? You take a hole and wrap tin around it; that's more or less what you do when you compose. But in all seriousness, how is one to describe the process? It happens in a hundred different ways. One minute it is the poem that is the inspiration, the next it is the melody, I often begin in the middle, often at the beginning, sometimes even at the end, and the rest of it gradually falls into place until it develops into a complete whole.

'Today, for instance, I had a theme in mind; I was leafing through a book, and soon came upon the lines of a charming song that would fit my rhythm. I call the piece "Tanzreime",'[8] (he later called it 'Rheinlegendchen') 'although I could christen it along with a group of other songs, or perhaps with "Um schlimme Kinder artig zu machen" ["To make bad children good"].[9] But this is quite different in type from the earlier songs that I wrote for Frau Weber's children.[10] It is much more direct, but whimsically childlike [kindlich-schalkhaft] and tender in a way that you have never heard before. Even the orchestration is sweet and sunny – nothing but butterfly colours. But, in spite of all its simplicity and folklike quality, the whole thing is extremely original, especially in its harmonization, so that people will not know what to make of it, and will call it mannered. And yet it is the most natural thing in the world; it is simply what the melody demanded.'

The work and its effect

'How much I lose through not being able to try out my things in live performance! How much I could learn from that! It would be so important for me, as my way of treating the orchestra is particularly individual. For example, when scoring I perhaps over-emphasize certain things for fear that they might become lost, or sound too weak.

'I am deprived of all living interaction between the external world and my inner world, between the work and the ultimate effect of this work. You can't imagine how that paralyses me!'[11]

A conductor's tribulations

Mahler said of his conducting in Hamburg:[12] 'I prepare my performances* in the minutest detail, and with the utmost exertion of all my powers, until everything really works and is all of a piece. And for whom do I take all this trouble? For this flock of sheep who listen mindlessly and pointlessly – everything going in one ear and out of the other, just like the sermon of St Anthony of Padua to the fishes!

'Sometimes I can bring off an exemplary performance in this way, putting all of myself, and all I know, into it – like the Wagner cycle last spring,[13] when even *that* audience sat evening after evening in complete silence, often for five hours at a stretch. The singers have to take curtain-call after curtain-call; but I go off all alone, without anyone to talk it over with or to calm me down after the excitement and the tension, and devour my ham sandwich alone in the café. I'd really be beside myself frequently over the futility and thanklessness of such work as mine if I didn't keep remembering that perhaps, after all, there will be a few on whom the seeds of my labours will fall – to grow and sometime, somewhere, to bear fruit. And that in itself is enough.'*

I told Mahler that I could not understand how his Hamburg orchestra players could be hostile towards him. 'For I've always found' I said 'even with people of no particular ability or seriousness, that they become most warmly and gratefully attached to the person who helps them along, lifts them out of themselves, and compels them to surpass themselves. In fact, they'd go through fire for him.'

'There you're quite wrong! Do you really think these people are interested in learning and making progress? For them, art is only the cow which they milk so as to live their everyday lives undisturbed, as comfortably and pleasantly as possible. And yet, there are some amongst them who are more willing and better than the rest; one ought to have more patience with them than I am able to manage. For if one of them doesn't immediately give me what is on the page, I could kill him on the spot; I come down on him, and upset him so much that he really hates me. In this way I often demand more of them than they are capable of actually giving; no wonder they don't forgive me for it!

'It's worst of all towards the end of the season, when everybody is played-out and exhausted. A musician shows less attentiveness and capacity at such times. But as a result, although I'm just as tired as they are – probably more so – I have to test my own strength to the limit and make even greater demands on the orchestra, in order to achieve the kind of perfection which alone can satisfy me. Rather unedifying scenes often result. It's true that I always keep the upper hand, but my anger nearly kills me!

'In spite of all this, I'm quite gentle today compared with what I used to be. In the first years of my career as a conductor, when I didn't yet quite know how to go about things and made people rehearse eight hours and more a day, matters once deteriorated in Cassel to such an extent that a real revolution threatened to break out in my orchestra.[14] A friend warned me that all the orchestral players and choristers were intending to come to the rehearsal armed with sticks and cudgels in order to beat me soundly. My friend advised me to plead indisposition and stay at home. Naturally, I went straight to the rehearsal, and began it immediately, as sternly and severely as possible! I never took my eye off a single one of the gentlemen, and never left them a moment's respite in which to collect their wits. As soon as the rehearsal was over, glaring around me furiously, I banged the grand piano lid shut – and without saying a word, or anyone having dared to approach me, let alone touch me, I left the hall.

'Looking back, I've often felt sorry for the poor fellows who were my first victims, and whose last breath and last energies I mercilessly extorted in my rehearsals.'

The brutality of noise

Mahler, who suffers so much from noise and disturbance even in the country, tells me that when he was a child he used to wish that the good Lord had equipped human beings in such a way that, the minute they got too noisy, something like an internal 'Jack-in-the-box' ['Knüppel aus dem Sack'] would pop out and, belabouring them vigorously, reduce them to silence. 'I am certain' he says in this connection 'that in some future age the human race will be as sensitive to noise as it is now to smells, and that there will be the heaviest possible penalties and public measures to forbid offences to the hearing. Nowadays, everything possible and impossible is protected – apart from the thinking person, who alone is exposed to every assault, every crude disturbance of brute force, and all kinds of unpleasant row.[15]

'Typical of this situation is the tale of Frederick the Great and the windmill, which has been made so much of in a furore about universal human and social justice.[16] It's all well and good that the peasant's rights are protected in spite of the King, but there's another side to the story. Let the miller and his mill be protected on their own ground – if only the millwheels didn't clatter so, thereby overstepping their boundaries most shamelessly and creating immeasurable havoc in the territory of someone else's mind!'*

Brahms and Bruckner

Gustav Mahler and his brother Otto were talking about Brahms and Bruckner. Otto insisted on ascribing greater importance to Bruckner; in his view, the content of Bruckner's works unquestionably excelled that of Brahms's, though Brahms did achieve greater perfection of form.

'In order to judge a work' said Mahler 'you have to look at it as a whole. And in this respect, Brahms is indisputably the greater of the two, with his extraordinarily compact compositions which aren't at all obvious, but reveal greater depth and richness of content the more you enter into them. And think of his immense productivity, which is also part of the total picture of an artist!'[17] With Bruckner, certainly, you are carried away by the magnificence and wealth of his inventiveness, but at the same time you are repeatedly disturbed by its fragmentary character, which breaks the spell. *I* can permit myself to say this, because you know how deeply I revere Bruckner in spite of it, and I shall always do whatever is in my power to have his works played and heard. That is what is so sad; that Bruckner never received his due in his lifetime, from his contemporaries. Now that he is just beginning to emerge from obscurity, he is over seventy;[18] and posterity, which inherits only what is complete and perfect in itself, will love and understand him still less. Look at Jean Paul,[19] who is, after all, such an extraordinary person, wittier and more extravagantly gifted than anyone else; yet who reads or even knows of him today?

'No, it isn't enough to judge a work of art by its content; we must consider its total image, in which content and form are indissolubly blended. It is this which determines its value, its power of survival, and its immortality.'

Evaluation of Liszt

Mahler told me that his opinion of Liszt is diametrically opposed to that of Strauss. 'The last time we met, Strauss told me that he used to think as little of Liszt as I do, but that lately he had come to have an extremely high opinion of his works. I shall never come to that. The paucity of content and the shoddy workmanship of his compositions are as obvious, if one looks closely, as the threads of a badly woven garment, which all too soon make themselves felt.'

The greatness of Wagner

Mahler said: 'Whenever my spirits are low, I have only to think of Wagner and my mood improves. How amazing that a light like his ever penetrated the world! What a firebrand! What a revolutionary and reformer of art such as had never existed before! But then he was born at the right moment, at the precise juncture of time when the world was waiting for what he had to say and to offer. And from this stems nearly half of the immense, world-shaking effect of such genius. "For the greatest power lies in the moment of birth and in the ray of light that greets the newly born", as Hölderlin says. How many lofty spirits may there be who, coming into the world at the wrong moment, go their way unused and unrecognized and vanish without trace!

'Those who are born after such great spirits as Beethoven and Wagner, the epigones, have no easy task. For the harvest is already gathered in, and there remain only a few solitary ears of corn to glean.'

Spiritual and physical birth

Mahler said that his works were always children of sorrow; of the most profound inner experience. 'And I think this is true of most artists, except perhaps for the really great geniuses, who could be numbered on a fingernail. To me, however, the creation of a work of art resembles that of a pearl, which, born of the oyster's terrible sufferings, bestows its treasure on the world.

'In this way, spiritual conception is very like physical birth. What struggles, what agony, what terror accompany it – but what rejoicing when the child turns out to be fit and strong!'

Mahler becomes furious if he suspects that anyone is listening to him, or even near him, when he is composing. 'Can't you people understand how disturbing it is, how it makes creative work quite impossible? How indiscreet and immodest to expose to other people's ears something that is still only in the process of becoming! It's as if one would expose the child still in its mother's womb.'

Steinbach am Attersee

Summer 1895[1]

Only just arrived here,[2] Mahler has already begun working on his Third Symphony. 'With it, I hope to earn applause and money,' he said to me jokingly on one of the first days 'for *this* one is pure humour and merriment, a great laugh at the whole world!' But the very next day, he took back what he'd said: 'You know as far as money-making goes, the Third won't do any better than the others! For, at first, people won't understand or appreciate its gaiety; it soars *above* that world of struggle and sorrow in the First and Second, and could have been produced only as a result of these.

'My calling it a symphony is really inaccurate, for it doesn't keep to the traditional form in any way. But, to me 'symphony' means constructing a world with all the technical means at one's disposal. The eternally new and changing content determines its own form. In this sense, I must forever learn anew how to forge new means of expression for myself – however completely I may have mastered technical problems, as I think I may now claim to have done.'

Coming thoroughly stirred-up and excited from his work, Mahler told me as we walked: 'It was like balancing Columbus's Egg[3] when I brought in the word and the human voice in the Second Symphony just at the point where I needed it to make myself intelligible. Too bad I didn't think of this in the First! But in the Third I feel no more hesitation about it. I'm basing the songs of the short movements on two pieces from *Des Knaben Wunderhorn*[4] and a glorious poem of Nietzsche's.[5]

' "Summer draws in"[6] will be the prelude. Straight away, I need a regimental band to give the rough and crude effect of my martial comrade's arrival. It will be just like the military band on parade. Such a mob is milling around, you never saw anything like it!

'Naturally, it doesn't come off without a struggle with the opponent, Winter; but he is easily dispatched, and Summer, in his strength and superior power, soon gains undisputed mastery. This movement, treated as an introduction, is humorous, even grotesque [barock], throughout.

'The titles of the movements, in order, will be:

1. Summer marches in.
2. What the flowers in the meadow tell me.
3. What the animals in the forest tell me.
4. What night tells me (Man).
5. What the morning bells tell me (the Angels).
6. What love tells me.
7. What the child tells me.[7]

'And I'll call the whole thing "Meine fröhliche Wissenschaft"[8] – for that's just what it is!'

Visit to Hamburg

January 1896

Mahler leads a wonderful life here with his sisters – a life such as one can live only in Hamburg. Hohe Luft [Mountain Air] is the attractive name of this quarter of the town: a name, as it were, symbolic for his work. A little house set in a garden with a view of meadows and orchards – all for just the three of them and their two maids. Mahler has the whole top floor, with a room for the piano, a study and a bedroom.

The performance of the
Second Symphony in Berlin

When I arrived, I found Mahler busy with the orchestration of his *Lieder eines fahrenden Gesellen*.[1] He was delighted to see me, although this didn't prevent him from immediately flying into a rage over the fact that I had not been at the performance of his Second Symphony on the 14[2] December in Berlin (which I could not possibly have attended because of our first quartet [concert] in Vienna).[3]

When he had calmed down, Justi and he began to tell me about the performance. By the end of the first rehearsal, the chorus and members of the orchestra were enthusiastically on his side (which is saying a lot, considering the unheard-of difficulties that he expected them to master in this work).

Justi, who had been present at the ghastly fiasco of Mahler's First Symphony in Budapest many years before,[4] and at the two recent controversial performances (of the Second Symphony in Berlin and the First in Hamburg, a year and two years ago respectively)[5] told how she entered the concert hall with the greatest trepidation. At first, indeed, she hardly dared look up from where she was sitting. But after the first movement a surge of applause burst from the audience, which was following the work in breathless suspense. It is true that, since paying customers had proved to be few, the hall was filled largely with Conservatory students and professional musicians on complimentary tickets – in other words, the best possible audience.

'The triumph' continued Justi 'grew greater with every movement. Such enthusiasm is seen only once in a lifetime! Afterwards, I saw grown men weeping and youths falling on each other's necks. And when the Bird of Death, hovering above the graves, utters his last, long drawn-out call – Mahler said he himself was afraid for a moment that the long unbroken silence, requiring, as it were, the whole audience to hold its breath, could not possibly come off – there was such a deathly silence in the hall that no one seemed to bat so much as an eyelid. And when the chorus entered, everyone gave a shuddering sigh of relief. It was indescribable!'

As for the musical effect, Mahler said that he himself had never imagined anything like it. There were sounds such as had never been dreamed of!

The meaning of the Second Symphony

One evening Mahler arranged a performance, by himself and Walter,[6] of Behn's piano reduction of the Second Symphony. This took place at Behn's house,[7] as a treat for me, in the company of a few close friends. Although I had already heard him play parts of it in Steinbach, its total impact on me now was tremendous.

The next morning Mahler spoke to me about this work: 'The first movement depicts the titanic struggles of a mighty being still caught in the toils of this world; grappling with life and with the fate to which he must succumb* – his death. The second and third movements, Andante and Scherzo, are episodes from the life of the fallen hero. The Andante tells of love. The experience behind the Scherzo I can describe only in terms of the following image: if, at a distance, you watch a dance through a window, without being able to hear the music, then the turning and twisting movement of the couples seems senseless, because you are not catching the rhythm that is the key to it all. You must imagine that to one who has lost his identity and his

43

happiness, the world looks like this – distorted and crazy, as if reflected in a concave mirror. The Scherzo ends with the appalling shriek of this tortured soul.

'The "Urlicht" represents the soul's striving and questioning attitude towards God and its own immortality.

'While the first three movements are narrative in character, in the last movement everything is inward experience. It begins with the death-shriek of the Scherzo. And now the resolution of the terrible problem of life – redemption. At first, we see it in the form created by faith and the Church – in their struggle to transcend this present life.* The earth trembles. Just listen to the drum-roll, and your hair will stand on end! The Last Trump sounds; the graves spring open, and all creation comes writhing out of the bowels of the earth, with wailing and gnashing of teeth. Now they all come marching along in a mighty procession: beggars and rich men, common folk and kings, the Church Militant [die ecclesia militans], the Popes. All give vent to the same terror, the same lamentations and paroxysms; for none is just in the sight of God. Breaking in again and again – as if from another world – the Last Trump sounds from the Beyond. At last, after everyone has shouted and screamed in indescribable confusion, nothing is heard but the long drawn-out call of the Bird of Death above the last grave – finally that, too, fades away. There now follows nothing of what had been expected: no Last Judgement, no souls saved and none damned; no just man, no evil-doer, no judge! Everything has ceased to be. And softly and simply there begins: "Auferstehn'n, ja aufersteh'n ..." ["Rise again, yea, rise again"] – the words themselves are sufficient commentary. And' cried Mahler 'I absolutely refuse to give another syllable of explanation!'[8]

'The increasing tension, working up to the final climax, is so tremendous that I don't know myself, now that it is over, how I ever came to write it.'

Orchestral technique and notation

At the Philharmonic concert, we heard a bad performance of the 'Pastoral' Symphony. Mahler was driven to despair by it, for he felt the lack of a 'sustained melodic line'.* When I asked him what he meant by this, he explained: 'The melodic [gesanglichen] and rhythmic passages which make up the whole must be clearly shaped at all times. Instead of that, these mechanics pound it into a sort of mush without substance or form, in which there is so little of Beethoven that I wonder how it ever became popular in such a garbled version!

'It is true that all Beethoven's works need a certain amount of editing.[9] For look here,' he said – explaining with the aid of the score of the 'Pastoral' which he had before him – 'Beethoven counted on artists, not artisans, for the conducting as well as the playing. He didn't write everything in such minute detail as Richard Wagner was later to do,* nor was he so experienced in orchestral technique as never to make a mistake in notating the sound he wanted, particularly later on when he lost control over this because of his deafness. So in order that the music should be played as it was meant to sound, one has to add all sorts of dynamic indications to the parts, so that the principal voice stands out and the accompaniment retires into the background. One must take care, too, that the bowing and expression produce the effect that the composer wanted.'

In this connection, he said of his own manner of notation: 'You wouldn't believe how anxiously and carefully I proceed in my compositions. In fact, I have worked out quite a new orchestral technique – the direct result of my long experience. For instance, when the musical meaning requires consecutive notes to be played disconnectedly, I don't leave this up to the common sense of the players. Instead, I might divide the passage between the first and second violins, rather than leave it entirely to the firsts or seconds. If I want a part to retreat into the background, I have it played by only one, two, or three desks, as needed. Only when all the stops need to be pulled out is everybody included. Also, in heavily scored passages, I take care that the strings bear the right relation to the wind and percussion, so that all parts are well balanced with each other. I have observed that the more accurate the intonation of the strings, the louder they sound. In order that there should not be the slightest inaccuracy in rhythm, I have racked my brains to notate it as precisely as possible. Thus, I avoid indicating the shortness of notes, or the space between them, by dots or other staccato marks. Instead, everything is spelled out in detail by means of the note-values and rests.

'Of course, I am referring to the things that *can* be written down. All the most important things – the tempo, the total conception and structuring of a work – are almost impossible to pin down. For here we are concerned with something living and flowing that can never be the same even twice in succession. That is why metronome markings are inadequate and almost worthless; for unless the work is vulgarly ground out in barrel-organ style, the tempo will already have changed by the end of the second bar. Therefore, the right inter-relationships of all the sections of the piece are much more important than the initial tempo. Whether the overall tempo is a degree faster or slower often depends on the mood of the conductor; it may well vary slightly without detriment to the work. What matters is that the whole should be alive, and, within the bounds of this freedom, be built up with irrevocable inevitability.'

Thus, when timing the movements of his Third Symphony in the summer, Mahler discovered to his amazement that he took one movement ('Die Nacht' [No. 4], I believe) a few minutes slower on one occasion than on another – he, the composer!

Concerning his introduction of new instruments into the orchestra, Mahler declared that he had borrowed several of them from military-band music – especially the E flat clarinet, whose sound had been considered rather vulgar and commonplace up till then. 'Even as a boy, I was thrilled by it. But at that time I didn't dare own up to my taste – all my friends poked fun at me for it. Now, I'm no longer embarrassed, for I know precisely what the orchestra has gained from the use of these clarinets.'*

In Hamburg again

Mid-February 1896

I felt as if I had never left Hamburg when, with Mahler and
Justi, who had met me at the station, I stepped into their friendly
home once again.

We spent a quiet evening there together, as Mahler was not
conducting. Our talk turned to amusing anecdotes about
Bruckner. For instance, there was the time when Frau
Krzyzanowski[1] (whose son Rudolf studied under Bruckner at
the Conservatory at the same time as Mahler)[2] visited Bruckner
in his bath! It happened like this: Bruckner, who had been
ill, had to take a daily hip-bath on doctor's orders. So as to pass
the time while sitting in the bath, he used to take music-paper
with him and compose. One day, deeply absorbed in this
occupation, he was surprised by Frau Krzyzanowski. She
knocked at the door, and was greeted by a friendly 'Come in!'
Imagine her shock when, on entering, she beheld Bruckner's
corpulent figure in the bath, as naked as the good Lord had made
him! The incident did not end there: while she stood as if
rooted to the spot, up got Bruckner with a polite greeting and a
smile. Dripping, and quite devoid of any kind of covering, he
approached the horrified lady – who rushed from the room with
a piercing shriek, thus finally bringing poor Bruckner to himself and to an awareness of his state.

And this had to happen to Bruckner, of all people – Bruckner,
who was paralyzed by self-consciousness in the presence of the
fair sex and blushed like a schoolboy if he so much as looked at
or spoke to a woman!

As an instance of Bruckner's incredible modesty and humility,
Mahler recounted the following tale. Whenever Mahler visited
Bruckner, the old man not only unfailingly accompanied him to
the door of the flat when he left, but would then embark on the
stairs with him, eventually making his way right down from the

third floor to the street door, insisting upon honouring his guest in this way.

'Is it true,' one of us asked, 'that he wanted to dedicate his last symphony to "the Good Lord"?'

'It's quite likely,' replied Mahler, 'and he would certainly have meant it in all seriousness and good faith – as could be expected, with his simplicity of nature.' Then Mahler remembered how Bruckner, already very ill, had said to him on his next-to-last visit: 'So, dear friend, it's a matter of getting down to things now. I must at least get the Tenth[3] finished, or I'll cut a poor figure when I appear before the Good Lord, as I soon shall, and he says to me: "Well, my boy, why did I give you so much talent, if not to sing to my honour and glory? But you've done far too little with it!"'

Mahler concert in Berlin
16 March 1896[1]

The rehearsals

To hear something conducted by Mahler is to feel that one had never really heard music played before. I was reminded on this occasion of a marvellous visual experience that I have sometimes had. When gazing up into the foliage and branches of a tree at sunset, I have suddenly perceived all the separate, transparent details of blossom and branch, down to the last leaf, in what usually appeared to be a wide-spreading, undifferentiated green covering. In like manner, every note, voice and rhythm of Mahler's infinitely rich and complex work became totally transparent and clear to me.[2]

I have always envied every single player his part in Mahler's symphonies. And they play this music with such enthusiasm and warmth that it is easy to see how they love their task, and are gripped and carried away by it.

How indescribably rich and pulsating with rhythmic vitality are the parts as they sing and ring out in his music! Again and again I noticed how he will allow not even the tiniest detail to get lost.

When he stands at the conductor's desk, he inspires the players with redoubled energy. They readily respond to his incredible demands, so fascinated are they and so much under the spell of his spiritual power [Geistesgewalt].

For sheer intensity, there is nothing to match his rehearsals. Naturally, not the slightest error escapes him. If even the most inconspicuous note is a shade off-pitch or late, he becomes wildly impatient, even furious. Relentlessly, he has the passage repeated until it is perfect: first by the offender alone, then by individual section – strings, wind, percussion – and finally by the whole orchestra.

I was fortunate that the complete programme was rehearsed on both days. Between the First Symphony and the first movement of the Second came the *Lieder eines fahrenden Gesellen*. (Mahler had arranged these with orchestral accompaniment especially for this concert.)[3]

The content of all these works is, in the main, profoundly tragic. Mahler himself said that anyone hearing them would be totally shattered. 'I'm not happy about it, for the aim of art, as I see it, must always be the ultimate liberation from and transcendence of sorrow. Admittedly this aim is achieved in my First, but, in fact, the victory is won only with the death of my struggling Titan. Every time he raises his head above the surging waves of life – and the conquering, transcendent motif accompanies him – he is struck down again by the blows of Fate.'

Mahler stopped the rehearsal at one point because a soft passage seemed too unclear to him. 'You must emphasize the entry somewhat, so that the listener's attention is caught, as if you were saying: "Look out, here I come!" Then you can immediately get softer again.'

He asked me, referring to his songs and other compositions with words, 'Have you noticed that, with me, the melody always grows out of the words? The words, so to speak, generate the melody – never vice versa. It is the same with Beethoven and Wagner. And this is the only way to achieve an indissoluble unity of word and note. The opposite process, by which some words or other have to fit arbitrarily to a melody, is the conventional relationship, but not an organic fusion of both elements.'

The concert

The sale of tickets for the concert was very poor indeed; I believe that takings at the box-office amounted to only 48 marks, whereas the performance cost Mahler thousands.

Mahler was not over-anxious before the concert. Everything went splendidly except for a false entry of the horns, which he soon had under control again. The reception by the audience, which half filled the Philharmonic Hall,[4] was a fairly warm and approving one, except for some hardly noticeable attempts at hissing after the first movement of the Second and the 'Bruder Martin'[5] movement of the First. In fact, one of the *Lieder* was even called for again, but Mahler did not respond. He was hurt by what seemed to him a rather cool reaction on the part of the public. Whatever people said to him, he only shook his head and repeated with intense sadness: 'No, they didn't understand it.'

Fortunately, there was at least one person present – apart from those of us who were closest to him – who understood Mahler and realized precisely what he had achieved. This was Artur Nikisch. On his way home from Moscow, he had stopped off in Berlin solely in order to attend this concert. He seemed sincerely and deeply moved by Mahler's work, and promised him to perform at least three movements of the Second during the coming winter season.[6]

Concern for the future

Together, we paid business calls on the concert-manager Wolff,[7] and an agent whom Mahler had commissioned to negotiate a post for him with the Court Theatre in Schwerin. Here, however, he heard news which depressed him intensely: they would be glad to have him if he were not a Jew. The manager of the Vienna Court Opera, too, had recently telegraphed, in answer to an inquiry, that there was no possibility of an appointment.

Mahler would have given anything to get to Vienna! In this depressed mood, everything looked even blacker to him than it really was. 'God! I could endure anything,' he told me 'if only the future of my works seemed assured. But after yesterday's experience it seems more hopeless than ever. I shall soon have spent everything I have on these expensive performances. And then it will be all over with my symphonies, for nobody else will perform them for me!'*

Easter visit to Hamburg
April 1896

'*What the flowers tell me*'

A short time ago, Mahler had been busy completing the more-or-less finished portion of his Third, and copying it out. While I was there, he was working at the movement 'Was mir die Blumen erzählen'.[1]

'You can't imagine how it will sound! It is the most carefree thing that I have ever written – as carefree as only flowers are. It all sways and waves in the air, as light and graceful as can be, like the flowers bending on their stems in the wind. Today, I noticed to my amazement that the double basses play only *pizzicato* – they don't have a single bowed note; and the powerful lower percussion instruments are not used at all. The violins – again including a solo instrument – have, on the contrary, the most supple, ethereal and graceful figures. (In copying the vast quantity of notes involved, I recently strained my hand again – because, as I've noticed, the only way I can write the innumerable sextuplets is by putting them down on paper as fast as possible, that is, in their proper note-value and speed. This happens quite unintentionally and unconsciously.) As you might imagine, the mood doesn't remain one of innocent, flower-like serenity, but suddenly becomes serious and oppressive. A stormy wind blows across the meadow and shakes the leaves and blossoms, which groan and whimper on their stems, as if imploring release into a higher realm.'

This is the movement that Mahler composed last summer directly after his arrival at Steinbach. On the very first afternoon, as he was gazing out of his summer-house that nestles amidst grass and flowers in the meadow, the music came to him. He sketched it quickly, completing the draft at one sitting.

'Anybody who doesn't actually know the place' said Mahler

'will practically be able to visualise it from the music, so
is its charm, as if made just to provide the inspiration for a piece
such as this.'

Uncanny visions

He confessed to me that, while writing this piece, he was struck
with the most uncanny sense of awe – far more so than if
working on a tragic subject, against which he could arm and
defend himself with both seriousness and humour. For here he
no longer contemplates the world from the point of view of
struggling and suffering Man, as he still did in the First and
Second Symphonies. Being transported into the world's inmost
being, he must now inevitably feel all the awe inspired by it, and
by God.

In his youth, he had had a similar experience with a seemingly
insignificant passage in *Das klagende Lied*. He could never get
through it without being profoundly shaken and overcome by
intense excitement. Whenever he reached it, he always had a
vision of himself emerging out of the wall in a dark corner of the
room. He felt such intense physical pain, when this 'double'
[Doppelgänger] tried to force its way through the wall, that he
could not go on with his work and had to rush from the room –
until one morning, while working on this same passage, he
collapsed in a nervous fever. (Admittedly, he had been working
for weeks under the utmost pressure, and at the same time had
undermined his strong constitution by a strictly vegetarian diet.)[2]

He had had another similar experience when he was working
on the funeral march in the first movement of his Second. He
saw himself lying dead on a bier under heaps of wreaths and
flowers (which had been brought to his room following the
performance of the *Pintos*). Frau Weber had quickly had to
remove all the flowers from his sight.[3]

No one can have any idea of the agonies of creation (together
with the ecstatic joys which come more in anticipation and as
an aftermath than during the creative act) who has not experienced them with him, being sensitive to every tremor of his
delicately strung soul.

Mahler said to me recently: 'Believe me, all creative work is closely linked to nervous excitement [Irritabilität]!' And the degree to which he possesses the latter quality is indescribable. I have never seen such a whirlwind succession of mood-changes in anyone else. His relationships with those nearest to him are at the mercy of this unpredictability. He can switch from the most passionate approval to the most violent disagreement without any transition whatever; and he can overwhelm you just as easily with unreasoning love as with unjust hatred.

Martyrdom

'You'll see: I shall not live to see my cause triumph! Everything I write is too strange and new to my listeners, who cannot establish contact with me. The compositions of my student days, where I still relied on inspiration from other sources, are lost or have never been performed. And what I did later, beginning with *Das klagende Lied*, is already so "Mahlerish", so distinctively and completely marked with my personal style*, that there is no longer any connection between them and the earlier works.* People have not yet accepted my language. They have no notion of what I am saying or what I mean, and so it all seems senseless and unintelligible to them. Even the musicians who play my works hardly know what I am driving at. Just lately, this dawned on me in Berlin, at the first rehearsal of the opening movement of the First Symphony. The players could not make head or tail of it at first – even I began to think that the difficulties facing me were insuperable. At that moment, I could gladly have shot myself! Something protested inside me: Why do I have to suffer all this? Why must I take this fearful martyrdom upon myself? I was overwhelmed with boundless grief, not only for myself, but for all those who were nailed to the cross before me, because they wanted to give their best to the world, and for all those who will suffer the same fate after me.'*

Steinbach am Attersee

Summer 1896[1]

The morning of 14 June dawned grey and unpromising. But, as the rain had stopped for an hour or so, I could not resist the chance of leaving my luggage on the boat and cycling the dear, long-familiar road from Weyregg to Steinbach.[2] I revelled in my freedom!

In the 'Schnützelputz-Häusel'

In Steinbach I woke up Justi and Emma long before the arrival of the early boat. Mahler was in the 'Schnützelputz-Häusel', the little summer-house named after a poem from *Des Knaben Wunderhorn*.[3] Here was his sanctuary for work,[4] where it was forbidden 'on pain of death' to visit or disturb him. From his sisters, I learned that so far everything had gone wrong in Steinbach. Mahler had left his sketches for the first movement of the Third Symphony in Hamburg, and was in despair because he could do nothing without them. Fortunately Dr Behn[5] was staying on the Baltic, not too far from Hamburg. Mahler sent him an express letter, begging him to go to Hamburg, find the papers and send them on at once. But, even so, five to six days were bound to elapse before they arrived, and the impatience and anxiety that Mahler (and all of us with him) endured during that time were indescribable. On top of everything else, the piano had not yet arrived from Vienna, so that Mahler sat in his summer-house like a grounded eagle, with pinioned wings.

Finally, the piano arrived, and soon afterwards the sketches. Mahler now worked hard at the symphony every day in the summer-house, in spite of all the unpleasantness and distractions from which, unfortunately, even his holidays were not free that year.

Certainly, the work was not going with the same impetus as

55

usual. But, even while complaining of his lack of mental freedom and freshness, Mahler would say to me: 'Who knows what purpose this may serve! Perhaps it is the ideal mood for the rigidity of the first movement. If it had gone the way I intended, I should have immediately evoked a whole summer, all sprouting and heady with life. This evidently is not how the work intends to turn out; it would probably have ruined the effect of all the following movements, and upset the balance of the whole. So we will put up with the unpleasantnesses, and entrust ourselves to the workings of a mysterious destiny and Providence – whose power I see ever more clearly in my life, the more I look back on it.'

War on the disturbers of the peace

No, Mahler is not so much 'up to his ears' in the work this year, not engrossed in it as if possessed by a divine madness.[6] This shows, too, in his greater tolerance towards the outside world. In earlier summers, he was engaged in a real life-and-death struggle with it. Anything that moved or made the slightest sound was chased away from the vicinity of the little house. We had thought out a whole system intended to keep the village children at a distance and quiet. They were not only forbidden to set foot on Mahler's meadow, or play and bathe in the lake, but they dared not so much as whisper in their houses or on the streets. We achieved this end with pleas, promises, sweets and presents of toys. If an organ-grinder or any other wandering musician came that way, we would rush out so promptly with money to move him on, that he would stop playing in the middle of a note. But even the animals, the dogs, cats, chickens and geese, couldn't enjoy life in our neighbourhood. They were driven away and penned in, or, if they refused to be quiet, they were bought and eaten. Anything to get rid of their voices! A real war was waged with the ravens, who besieged and encircled Mahler's peninsula. We offered a reward of a guilder to have their nests taken down and removed. Near the 'Schnützelputz-Häusel', one dead raven was hung as a warning to ward off the crowing flock. Such were the drastic

measures to which Mahler was forced by his need for peace –
he, who cannot bear to see a fly or a beetle unnecessarily killed,
and who detests the horrible barbarity of hunting. On the other
side of the summer-house, a hideous scarecrow was erected,
put together with a bundle of hay for a body, a broomstick
stuck through it for arms and a pumpkin for its head. It was
dressed in a swimsuit of Justi's, a coat of Emma's, and a gigantic
hat belonging to me. Truly, a sight to scare away man and beast!

But, in spite of these measures, it often happened that Mahler
sent for me to come from my violin-playing to his rescue 'as
fast as I could'. Perhaps whistling reapers had turned up in some
neighbouring meadow, or farmers, all too ready for a song or a
fight, had gathered in the garden of the inn[7] whence he could
hear their disturbing voices. So I had to muster all my cunning
and my powers of persuasion to make these disturbers of the
peace understand what we wanted of them, and to reduce them
to silence with bribes of beer, money and God knows what else.
If nothing else worked, I used to tell them that the gentleman
was not quite right in the head.

But, this summer, such incidents are much less frequent than
they used to be before he had the little summer-house.

Early works
21 June

On an evening walk, Mahler and I talked about the compositions
of his youth. He was so careless with these manuscripts that only
a few of them remain. 'The best of them' he told me 'was a
piano quartet, which I wrote at the end of my four Conservatory
years and which proved a great success. Grädener[8] kept it for
months, and he liked it so much that he performed it at
Billroth's.[9] I sent it to a competition in Russia, and somehow it
was lost.'[10]

A number of these works were never fully written out: a
piano quintet, two symphonies, a prelude to *Die Argonauten* (an
earlier work) and a prize-winning violin sonata.[11] 'In those days,
I couldn't be bothered with all that – my mind was still too rest-
less and unstable. I skipped from one draft to another, and

finished most of them merely in my head. But I knew every note of them, and could play them whenever they were wanted – until, one day, I found I'd forgotten them.

'Three movements of an A minor symphony still exist;[12] the fourth was finished, but only in my head that is, on the piano. In those days, I still composed at the piano; one should *not* do this, and later I gave it up.

'The songs I wrote at that time were inadequately worked out, as my imagination was still too wild and undisciplined. For it's the hardest of tasks, and requires the highest art and skill, to achieve something great in a small space.'

Truth and simplicity
22 June

In the afternoon, Mahler and I cycled to Unterach, and on the way spent an hour or so over coffee in the Burgau.[13] Speaking of conducting and musical interpretation, Mahler said: 'What a long time it takes, what an accumulation of experience and maturity is necessary, before one can perform things quite simply, just as they stand, without adding anything or wanting to read anything in that is not there! For additions can only detract. In my early years as a conductor, I made this mistake. My interpretations of the great masterpieces were too artificial, too contrived; I added too much of my own – even though with understanding and in the spirit of the thing. Only much later did I find my way to complete truth, simplicity and economy. Then I realized that genuine art is to be found only in what is absolutely free from artificiality.'[14]

Conversations about the Third Symphony

Although initially without his sketches, Mahler could not waste those first few days in his summer-house. So he set to music a song from *Des Knaben Wunderhorn*: 'Lob des hohen Verstandes' ['In praise of great understanding'], a priceless piece of satire on criticism. 'Here,' he said to me, 'I merely had to be careful not to spoil the poem and to convey its meaning exactly, whereas with other poems one can often add a great deal, and can deepen and widen the meaning of the text through the music.'

He also drafted the introduction to the first movement of the Third. Of this, he said: 'It has almost ceased to be music; it is hardly anything but sounds of nature. It's eerie, the way life gradually breaks through, out of soulless, petrified matter. (I might equally well have called the movement "Was mir das Felsgebirge erzählt" ["What the mountains tell me"].) And, as this life rises from stage to stage, it takes on ever more highly developed forms: flowers, beasts, man, up to the sphere of the spirits, the "angels". Once again, an atmosphere of brooding summer midday heat hangs over the introduction to this movement; not a breath stirs, all life is suspended, and the sun-drenched air trembles and vibrates.* At intervals there come the moans of the youth, of captive life struggling for release from the clutches of lifeless, rigid Nature.[15]* In the first movement, which follows the introduction, *attacca*, he finally breaks through and triumphs.

'The title "Summer marches in" no longers fits the shape of things in this introduction; "Pans Zug" ["Pan's Procession"] would possibly be better – not the procession of Dionysus! It is not in dionysian mood; on the contrary, satyrs and other such rough children of nature disport themselves in it.'[16]

On another occasion, Mahler remarked while talking about the symphony: 'Nothing came of the profound interrelation-ships between the various movements which I had originally dreamed of. Each movement stands alone, as a self-contained and independent whole: no repetitions or reminiscences.[17] Only at the end of the "animal" movement [movement 3], does there fall once more the heavy shadow of lifeless Nature, of as yet uncrystallized, inorganic matter.* But here, it represents a relapse into the lower forms of animal creation before the mighty leap towards consciousness [zum Geiste] in the highest earthly creature, Man. There is another link, between the first and last movements – which will, however, hardly be noticed by the audience. What was heavy and inert at the beginning has, at the end, advanced to the highest state of awareness: inarticulate sounds have become the most perfectly articulate.'

28 June

As I was coming from practising this afternoon, Justi ran to
meet me: 'What do you think! Gustav has finished his sketch
of the first movement!' As I stood there speechless with
astonishment, Mahler called from his room, 'Natalie, Natalie!'
and told me how, to his own great amazement, he had suddenly
found his draft complete this morning. (He had been speaking
of this work as if it would take weeks longer.) He was so
delighted about it that he could hardly contain himself for joy.
'How did it happen? How is it possible?' I asked. 'I don't know
myself – of course, I had the stones to build with, but the whole
thing must have suddenly come together like a jigsaw puzzle.
For a long time, you try in vain to put the picture together out
of the confused heaps of separate pieces. Suddenly, when a few
important pieces are grouped together, everything begins to
fall into place until – the picture is before you!

'But what I have now is merely a skeleton. All the flesh
and blood, the living content, is still to come; and that will
take a good three weeks. Still, the main outline is there and I
can face what remains for me to do with greater peace of mind
and confidence.'

Later, he repeated in his joy: 'Having such a draft finished is
like being a girl with her dowry in her pocket. I've also now
found the right title for the introduction: "Pan's Awakening",
followed by "Summer marches in". I wonder how on earth it
will turn out! It is the maddest thing I have ever written!'

Going through the order of the movements, he said: 'Five of
them are humorous; only two, the fifth and the seventh –
"What night tells me" and "What love tells me" – are deeply
serious.[18] The humour will be understood least, as I realized
from the reaction of a friend to whom I played the work. The
"Night" made an enormous impression on him, whereas he
disapproved of the subsequent "Angels" movement on the
grounds that the music was too slight after such solemnity. He
didn't understand (and, incidentally, only the fewest of the few
can grasp such a thing) how the humour here has to aim at such
heights of expression where all other means fall short.'

29 June

'The scoring is going much more smoothly than I had expected, because even in the first sketch I find that I had already thought out the instrumentation – horns or violins or percussion. So I've hardly anything to add as I work it out more fully.'

Nevertheless, he has as usual filled a pile of sketch-sheets and his pocket music notebooks with a hundred variants of a motif or a modulation, until he has found exactly what he needs and exactly how it is to fit into the whole.

'A score by Weber looked very different', said Mahler to me. 'He often wrote down practically the whole work straight away in fair copy. People reach their goals in such different ways.'

He confessed to me that, even now in the Third, he still did not quite dare give a big part to the *Flügelhorn* – an instrument which he had been fond of ever since he heard it in military bands as a small child.[19] 'I'm always afraid that it might not be available in some performance here or there. Berlioz was just as cautious and anxious about using the E flat clarinet – actually just to give an effect of vulgarity – whereas I have two E flat clarinets playing throughout this symphony. And I must have twenty fiddles too! Heavens, perhaps I'll get to feel embarrassed about it after my death – for they'll certainly never perform me in my lifetime!' he exclaimed with mock indignation.

4 July

Today, Mahler came to my little practice-house, quite exhausted and yet as if intoxicated with his work, to take me for a walk before lunch.

'It's frightening the way this movement seems to grow of its own accord more than anything else that I have done. The Second seems to me like a child in comparison. It is in every sense larger than life, and everything human shrinks into a pygmy world beside it. Real horror seizes me when I see where it is leading, the path the music must follow, and that it fell upon me to be the bearer of this gigantic work. As sometimes a personal experience will illuminate and fully bring home to one the significance of something long known, so today it came to me in a flash: Christ on the Mount of Olives, compelled to drain the cup of sorrow to the dregs – and willing it to be so. No one for whom this cup is destined can or will refuse it, but at times a deathly fear must overcome him when he thinks of what is before him. I have the same feeling when I think of this movement, in anticipation of what I shall have to suffer because of it, without even living to see it recognized and appreciated for what it is.

'Whereas I could clarify and to a certain extent "describe" in words what happens in the other movements, that is no longer possible here; you would yourself have to plunge with me into the very depths of Nature, whose roots are grasped by music at a depth that neither art nor science can otherwise reach. And I believe that no artist suffers so much from Nature's mystic power as does the musician when he is seized by her.'

'It must be terrifying,' I exclaimed 'like the Earth Spirit appearing before Faust.'[20]

'Not only the Earth Spirit, but the Universe itself, into whose infinite depths you sink, through whose eternal spaces you soar, so that earth and human destiny shrink behind you into an indiscernibly tiny point and then disappear. The greatest human questions, which I posed and attempted to answer in my Second: "Why do we exist?" and "Will we continue to exist in an after-life?" – these questions can no longer concern me here. For what can they signify in the totality of things, in which *everything* lives; will and *must* live? Can a spirit that has dwelt upon the eternal creation-thoughts of the deity in such a symphony as this, die? No, one grows confident that everything is eternally and unalterably born for the good [ewig und unvergänglich wohlgeboren]. Even human sorrow and distress has no place here any more. The most sublime cheerfulness prevails, an eternally radiant day – for gods, to be sure, and not men, for whom it is the great and terrible Unknown, something eternally ungraspable.

'Such regions does this work inhabit. You can imagine that

its external dimensions too are vast. To my real horror, I discovered only today that this first movement will last for half an hour, perhaps longer. What will they say to that? Not a hair of my head will be left unscathed! But I can justify myself. Because of its manifold variety, this work, in spite of its duration of two hours, is short – even concise in the extreme. I shall style the first movement "Part 1", and will then have a long pause. But I now want to call the whole thing "Pan, Symphonische Dichtungen" ["Pan, Symphonic Poems"].[21]

'Only I will be able to conduct it; I can't imagine anyone else ever being able to do it. If only a few people can hear me conduct it, and understand it. I am almost afraid that even the faithful and initiated few will find it too much for them – this movement is so difficult, so incomprehensibly vast, and developed in a polyphonic style that is new even to me. Whoever fails to comprehend it in terms of the Grand Manner [im grössten Stile] will be like a dwarf faced with a mountain giant; at best, he will see details, but never grasp the whole.

'And people will be sure to say: "What a nerve, to think he can palm this off on us! He must have deliberately set out to offer us something still more extravagant than he had in the Second!" If they only knew how little it is a matter of audacity on my part! On the contrary, I am driven to it against my will; I am anything but happy at having to tread this path, because the work unconditionally demands it. After the seriousness and weightiness of the Second, I wanted to relax with this work – and now look how it's grown! It sweeps me along irresistibly. It's as if the creative surge were breaking through in remorseless spate after being dammed up for so many years. There's no escaping it!

'It's frightening that, along with the content, the means of expression have also had to expand again. I need five trumpets, ten horns and six clarinets;[22] I have never come across such things, and nowhere will I be permitted them willingly. The choice is before me: I can adapt my scoring for an orchestra which is inadequate and obsolete for my music (as Beethoven naïvely did with his Ninth; for the orchestra of his day was totally insufficient for it – it was cramped and restricted until someone suitably competent came to loosen its bonds, as I did, much to its advantage, in my performance a year ago).[23] On the other hand, I can simply use what I need – and run the double risk of being attacked everywhere because of my immoderate requirements, and of not being performed at all.

'It all tumbles forward madly in the first movement, like the gales from the south [der Südsturm] that have been sweeping over us here recently. (Such a wind, I'm sure, is the source of all fertility, blowing as it does from the far-off warm and abundant lands – not like those easterlies courted by us folk!) It rushes upon us in a march tempo that carries all before it; nearer and nearer, louder and louder, swelling like an avalanche, until you are overwhelmed by the great roaring and rejoicing of it all. Meanwhile, there come mystical presentiments – "O Mensch, gib acht" ["O Man, take heed!"] (from the "Night")[24] – as infinitely strange, mysterious interludes of repose.

'After this first movement – an enormous undertaking for which I don't think I should have had the courage, had the rest not already been completed – the others follow on a quite different plane. They are as infinite in their variety as the world itself, reaching their final culmination, their liberating resolution, in the "Love" movement.[25] And in return for this – I can see it now – all the critics will throw stones at me, and one of them (as after the First, to Marschalk)[26] will say: "This Mahler is either a genius or a crackpot!" But I am certain – a crackpot!'

5 July

We do not have lunch these days until one o'clock; for Mahler works intensively from eight till twelve, after which he has to wander around for an hour or so in order to relax and find his way back to the everyday world and to people. The intensity of his work is unparalleled, and holds him so fast in its spell that everything else ceases to concern him. I do not wonder that he is nervous and excessively irritable. He is preoccupied with his work all the time, not just during the four hours in the summer-house. You can see this when you're walking or cycling with

3. Mahler's dedicatory inscription on some early sketches of the Third Symphony which he gave to Natalie Bauer-Lechner in July 1896 (see p. 67)

4. Two pages, with evidence of her corrections and alterations, of Natalie Bauer-Lechner's letter of 16 November 1900 to Ludwig Karpath (see Appendix II)

5. *Mahler's villa on the Wörther See*

him. He's constantly losing himself in his thoughts, or else he lingers behind and pulls out his manuscript notebook to jot something down – only you mustn't notice this, or he becomes furious!

Today, when Mahler came up from the summer-house, he said to me: 'I must have a few days' break from my work so I can approach it freshly and with a clear eye – like the painter who stands back from his handiwork to survey it from a distance and correct it afterwards. I don't know what it's like any more, and nothing about it seems right to me. So I'll merely finish the orchestral rough draft now and then go to Ischl[27] for a few days before I start working out the details.'

6 July

At last, today, the weather has begun to clear up; for eight or ten days it has been as frightful as it can only be in the Salz-kammergut.

I have been fiddling away on my own, in my practice-house, almost the whole day. For when you live in the same house with Mahler, you often feel the need to recover from the constant inner and outer excitement and tension that surrounds him and everybody with him. It's like being on a boat that is ceaselessly rocked and tossed to and fro on the waves. You have to get away from it, to find your feet and yourself again.

10 July

When I was cycling to Unterach with Mahler this afternoon, he said: 'It's a strange thing: the passages that I jot down rapidly, provisionally, just so that I can get on with the work – passages that I expect to cut later or to change completely – these are the ones that eventually turn out best of all. They're so important and essential that I can neither add nor subtract a single note without spoiling them.

'Something even stranger has happened with one passage that I just could not get right, and that has been worrying me for days. Suddenly, this morning while I was still asleep, a voice called to me: "Why don't you bring the horns in three bars later?" It was either Beethoven or Wagner speaking, for I usually spend my nights with them – not such bad company! Anyway, this was such a simple and marvellous solution to the difficulty that I could scarcely believe my eyes!'

25 July[28]

Mahler was in high spirits when he came from his summer-house, because he's finally seeing daylight in his work. 'It's like the enormous stretch that a swimmer has to cover to get to the opposite shore.' (He and I had swum across the Attersee together, the previous summer.) 'At first, the goal isn't even in sight; water everywhere, and seemingly no end to it. And even halfway across, how distant and unattainable the goal still seems! But finally it comes nearer and nearer; suddenly, the waves are smaller and in a couple of strokes you are there.'

27 July

Only another sixteen bars to go, and Mahler will have finished!

Chatting about it, he said: 'Now I see that without my having planned it, this movement – just like the whole work – has the same scaffolding, the same basic groundplan that you'll find in the works of Mozart and, on a grander scale, of Beethoven. Old Haydn was really its originator. Its laws must indeed be profound and eternal; for Beethoven obeyed them, and they're confirmed once more in my own work. Adagio, Rondo, Minuet, Allegro – and within these forms the traditional plan, the familiar phrase structure. The only difference is that, in my works, the sequence of the movements is not the same, and the variety and complexity within the movements is greater.'

28 July

What a joy and relief: Mahler's Third is finished!

When I came back from my morning ride and my hour in Attersee,[29] Mahler came to meet me. I jumped off my bicycle, and as we walked home he told me that he was happy and satisfied with the work, except for the beginning, which still did not altogether please him. (A miracle indeed! For up until now, he has always been wretchedly unhappy on the longed-for day of a work's completion, because he was never satisfied with it. Even less could he bear to lose the constant companionship of something that had filled his life with meaning for so long.)

At home, to my great joy and surprise, I found the sketches for this first movement[30] on my table – laid there by Mahler. They bore the following charming dedication:

On 28 July 1896, a curious thing happened: I was able to present my dear friend Natalie with the seed of a tree that, nevertheless, is now grown to full size – flourishing and blossoming in the open air with a full complement of branches, leaves and fruit.

30 July

Overcast weather; meaning that our intended trip to Berchtesgaden (to visit the Lipiners)[31] had to be held over.

However, Mahler succeeded today in revising the beginning of the first movement so that it follows logically upon the climax of that monumental introduction. 'In fact,' he said, 'I had to set about it exactly like a master-builder arranging the units of his building in the right relationship to each other. By doubling the number of opening bars (that is, by making it go at half speed in an adagio tempo) I have now given this part the necessary weight and length.'[32]

? August[33]

On our walk today, Mahler said to me: 'In the Adagio, everything is resolved into quiet "being"; the Ixion-wheel of appearances has at last been brought to a standstill. But in the fast movements, the Minuet and Allegro (and even in the Andante, according to my tempi) everything is flow, movement, "becoming". So, contrary to custom – and without knowing why, at the time – I concluded my Second and Third Symphonies with Adagios: that is, with a higher as opposed to a lower form.[34]

On instrumentation
9 July

I was discussing Mahler's instrumentation with him. 'Where I think I am ahead of other composers, both past and present,' he remarked 'is in the matter of what one might call clarity [Deutlichkeit]. I demand that everything must be heard exactly as it sounds in my inner ear. To achieve this, I exploit all available means to the utmost. Each instrument must be used only in the appropriate place, and according to its own individual qualities. Yes, I even go so far as to make the violins play on the E string for *cantabile* passages [an Gesangstellen] and moments of high flight [im höchsten schwunge], but on the G string for sorrowful and sonorous tones. When I want passionate expression, I never use the middle strings, which do not sound effective. They are much better suited to softly veiled, mysterious passages. It doesn't do, in these matters, to have preconceived ideals which simply do not correspond with reality.

'I sometimes get annoyed at having to work all this out in such minute detail – and I can't tell you how often I rack my brains, fuss and split hairs in order to get exactly what I want. Then I tell myself: if it's worthy to exist, it's worth this trouble – and at least the maw of time will not devour it quite so easily.

'When, in my earlier years, I didn't know any better and worked less carefully and skilfully – as in my First Symphony – I paid for it dearly. What came out was not what I wanted; what one heard was not nearly as transparent and perfect as it could and should have been, so that I had to re-score it later.

'The "modernist" twaddle that art can dispense with the highest artistry in every detail, is just nonsense. On the contrary, such a tremendous amount of artistic technique is needed to perfect a work of art, from its first conception to its final detailed realization, that those worthy "Naturalists" – "Impotentists" [Impotentisten] rather! – have no conception of it. And whatever is not imbued through and through with this highest artistic mastery is doomed to die even before it is born!'*

Home and childhood

In the evening, under starry skies, Mahler and I walked along the lake on the road to Weyregg. We passed a few miserable-looking peasant cottages. Near one of them, Mahler said: 'Look, I was born in just such a wretched little house; the windows didn't even have glass in them. There was a pool of water in front of the house. Nearby was the tiny village of Kalischt – nothing but a few scattered huts.[35]

'My father (whose mother had kept the family going by hawking drapery around) had, with his extraordinary energy, worked his way upwards by every possible means of making a living. At first, he had been a carter. While driving his horse and cart, he had read and studied all kinds of books – he had even learned a bit of French, which won him the mocking nickname of "coachman-scholar" ["Kutschbokgelehrten"]. Later, he was employed in different factories; and then he became a tutor in a family. Finally, he married my mother for the sake of her small property in Kalischt. She was the daughter of a soap-maker from Leddetsch. She did not love him, hardly knew him before the wedding, and would rather have married someone else whom she preferred. But her parents and my father were able to break her to his will. They belonged together like fire and water. He was all stubbornness, she gentleness itself. And had it not been for that union, neither I nor my Third Symphony would exist – that thought is always remarkable to me.'

Trials of strength

Mahler's motto is: 'Whatever you do, do it as well as you can!' – or, as he sometimes puts it: 'Everywhere and always, my motto is "Hic Rhodus, hic salta!"'[36]

He proved that he meant it last winter, when, besides his many other professional activities, he took on the burden (if admittedly a welcome one) of conducting the Bülow concerts.[37] Then, just when he was working hardest, there came the performance of the first three movements of his Second Symphony in Berlin, which kept him busy checking parts and attending to a host of other details. At the same time Pollini[38] was maliciously making him conduct opera every evening. On top of all this, Mahler was preparing Beethoven's Ninth Symphony in Hamburg for the last subscription concert! In order to conduct the rehearsals for his symphony, he regularly travelled all night to Berlin *after* the opera, rehearsed for several hours in the morning with the Philharmonic, and then travelled back to Hamburg in time for the evening performance.

Mahler could well have broken his neck as a result of this frenzied chasing about, in the course of which he conducted the Ninth from a particularly high podium. In order to have a better view of the greatly enlarged orchestra, he had in fact ordered a special and unusually high conductor's platform to be built. But the carpenter did not finish it until the day of the performance, and Mahler, in a mad rush as always, was not able to inspect it in advance. So, on the evening of the concert, he approached it for the first time – and saw, to his horror, a scaffolding that looked to be a full storey high! At the top of the steps, the height and narrowness of this wobbly trestle made him feel so violently dizzy that he thought he would crash to the floor unless he came down at once. But, summoning all his energy and all his strength – 'If I hadn't been so continually bracing myself against things lately, I don't think I could have done it' – he took a firm foothold on the narrow ledge. He remained as if rooted to the spot, the lower half of his body as immovable as a statue, throughout the Ninth. The audience, however, were so fascinated by the performance that after the first bars they became completely oblivious to the terrifying spectacle.

Mahler gave another demonstration of his energy and stamina last winter, when he conducted his Second Symphony[39] while suffering from one of his worst migraines. It had reached the stage at which he cannot remain lying down, but has to get up, even if it is the middle of the night, and run up and down incessantly to relieve the intolerable pain. That this had to happen, as if by the calculated malice of fate, just at this longed-for hour of his life when he was able to hear his work and perform it for others! Usually, in the excitement of such a moment, the pain would abate, at least for as long as the exertion lasted. This time, however, the maddening headache never left him, so that he hardly dared move. He conducted with such unparalleled outward calm that those who did not know the reason were mystified, and all those who did were filled with admiration. He could scarcely bow in response to the endless acclaim of audience, orchestra, and choir. At home, he sank down on the couch as if dead. Yet half an hour later the attack was quite over.

Today in the train from Mondsee to Salzburg,[40] Mahler said to me: 'May Heaven preserve me from ever failing to realize when my works are becoming weaker. As far as my compositions are concerned, one bad work would destroy the lot – it is otherwise for those who would spare all Sodom and Gomorrah for the sake of one just man. Far better to be carried off at the height of one's powers, with the promises of still greater and finer things to come and no limit to one's achievements in sight. A mountain whose top is veiled in clouds seems higher than even the highest peak that can be seen against a clear sky. But then Nature has set limits to the growth and power of a mind, and perhaps it is merely sentimental not to want to admit to these limits.'

Lipiner[41] and Mahler
1 August

Early in the morning, Mahler and I had set off on our bicycles from Salzburg to visit the Lipiners in Berchtesgaden. We spent an extremely stimulating and pleasant day with our friends. Lipiner spent four hours outlining the whole of his *Christus* to Mahler.

In the afternoon Lipiner, Mahler, Clementine[42] and I took the lovely walk to the Achau Pond, but were caught in a cloudburst. While Clementine and I sheltered under the roof of a coffee-bar terrace, Lipiner and Mahler stood out in the heaviest of downpours, protected only by their umbrella, absorbed in their discussion of *Christus*. Lipiner, talking incessantly, was leaning slightly towards Mahler and gesticulating animatedly, as much with his one free arm as his head and body. Mahler, meanwhile, stood still, in the attitude of one listening intently, as if rooted to the ground. Occasionally, as happens when he is deeply moved and excited by something, he would give the ground a kick and stamp like a wild boar. All this took place to the great mystification and delight of the many onlookers on the terrace. With steadily increasing curiosity, they watched the animated silhouettes of the two little figures below in the streaming rain. In the end everyone was standing up; pressing forward and staring down at them as if at two escaped lunatics! So in spite of the appalling downpour, Clementine and I thought it best to forsake our shelter, collect our two menfolk and make our way back.

Reunion in Hamburg

September/October 1896

Mahler's way of life

This time I learned more about Mahler's town and theatre life than on my earlier brief visits.

His daily schedule is more or less regularly as follows: at 7 a.m. – in spite of going to bed late – he gets up. On the way to the bathroom for a cold shower, he rings impatiently for his breakfast. A moment later, he appears already fully dressed; then he takes breakfast alone in his room. If he is feeling well, these early-morning hours are his hours with the gods – the only time, even in winter, that belongs entirely to him and his work. With his coffee and cigarette, he reads a little. (*Des Knaben Wunderhorn*, Goethe and Nietzsche occupied him at that time – though he would have nothing to do with newspapers.) After this, he turns directly to his work. When things are going well, he makes such good use of the short time till 10.30 (when he has to go into town for a rehearsal) that, during my visit, the detailed working-out of the gigantic first movement of the Third, as well as a fair copy of it, was completed.[1] Then, he dashes into town on foot – a trek of some three-quarters of an hour – to return home in the mid-afternoon.

The intervening hours are filled with rehearsals for orchestra, chorus, and soloists, in which he drives and drills his people until they achieve such things as never before. 'I can bring it off only by playing the part of an animal tamer,' he said. 'I constantly apply the lash of the sternest demands to their powers of concentration and their capacity. And I treat them very roughly indeed the moment the beast of impotence and indolence rears its ugly head!'

Very hungry and impatient, Mahler arrives home at half past two. His signal, heard from afar [from Beethoven's Eighth Symphony] –

73

Ex. 1

– heralds his arrival, calling everyone to the table, where the soup awaits.

The arrival of the post plays a great part in the day's events; for Mahler never tires of expecting what he jokingly terms 'the call to the God of the Southern Climes' ['die Berufung zum Gott der südlichen Zonen'].[2] In other words, he longs for a call from anyone to go anywhere – just as long as it's away from Hamburg. This is all too indicative of his considerable dissatisfaction with his present position.

Mahler is very fond of bringing home various unexpected guests, and would offer his hospitality a good deal more if his poor financial situation did not prevent him. He brought Brüll[3] back for lunch almost daily, when the latter was in Hamburg for the rehearsals of his operas. Later, after I had left, he did the same with Goldmark.[4]

After lunch, Mahler's short nap is usually interrupted by the visits of other musicians – opera composers, librettists, singers and so on. Then he goes, almost daily, to see the copyist Weidik.[5] I usually accompanied him on these visits, after which we would continue with our walks – further into the outskirts of Hamburg, if Mahler did not have to conduct that evening, otherwise just around the neighbourhood for half an hour or so. On these occasions, whatever happened to be preoccupying Mahler and his companion of the moment would be thrashed out in conversation – anything between eternity and yesterday, from the infinite to the most mundanely finite, whatever was in the air.

At six o'clock, if he had a performance to conduct, Mahler would go to the opera. He would often come home profoundly depressed – nobody was doing good work, nor were they even capable of doing so. 'It's an Augean stable which Hercules himself wouldn't be able to clean out!' But if he had a free evening, we would spend it at home, chatting or playing; sometimes moping, sometimes making merry.

Clarity of line

After a performance of *Carmen*, which I have now heard three times in Hamburg, I told Mahler that I felt one should not hear this work of genius too often – or one might become tired of it, as of a too highly spiced dish. 'That will never happen,' he replied 'because of the wonderful orchestration. This is one of the most meticulously worked-out scores that you can possibly imagine. It always gives me the greatest pleasure. When I am conducting, I observe and analyse all its little details; I am constantly learning something new from it, finding out how this or that effect is turned to the best advantage.'[6]

In this connection, he said: 'The most important thing in composition is clarity of line [der reine Satz] – that is, every voice should be an independent melody, just as in the vocal quartet, which should set the standard here. In the string ensemble, the texture is transparent enough in its own right. This becomes less and less true as the orchestra grows bigger, but the need for a similar clarity must remain. Just as the plant's most perfect forms, the flower and the thousand branches of the tree, are developed from the pattern of the simple leaf[7] – just as the human head is nothing but a vertebra – so must the laws of pure vocal polyphony [der reinen Führung des Vokalsatzes] be observed even in the most complex orchestral texture.

'In my work, the bassoon, the bass tuba, even the kettle-drum must be tuneful! And this has always been true for all genuine artists, especially Richard Wagner. Unfortunately, because of the imperfections of the natural instruments, earlier composers often had to resort to makeshift devices which led to sloppiness in the part-writing, even where it could have been avoided.'

The first movement of the Third Symphony

Finally, one evening, the longed-for opportunity came: Mahler was able to play the first movement of his Third Symphony for me. In spite of all that I had heard him say about it while he was working on it last summer – and in spite of having heard Walter play some of it in Steinbach[8] – it struck me as something totally unexpected, almost inconceivable. Mahler was quite beside himself, completely carried away by it.

Trying, as he does, to interpret his creations after the event, he hits on all sorts of programmatic explanations. This time he told me: 'It is Zeus destroying Kronos, the higher form overcoming the lower. More and more, I see how the Greeks' vast conception of nature underlies it.'

Later, when Mahler's thoughts were roving farther afield to the creative impulse in general, he said, 'A magnificent symbol of the creator is Jacob, wrestling with God until He blesses him. If the Jews had been responsible for nothing but this image, they would still inevitably have grown to be a formidable people – God similarly withholds His blessing from me. I can only extort it from Him in my terrible struggles to bring my works into being.'

The printing of the Second Symphony

One of the chief successes of my visit to Hamburg this year was that, through using my powers of persuasion on a few of Mahler's patrons and admirers there, I got the score of his Second Symphony printed.[9] One day, we had been invited to Berkhan's[10] for lunch, but Mahler had been unable to come because of an attack of migraine. Enlivened by the champagne we had been drinking, I began to paint for Berkhan a vivid picture of Mahler's troubles with his unpublished works. I told how he would always drag the heavy trunk of manuscripts around with him on his summer holidays, never daring to let it out of his sight; how he never went off for a day's excursion without worrying about the dangers of fire, flood, or theft, and, above all, how difficult it was for him to circulate his works and get them performed because he did not have multiple copies to send out. Berkhan was so impressed by all this that, in his great magnanimity, he not only promised to pay for the major part of the printing costs, but also undertook to find a donor for the remaining sum. Some time after this, he came to Mahler's house in person, to announce solemnly, joyfully, and yet with all the modesty becoming such a genuinely open-hearted person, that the printing of the C minor Symphony was, happily, to be undertaken.

Mahler was beside himself with joy, knowing that at least this 'favourite child' was in safekeeping and preserved from destruction. Furthermore, Behn and Berkhan offered the kind assurance that if the Third Symphony did not find a publisher by next year they would be responsible for printing that as well.[11]

Trial concert in Munich
24 March 1897

The two concerts[1] which Mahler now conducted with the Kaim orchestra in Munich gave him a great deal more pleasure than his successes in Moscow.[2] The Kaim players were a group of young musicians whom he won over from the start and who followed him through thick and thin. They responded to his every suggestion and, after a few (admittedly very intensive) rehearsals under his leadership, they were able to fulfil all his demands in the performance itself.

'Even here' said Mahler 'I wasn't spared the ghastly abuses or rather, imperfections that I have never yet failed to find in any orchestra. You see, people just can't observe the printed signs, and so they sin against the sacred laws of dynamics as well as against the inner rhythm that lies at the heart of any work. As soon as they see a *crescendo*, they immediately play loudly and get faster; for a *diminuendo*, they immediately play softly and hold back the tempo. In vain you may seek for the finer nuances of *mezzo-forte*, *forte*, *fortissimo*, of *piano*, *pianissimo*, *pianississimo*. Much less do *sforzando*, *fortepiano*, or any shortening or lengthening of the notes ever register. And if you go so far as to do something that isn't in the score – as is necessary again and again when accompanying an opera singer, when they must respond to your slightest gesture – you are lost with any orchestra. But the Munich musicians grasped all this surprisingly quickly, so that it was a joy to play with them.'

The mastery with which Mahler led this orchestra after having worked with it for so short a time was recognized everywhere. Even his interpretation of Berlioz and Liszt[3] was accepted. Not so Beethoven's C minor Symphony! Since Mahler's interpretation was different from what they were used to hearing, they found it 'extremely unclassical and arbitrary'.

Mahler said irritably: 'I could have done what they wanted –

played Beethoven in their soulless and senseless way, and spared myself a lot of effort in the process. But in music at least I will maintain my standards even if my life is a struggle in other respects.'

The result of this trial concert was that Mahler was *not* offered the post.

The call to Vienna

1 May 1897[1]

All his hopes were now centred on Vienna. There, after many negotiations, vacillations, and stopgap expedients, the urgent problem of finding a conductor was still no nearer to a solution.

Ever since Mahler had left Vienna – his spiritual home as man and artist – he had been possessed by a single longing: to return there. With every change in the musical constellations of Vienna, this longing stirred in him afresh. There was nothing that he would not have attempted in order to satisfy it.

For a long time, the question of finding an opera director in Vienna had been hanging fire. Finally, this winter, the problem became acute. Besides Mottl, Schuch and others, Mahler was being halfway considered for the post.[2] For a long time things did not look too favourable for him. Then, just at the right moment, he stopped off in Vienna on his way from Munich to conduct some concerts in Budapest. Within two days his decisive and forceful personality had settled the matter in his favour. On his return from Budapest,[3] he was appointed conductor at the Vienna Opera – at first for a provisional year only.

Mahler's personality and appearance

Mahler, whose outward appearance gives so much cause for criticism, used to reply to reproaches about it: 'I can't live an aesthetic life; my personality and temperament are otherwise inclined. And if I weren't what I am, I couldn't write the symphonies that I do.'

Recently, coming to fetch me at a friend's he rushed into the house like a whirlwind. He talked brilliantly, in the most exuberant mood, and swept everyone off their feet with his high spirits and sparkling merriment. But after a short time – who knows what had come into his head! – he suddenly fell silent as the grave, sat there lost in his own thoughts, and uttered not another word until he left.

So changeable and inconsistent is he by temperament, that he is never the same for an hour at a time; and with each shift in his own view of things, he seems to see everything around him – particularly where his closest friends and relatives are concerned – in a new light. But in spite of these changes of mood his loyalty is one of his strongest characteristics. Like the indicator of a pair of scales finding the point of balance, he always returns to anyone he has once chosen and taken to his heart. In this respect one could count on him utterly.

He is extremely forgetful and absent-minded, because inwardly preoccupied and distracted. In fact, he used to be much more so. The strangest things would happen to him! The most extreme instance occurred in his youth, while drinking black coffee at a party. Without thinking, he stirred the cup with his cigarette instead of his spoon and then, imagining that he had smoke in his mouth, blew coffee across the table right into his hostess's face!

Innumerable tales of this kind are told of him. His Conservatory colleague Winkler told me that once, after a rehearsal of his piano and violin sonata, he ran out of the Musikverein – this was in winter – so lost in thought that he forgot his coat, stick and hat. In fact on the Ringstrasse he even dropped half his music! Luckily some of his colleagues were following, picked up the manuscript and returned it to him safely, along with his clothing.

Needless to say, the neatness and cleanliness of his dress leave everything to be desired. His bootstraps are always sticking up, or a bit of shoelace is hanging out. If he goes out in the morning without being looked over, he often comes back at noon with the white traces of tooth-powder or shaving-soap still on his mouth or cheeks. Sometimes he even forgets to comb his hair, and runs around all day like a Struwelpeter.[1] However, this happens only when he's travelling; at home, he washes daily from head to foot, including his hair.

Naturally, he is just as untidy in his room. When he leaves it in the morning, it looks as if the Devil had camped out there! The bed is in the most disordered state possible: bolster and bedspread on the floor, the sheet rolled up in a ball in some corner of the bed. Comb, toothbrush, towels and soap are strewn about the room or on the bed, envelopes and bits of paper in the washbasin, nightshirt and dirty linen from one end of the floor to the other.

Most characteristic of Mahler is his walk. It excites notice everywhere – even the children poke fun at it. As he stamps along, he twitches with impatience with every step he takes, like a high-stepping horse, or a blind man feeling his way. If he is engaged in lively conversation with anyone, he grabs him by the hand or by the lapels and forces him to stand where he is. Meanwhile, he himself, growing more and more excited, stamps the ground with his feet like a wild boar.

It's most extraordinary that Mahler – with his fine sense of rhythm – cannot walk two successive steps at the same pace. Instead, he changes his speed so often that it is utterly impossible for anyone to keep in step with him. Rowing in a boat is even worse, for he makes wildly irregular strokes – now in quick succession, now quite slowly. What's more, he becomes quite furious if his rowing companion – who is always to blame for everything – bumps oars with him.

Mahler, who is of less than average height, has an apparently delicate frame, being slight and lean in build. But many a more powerfully-built person might envy him his extraordinary strength and suppleness. For example, he shows great skill and stamina in athletics; he's an outstanding swimmer, cyclist and mountaineer. I have myself never seen him skate or do gymnastics. In Budapest, when Justi was quite ill, he used to carry her up three flights of stairs in her winter clothes and furs, in order to spare her the climb. And she's heavier than he is! And no giant could compare with him in his effortless control of the mightiest pianos.

It is almost impossible to judge Mahler's age from his face. One moment it seems as youthful as a boy's; the next, it's furrowed and aged far beyond his years. In the same way, his whole appearance can change from one extreme to the other within a few days, even a few hours. Sometimes he looks full in the face, sometimes strained and haggard. This all depends on the perpetual and swift transformations of his whole spiritual and physical nature. Each transformation possesses him completely, spontaneously and with utmost intensity.

When he is in good spirits, he often looks boyishly young, perhaps because he does not wear a beard. Actually, when he was a young man he had quite a luxuriant, bushy black one. He was wearing it some seventeen years ago when I first met him, and did not have it shaved off till he moved to Prague. Now that the beard's gone, there's something about his face, to a superficial eye, that reminds one of an actor's. But I hate to hear people say so. Actually, nothing could have less in common with the empty, artificial and impersonal expression of an actor than Mahler's features – so intense, so clearly reflecting his spirit and soul in their every configuration, so frank and striking. Is it possible that the outward appearance would not faithfully reflect the inner man?

In earlier years, I used to urge Mahler to let the beard grow again in some form. He protested vigorously: 'What are you thinking of? Do you imagine that I go clean-shaven out of whim or vanity? I have a very good reason for it. When I am conducting, I communicate with singers and orchestra not only through hand-movements and glances, but also through mouth and lips. I secure the notes with every expression, every tiny facial movement. I can't do that with my face hidden by a beard. It must be quite free.'

His small, brown eyes are fantastically alive and fiery. I can well believe that some poor devil of a player or a singer might be ready to sink through the ground when Mahler turns his sharp gaze upon him. Neither glasses nor pince-nez (which he wears because he's short-sighted) can in the least dim those eyes, above which rises his tremendously powerful forehead, in whose bumps and lines you can literally read his thoughts. Two blue veins run jaggedly over his temples (I call them the 'zigzag lightning veins') and herald the storm brewing within, by protruding threateningly and conspicuously when he is angry. There can be little more terrifying than Mahler's head when he's in a rage. Everything about him burns, twitches and emits sparks, while every single one of his raven-black hairs seems to stand on end separately.

I mustn't omit to mention a peculiarity in the shape of his head: the straight line from the back of his head to his neck, which reminds one of the head of an otter. Imperious is the hooked nose with its finely sensitive nostrils, and the energetic, rather wide and firm-shutting mouth that conceals a row of irregular, but sound, snow-white teeth. The delicate, rather thin lips, however, are said to betoken a lack of sensuality.

The expression of this mouth, slightly drawn down at the corner – half scornfully, half in anguish – reminds me of Beethoven. But I mustn't say so in front of Mahler as he is too modest. (He possesses an authentic plaster cast of Beethoven's features, taken during the composer's lifetime.) The dourness and severity of Mahler's mouth are, nevertheless, immediately transformed into their opposite when anything excites his good-natured and humorous laughter. You cannot imagine a more naïve, hearty, Homerically boisterous laugh than his. Often, if I hear him laughing in the next room or wherever, even without knowing why, I have to laugh aloud myself – so convincing and infectious are his salvoes of merriment.

He must have been like that even as a child. One day, when he had hurt his finger very badly and cried for hours, refusing to be comforted, his father brought him *Don Quixote* to read. Suddenly his parents heard little Gustav roaring with such loud laughter that they thought he must have gone out of his mind. They rushed to his side, only to find that the adventures of Don Quixote had so taken him out of himself that his really severe pains had quite gone.

PART II

Mahler in Vienna

The opera season, May to summer 1897

Début
11 May 1897

The chief opposition was to be feared from the orchestra. Mahler had the reputation of demanding the utmost from his players in his painstaking and detailed rehearsals, and the rumour went around that the orchestra members would revolt, and wreck the first performance for him through open defiance. But after the first rehearsal he had not only overcome all resistance, but won over the entire orchestra.

For his début, Mahler was to direct *Lohengrin*, for which he had been allowed but a single rehearsal. In this first rehearsal, he was afraid of one thing only: the address which he had been told he must deliver to the musicians. A vivid and highly animated impromptu speaker, he nevertheless had a positive horror of 'speechifying', and would not consent to do it at any price unless it was absolutely necessary. On this occasion he went about for days beforehand, racking his brains and cursing this speech. But in spite of his self-consciousness, it went quite well, he told us. With the first notes of the *Lohengrin* Prelude, every trace of nervousness had vanished. After he had gone straight through it with them once, he explained exactly what he had in mind and went through all the details from A to Z.

He subsequently said that he had never yet encountered an orchestra with such ability to grasp and to execute his musical intentions. 'I got further with them in one rehearsal than after years with the others. It's true that the acoustics of the Vienna Opera House idealize the tone in a quite unbelievable way, whereas elsewhere bad acoustic properties make it less spiritual, coarser. But the chief credit must still go to Austrian musicianship: the vitality, the warmth, and the great natural gifts which each man brings to his work.'

In spite of the inadequacy of this single rehearsal, in which, apart from the Prelude, he could go over only a few points with the chorus and practise a little with the soloists, the performance of the whole work went as if Mahler had himself breathed something of the Holy Spirit into *Lohengrin*. After the Prelude and after all other passages where the differences between this performance and others were most obvious, there broke forth spontaneously a storm of jubilant applause.

When Mahler was leaving the Opera House after the performance, by the stage door, he found that a crowd of young people (probably Conservatory students and other young musicians) had gathered there. They surrounded him, stretched out their hands to him, and greeted him with enthusiastic cheers. This made him happier than anything else – more even than the unanimously glowing reviews which appeared the next day. 'Those young people' he said 'have just had the same experience as I did at their age. Almost always, I was bitterly disillusioned in my longing to hear in live performance the works that I knew only in imagination from the score. For, as a rule so little of what is in the work is really brought out! But if you finally do hear it in all its perfections, if – better still – its effect even surpasses your idea of what it should be like, then your enthusiasm and gratitude for the one who had made this possible knows no bounds.'

An anonymous letter

(This letter, inspired by no ulterior motive, offers a real first-hand account of Mahler's début, and is thus surely entitled to a place here.)[1]

12 May 1897

Your Excellency!
Most esteemed Herr Kapellmeister!
  The following lines are written by one who has good reason to remain nameless. Perhaps in fact, he cannot answer to a name at all, since life, position, etc., often make of one what one would rather not be. At least, one cannot often speak freely, and must therefore resort to

writing – and writing anonymously, at that. I hope that you will forgive me for doing so, since the only purpose of this letter is to tell you with what joy and enthusiasm your conducting of Lohengrin *yesterday filled, not only this old musician and even older Wagnerian, but everyone who is an artist at all in the true Wagnerian sense. For twenty-one or twenty-two years, the writer of these lines has not heard a good two-thirds of this work played as it was yesterday under your baton.*

Your tempi, your nuances and accentuation – all these were 'Wagnerian' in the fullest sense of the word. The Master himself conducted in this way; that is how it used to be played under his baton – no more, alas!

To start with, the Prelude was just as slow as it should be. The chorus after Lohengrin's farewell to the swan was wonderfully tender in yesterday's performance; tender, too, was the interpretation of the passage 'Seht, seht, welch seltsam Wunder'.[2] The climax of the prayer was magnificent, the unaccompanied portion being sung with pure intonation, though yesterday's performers were a little hesitant. Then, in the second act, there was the passage 'In ferner Einsamkeit des Waldes',[3] which nearly always drags. I would also mention Lohengrin's special emphasis on the words 'O Himmel schirme sie vor Gefahren'[4] and 'Euch Helden',[5] then the Prelude to the third act, the wonderfully refined interpretation of the love-scene, and so much else besides. Nothing of this has been experienced here for years.

Your conducting is truly Wagnerian, for you know how to modify the tempo with perfect fidelity to the Master's intentions. No detail is lost, yet nothing is out of proportion within the framework of the whole. A fine example was the almost imperceptible slowing-down in the opening chorus of the third act, in the passage 'Rauschen des Festes seid nun entronnen'.[6]

Herr Kapellmeister: as a connoisseur of Wagner's art, you will certainly remember the following incident which the Master describes in his essay 'On Conducting'. Eighteen years after Weber's death, he conducted Der Freischütz *for the first time in the Dresden Court Theatre. He took the Adagio at the beginning of the overture much more slowly than his immediate predecessors had done. Then, recounts Wagner, 'a veteran of Weber's day, the old cellist Dotzauer, turned*

to me with serious mien and said: "Yes, that's how Weber took it too;
This is the first time I have heard it done correctly since then." '

*Yesterday, this writer felt just as Dotzauer felt then. Since Wagner
and Bülow, I have never experienced conducting of such significance as
yours.*

*Accept my most heartfelt gratitude, and my best wishes and
blessings on your future.*

With great respect,

An Old Musician.

Size of the orchestra

Along with the preparation of *The Flying Dutchman*, the
next work to engage Mahler's attention in Vienna was *The
Magic Flute*. In the course of the first rehearsal of the opera, a
delicate cello passage continued to sound far too loud, in spite of
his repeated exhortations. He suddenly realized, to his amazement, that he was surrounded by an orchestra large enough for
a Wagner opera. This had been customary here, year in and
year out, and the fine bloom that lies on the work had naturally
been worn away. Mahler at once sent half the orchestra home,
whereupon they applauded him and cried 'Bravo!' 'I see I am a
success!' he exclaimed laughingly. 'But don't think I am doing
this as a favour. On the contrary, I am convinced that such a big
orchestra destroys the fragrance and the magic of a work by
Mozart.'

'Der Freischütz'

The same evening, Mahler took a box for us both at a performance of *Die Meistersinger* under Hans Richter.[7] Afterwards,
he said to me, 'He conducted the first act, in which I enjoyed
him enormously, like a master; the second like a schoolmaster;
and the third act, like a master cobbler.'

'How many works,' he went on 'even the best-known ones,
are violated and ruined in performance! You should hear me
conduct Weber's *Freischütz* once; you wouldn't recognize it,
simply because I take quite different tempi – and the right ones!
For example, the second Finale is always played loud and fast,

whereas I take it quite slowly and softly; this has a magnificent effect. It should rise up like a breath to heaven, the quiet confession of personal guilt. And only then does the prayer burst in with great force: a wonderful contrast, which is otherwise quite lost. Weber has always been performed with such lack of understanding that what is heard bears about as much relation to what he intended as if the painter of a woodland scene, instead of creating an idyll full of repose and peace, were to turn it into a wild hunt or a vision of Wotan with his warlike host.

'If I become Opera Director, I shall put on a new production of *Der Freischütz*. And you'll be surprised! Not one of the soloists would retain the part he has now. In allotting a part I don't consider the voice alone, but the whole person, and if I didn't have the right people, I would engage a guest singer[8] for every part rather than leave it in the wrong hands.'

'In this connection' he continued 'there would be damned little emphasis on sets and costumes, under my direction. I would force the misguided public and its jaded taste along quite a different path. It would be a blessing if much more – in fact, practically everything – could be left to the listener's fantasy and powers of imagination. In this respect, I'd like to take Munich's Shakespeare Theatre as a model. They would really get to *hear* the thing with me, which they haven't done yet.'

Musical involvement

One evening – it was marvellous spring weather – Mahler came to pick me up for a walk in the Prater. We drove to the Sophienbrücke, and from there walked a long way down into the 'wild Prater'[9] with its magnificent meadows, ancient copses, and dreamy pastures along the bank of the Danube.

We were still excited over the *Flying Dutchman* performance of the day before.[10] I told Mahler that I thought it was quite remarkable how he had transformed soloists, chorus and orchestra almost without rehearsals, and set his personal seal upon them. 'That comes from passionate involvement,'[11] he replied 'something which I cannot imagine a real conductor being without. It drives him to bring out what he feels in a work, to extort it from his performers, even from the most clumsy or incompetent amongst the orchestra, chorus and soloists. Hence my indescribable rage when they don't do what I want, but play or sing badly and incorrectly.

'This has often, in the course of my life, prevented me from forming intimate relationships. For if a girl I liked sang a wrong or unmusical note, it was all up with my feelings for her – in fact, my love at once turned into hatred. It is true, on the other hand, that I would often be deeply attracted by a beautiful voice or other manifestation of musical talent. I remember hearing Wilt[12] once when I was a little boy (I probably couldn't even see her from my seat in the fourth gallery). I was quite beside myself and ran around for days madly in love with that voice – for it is only with love that such feelings can be compared.'

Uneven tempo

Mahler seems to have brought on a nasty complication of his angina, from which he had just recovered, by starting to rehearse *Die Walküre* too soon. Instead of the inflammation, which had barely subsided, there developed an abscess which was even worse and more painful. In this condition he had to conduct *The Magic Flute*.[13] He got up from his sickbed to do it, although he was feeling unusually miserable and exhausted. He could scarcely speak out loud and was so depressed that – contrary to his usual custom – he got up at the last possible moment. I accompanied him in the carriage to the Opera. But no sooner was he seated at his conductor's desk than I could see that he looked fresh, full of vitality, and relieved of all discomfort. As I listened, all my anxiety and agitation vanished, and I was able to follow the enchanting performance from beginning to end with unimpaired enjoyment.

On the way home, I remarked how wonderful and how different from all other performances this one had been. 'Did you notice?' he exclaimed 'right away I took the overture nearly twice as slowly as the others do. And yet, it sounds faster because you hear the quavers:

Ex. 2

Otherwise, it's quite lost and all you get to hear is:

Ex. 3

The most extraordinary thing about this is that, although Mahler has every *cantilena* and every melodic passage very *sostenuto*, never rushing like other conductors, his performances are usually shorter than theirs. (In a Wagner opera, this can sometimes make as much as half an hour's difference!) 'That' Mahler told me 'is because most conductors don't understand how to distinguish what is unimportant from what is important. They put the same emphasis on everything, instead of passing more lightly over what is less significant.'

Summer 1897

Mahler and his party (including his sisters, Justi and Emma, as well as the writer) spent the holidays in various places in the Tirol (Kitzbühel, Steinach and Gries am Brenner) and went on a walking and cycling tour of the Ridnaun Valley (near Sterzing), before finally stopping in Vahrn (South Tirol).

Deputy Director

It was in the last days of the vacation, when Mahler and I had just set off on a wonderful cycling tour into the Pustertal, that word came of his appointment as Deputy Director of the Opera. Of course, he had to rush post-haste to Vienna, via Trofaiach, where he looked up Jahn.[1] Justi and Emma stayed on in Vahrn, and I went with Mahler to Toblach.[2]

Natural sounds as the source of music

Let me recall here a conversation that I jotted down on 12 July in Ridnau.

Mahler has a very sensitive ear for all the sounds of nature, and has to listen to them whether he wants to or not – the cuckoo's call, for instance, which plays such an exuberantly cheerful role in his First Symphony, and the cries of peacocks and farmyard fowl. In Steinach am Brenner he was nearly driven mad by a cock that crowed indefatigably with the most peculiar modulations. In the same way, two years ago in Steinbach, the cawing of ravens, that could not be silenced, crept into the last movement of his Second Symphony.*

On this subject, he tells me: 'We probably derive all our basic rhythms and themes [Urrhythmen und –themen] from Nature, which offers them to us, pregnant with meaning, in every animal noise. Indeed, Man, and the artist in particular, takes all his materials and all his forms from the world around him – transforming and expanding them, of course. He may find himself in a harmonious and happy relationship with

Nature, or alternatively in painful and hostile opposition to her. He may even seek to have done with her, looking down upon her with humour and irony from a superior vantage-point – and this attitude provides the basis, in the most precise sense, for the sublime [schön-erhabenen], the sentimental, the tragic and the humorously ironic styles in art.'

The 1897–1898 season
The 'Ring' Cycle

August 1897

I arrived in Vienna early on 24 August for the series of performances beginning on the 25th. I found Mahler working full tilt at his musical tasks – and also, unfortunately, at his wretched administrative ones. He works at the Opera from nine till two, and from six till ten.

In Vienna, Mahler was usually spared artistic torments. The level of musical accomplishment, particularly in the orchestra. delighted him. 'Even so, I want much more out of them, and at close range I find masses of offending features and imperfections. These perpetual *portamenti* (*crescendi* in mid-bow)[1] of the cellos are horrible; they cannot hold *a single note* evenly! And, instead of taking *piano* as the mean, their natural dynamic [der Sprechton] is always *forte*, except when they want to achieve a special "effect" by playing *pianissimo* – no matter how violently I signal to them to desist. If a string player has a solo, he thinks it is there only so that he can play as loudly and prominently as possible. Their rhythm is sloppy, too. But I shall drive all that out of them in time!'

On the day of the *Rheingold* performance, Mahler could hardly wait for seven o'clock. He was as excited about the coming performance as a child just before Christmas. At Mahler's instigation, the work was played right through without interruption – as Wagner directed – for the first time in Vienna, so that the tension would be maintained throughout. Furthermore, under Mahler's leadership the elemental force of this poetic work, so profoundly inspired by Nature, made itself felt with unforgettable impact. Perhaps only Wagner could have done it this way! Mahler had had no orchestral rehearsals for the entire tetralogy, except for the restored passages which had previously been cut. That was why one seemed to be present at the very creation of the work. Under Mahler's hands, *Das Rheingold* seemed to come to being as stone is wakened into life by the blows of the sculptor, who impresses upon it the form of his inner vision. It was the absence of rehearsals which made this creative work, these creative gestures, so noticeable. This way, he must, in the very moment of performance, impose his musical will on the players and singers to the exclusion of all else, inspiring their playing with it. And from his expressions and gestures I can myself read what the performers have not yet managed to achieve. I can see and hear (with the inner ear) the Inaudible that twitches and throbs in the motions of Mahler's every muscle. His whole being appears dissolved into sound and rhythm. Just as the beat vibrates in every fibre of his body, the notes and words quiver on his lips. Almost constantly he anticipates the singers' and actors' words. Indeed, he almost communicates by look and gesture the very expressions and movements that he wants of them. After the performance of *Die Walküre*, Frau Sedlmair,[2] the Brünnhilde, came up to him, wanting to kiss his hands in gratitude. She confessed that she owed him her entire performance; she could read every note and every syllable from his expression.

Yet still he struggles heart and soul against imperfection. More than in the case of *Das Rheingold*, the day of the *Walküre* performance caused him much annoyance and distress. This time his dissatisfaction and anger were directed at the orchestra to some extent as well. On the evening before the performance, the leader[3] had in fact assured him that everything was much more secure in this opera than in *Das Rheingold*, which had been given so seldom. But the 'secure' sections were hardly to Mahler's liking. 'The dust of sloppiness and inaccuracy lies an inch-thick over the whole thing – much more so than in the case of *Das Rheingold*, where the rust has not yet eaten so deep!' exclaimed Mahler afterwards, in despair.

On top of this, there occurred the following incident, which throws a sidelight on the disorderly conditions prevailing in the Opera. In the last act, there is a very important timpani-roll.

Mahler gives the sign – no roll! When he looks in that direction, he finds the timpanist missing. An incompetent substitute sits in his place, and has missed the entry. When, after the performance, Mahler inquires the reason, he is told that the timpanist lives in Brunn (a suburb of Vienna), and so as not to miss the last train home had, as usual, left the Opera before the end, handing his timpani-roll over to somebody else. Mahler was so furious at this that, although it was midnight, he ordered a telegram to be sent to the offender (in the hope that he would spend a sleepless night and learn a lesson from it), commanding him to report to him in the office next morning by the first train. Then he gave him a thorough dressing-down. He also, of course, learnt on this occasion that an orchestral player of this standing had a salary of only 63 guilders a month.[4] He alone, to say nothing of a wife and child, could not possibly live in Vienna on this amount. This incident confirmed Mahler in his resolution to effect an improvement in the orchestra's pay as soon as he could, and to economize on equipment, costumes and the like, to this end.

In spite of such occasional lapses of discipline in the orchestra, and the inadequacy of many of the singers, the Prelude was on a grand and powerful scale, so profound and yet delicate in its detail, so sensitive, that it had probably never sounded as impressive and moving since Wagner. Even in the first act, there were such magnificent and overwhelming moments that Hugo Wolf, who attended all the performances, said, 'Now for the first time – as with this whole *Ring* cycle – we could hear things that nobody had heard before; things that we had given up all hope of hearing except inwardly, from the score [als in der Partitur zu sehen].'

It is sad when Mahler, instead of being pleased after an evening like this, is profoundly unhappy and depressed because he is still dissatisfied with the whole thing. 'It's a trick of Fate' he exclaimed in one of these moods 'that the greatest composers had to write their works for that pigsty, the theatre, which excludes all perfection by its very nature.'

Mahler derived most pleasure from *Siegfried*, and met with fewer obstacles. The second act, particularly the 'Forest

Murmurs', breathed the very magic of nature. It could be felt, but cannot be described. The introduction to the awakening of Brünnhilde was filled with a solemnity and grandeur not of this world; it radiated the sunshine of a truly godlike splendour. At last, the cut, that in Vienna had done such violence to that love-scene of all love-scenes, was finally restored. Mahler said to me beforehand: 'This cut was scandalous, making Brünnhilde appear to be a harlot who resists Siegfried's wooing for a moment at most before flinging her arms about his neck. The whole transition, in which she makes him understand what she is giving up, and all the intermediate stages leading up to the final climax, have simply been left out up until now!'

With the restoration of the Brünnhilde-Waltraute scene, the first act of *Götterdämmerung*, played on the following evening, gained enormously. Unfortunately, this time Mahler still had to resign himself to doing without the Norns' scene, as he had not yet secured the necessary performers; but next time he will certainly have them.[5]

Mahler's success with these performances was extraordinary. His name was repeatedly called at the end, amid thunderous applause. His 'bodyguard' of Conservatory students and other young musicians had also gathered at the stage door in ever-growing numbers. There they waited tirelessly until he came out after the performance, to greet him with renewed cheers.

'Dalibor'

On my arrival in Vienna (at the beginning of October 1897) I found Mahler deep in preparations and rehearsals for his first new production here, Smetana's *Dalibor*.[6] He has been personally responsible for everything in it, having chosen and suggested the sets, costumes and lighting – not to mention his attention to the dramatic and musical aspects. In fact, he has even reworked the final section of the opera. Instead of the incongruous ending with Dalibor's departure to his death, Mahler has now altered the final scene so that it ends where Dalibor is set free and Milada dies. He has then added about 20 bars which bring the work to a moving conclusion.

Even apart from all this, I have perhaps never seen anything more perfect on the stage in every detail of performance and conception. Whereas formerly Mahler never ceased to complain about the bad casting and the inadequacy of the performers, all were now splendidly convincing. In *Dalibor*, everyone was so marvellously and ideally cast that many an actor was simply not recognized. All the choruses were masterly. No longer did they stand stiffly and unconcernedly apart from the action, but participated fully, as an integral part of the whole.

Now, for the first time under Mahler's direction, the orchestra gave of its best without his having to struggle and rage perpetually. Mahler had accentuated and even altered many expression marks and had touched up the orchestration here and there. As Rosé observed to me recently, no other conductor, however outstanding, has ever done such perfect justice, not only to the broad outlines but also to the most delicate, finest and subtlest points of a score.

Thus, although *Dalibor* had never been able to get a footing elsewhere, Mahler not only gave it a brilliant first night, but also assured it a genuine success.

In connection with this performance, Mahler asked me: 'Do you remember the end of the second act, where Milada leaves the prisoner, and I staged it so that at the very moment when she vanishes with her torch, night falls? With the departure of the Beloved, every light goes out. The music expresses this gloriously in the violent chords that suddenly break in upon the tender, intimate melody of the love duet. When I first saw this passage in the score, I could not accept the sudden violent contrast, which went against my musical instinct. I even altered the passage to suit my feeling. However, the first time I tried it on the stage, the full significance, indeed the inevitability of this musical setting was borne in upon me. I immediately restored it, and it turned out to be the most effective thing in the whole opera. This is a striking example of the difference between dramatic and pure music [zwischen dramatischer und der reinen Musik].'

Appointment as Director

On the evening of 9 October, after *Zar und Zimmermann*,[7] I went to meet Mahler under the arcades of the Opera House. 'My appointment has gone through!' he exclaimed, as he rushed to meet me.

At the first performance after his appointment (it was *Dalibor*), the audience wanted to give Mahler an ovation. But, fighting shy of any demonstration of this kind, he made his appearance with lightning speed and had raised his baton even before he was properly in his place. Similarly, in the pause after the overture before the curtain went up, he kept his arms raised for the beat so that there was no time for continued applause. Nor did he appear on the stage at the end, in spite of repeated shouts of 'Mahler' and the frenetic applause. (In any case, he never did this after the performance of a new work.)

The newspapers at home and abroad were full of Mahler's name and praises for him. (Even the anti-Semitic papers could do nothing to him but withhold the announcement of his appointment for twenty-four hours.)

Mahler's appointment, which carried various titles with it, was not on a contractual basis, but was a lifetime office. It carried a salary of 12,000 guilders, together with a bonus of 1,000 guilders. But much more valuable to him than this high salary was a pension of 3,000 guilders payable on retirement from the post. This freed him from the financial anxieties which up till then, had always tormented him because of the uncertainty and instability of his life. What concerned him above all was the possibility of eventually being able to retire and devote himself to his own compositions.

In the meantime, his joy and satisfaction in what had been achieved and what could be achieved within the given limitations alternated constantly with the profoundest dissatisfaction and torment over his nerve-racking existence. He often exclaimed in despair: 'You'll see, I shan't be able to hold out in this ghastly state of affairs long enough to feel justified in taking up my pension. I should really like to be up and away right now. If only there were some purpose to it all. If only I could prepare a number of works flawlessly and present them as real festival performances, the way it's done in Bayreuth! (For that matter, I could put on ten times as many works as they do.) But the arrangement in our theatre is such that there must be a performance every day! I constantly encounter the most extreme laxity and deep-rooted weaknesses in the whole company with whom I have to deal. Often I have to tear down everything and build it up afresh with the greatest difficulty during the very performance itself. I have a repertoire in which the noblest works stand beside the most commonplace. The stupidity and narrow-mindedness of the performers and the audience usually confronts me like an impenetrable wall. I have to labour like Sisyphus, consuming my best energies, my very life, but without being able to look to any goal or success! The worst of it is that my thousand worries never leave me time for myself.'

When I once urged Mahler to do something about getting his symphonies performed, he rejected the idea: 'At the moment, I don't care whether my works are accepted a few years earlier or later; I am such a stranger to myself these days that I often think I'm no longer the same person.'

And yet ... a successful evening; the achievement of a masterly performance; the progress of the orchestra and the endless trouble to which the entire opera company went to satisfy him; the fact that he could work with the fullest resources he had ever had in his life, perhaps more than in any other theatre in the world; that he had to account for his decisions to practically nobody – all this would lift him above pain and disappointment once again.

Then, too, he derived pleasure from the phenomenal approval and admiration that met him on every side. In moments like these he could rejoice and marvel at his fantastic position. Once, as we were just passing the Opera House, he said: 'It's like a dream to think that I really rule there as Lord and Master!'

'The Magic Flute'

After an enchanting new rendering of *Zar und Zimmermann*, *The Magic Flute* is now being largely restaged.[8] Mahler told me that he wanted to bring out its fairy-tale quality as far as possible. For example, he intended to treat the flute aria of Tamino like the Orpheus and Arion legends,[9] with every conceivable animal wandering up to listen. And a few days later, coming from a rehearsal, he told me: 'My animals are marvellous! I have shown all the extras what they have to do. It will really be quaint and amusing. First a lion appears, followed by his mate, and they lie down affectionately beside each other. Then a tiger peeps out from behind a bush, and slinks slowly forward, ears alert. Birds come flying up; a hare lopes by, pricks up his ears (how I manage that is my secret!) and listens. Then, a giant snake slithers up, and, to top it off, a crocodile flops out of the Nile. You can imagine the naïve effect when, after all this, Tamino complains that everybody is coming except his Pamina. But the moment Papageno's piccolo sounds, the whole company takes to its heels. I hope people will understand it, and not take it as an insult to their "classical" Mozart! I am not introducing anything which isn't in the text, and I've brought the boring stage-business to life.

'The Three Boys, who always used to enter so stiffly and insipidly, are now part of the new staging as well; I have them floating through the air in a winged carriage drawn by doves. At first, one of the girls objected that it made her dizzy. As she is not a particularly good singer, I immediately took the part away from her and gave it to someone else. But she cried for so long that I felt sorry for her and gave her the part again – on condition, of course, that she took to the air. And now all three of them sail around as boldly as if in an airship!'

Mahler has also restored the text, which had been smoothed down and refined in 'salon' style, to its original bluntness and naïveté. The passage 'Kommet lass uns auf die Seite geh'n, damit wir, was sie machen, sehn!'[10] which Mahler had restored without giving it a second thought, brought volleys of laughter from singers and players in the first rehearsal. Wlassack[11] told Mahler that this was too much – it would have to go. But Mahler replied that the public, cossetted [geleckte] and misled as they all were, had better get used to simplicity and naïveté again.

The effect of *The Magic Flute*, revitalized in this way, was extraordinary. Everybody thronged to the performances of this enchanting work. The most confirmed and diehard 'Mozartians' were transported to seventh heaven by the ravishing chamber-music effect of the orchestra and the unexpected stage-effects. Uncontrollable merriment and bursts of laughter that lasted for minutes were excited by Mahler's animals, and gave him much child-like pleasure.

Some further improvements would still have to be made. For example, Mahler mentioned the Boys, whose parts he felt should be sung by real boys (not girl singers). Above all, he wanted an altogether different Queen of the Night. 'She ought to be a more than life-sized figure (as Mildenburg will be for me) – this giant Mother of the Gods, who must shelter all the characters of the play in her nocturnal lap. She must descend from the night sky in a flowing black cloak, with her hair streaming loose – she must not step out of a grotto as hitherto.'

The claque

The Opera has been thoroughly transformed, from top to bottom, by Mahler in the few months during which he has been working here. From a state of decline, it has been restored to the most flourishing health and growth. The full houses – sold out on the days when he conducts – have put an end to the deficit; in fact, there is even a respectable profit.

One of the reforms which Mahler has put through is the elimination of the claque. This noisy element has often caused the most appalling interruptions. Besides, the shameful practice has meant a burdensome expense for the singers; it could run, to a considerable figure per head each month. Mahler made everyone promise on his honour to renounce the claque from a given day. In a letter, which was also published in the newspapers, he pointed out the unworthiness of this practice, so discreditable not only to the individual artists but also to the whole Opera House. They gave their word of honour, and the new era opened without incident (a few detectives had been stationed in the fourth gallery, in case the claque decided to take its revenge by hissing). Shortly afterwards, the Raimund Theatre followed the Opera's example.[12]

'Master in his own house'

Mahler's ban on late-comers[13] elicited violent discussions pro and con in all the newspapers and society circles. Nevertheless, it established itself without the anticipated scandals and disturbances.

But, even without such regulations, Mahler has already disciplined his audience marvellously through the power of his personality, his dedicated seriousness, the severity of his whole manner and bearing, and the sovereign mastery which he reveals in every one of his achievements.

When he conducts, the behaviour of the whole audience is different. Even in the boxes, where there is no ban on late entry, the people are far more punctual. If someone comes late or leaves early in the *parterre* and Mahler notices it, he turns completely around towards the offender and pierces him with a baleful glance. And, although the theatre is three times as crowded as it used to be, everything runs with military precision.

Everybody realizes that Mahler has made himself absolute ruler of his kingdom. Even the Emperor remarked to him recently, when Mahler was being received in audience: 'It hasn't taken you long to establish yourself as master at the Opera House!' – and Prince Liechtenstein[14] is delighted with Mahler's energy and the success with which he tackles everything. 'You are really a success!' he exclaimed on Mahler's recent visit. 'All Vienna is talking about you and is full of your doings. Even the old diehards are saying, "Something's always happening at the Opera now, whether you like it or not." '

'The Flying Dutchman'
(*Performance on 4 December 1897*)

Yesterday there was a splendid new production of *The Flying Dutchman*. Mahler had already told me: 'I had not initially intended a new production, but merely wanted to improve on a few unsatisfactory aspects of the old one. But once I got started, I found that one thing after another had to be changed, and I couldn't leave off. I found I had to redistribute the parts which were shockingly cast. I had to restore the recent cuts. The sets, costumes and lighting were ghastly; I had to try to change them into something more credible and natural – at least, so far as the modest amount of time and money at my disposal permitted.' With his extraordinary talents as producer, Mahler succeeded, in no time at all, in creating the most surprising scenic effects. How ghostly was the opening of the third act! The fisher-girls arrive in a merry, festive crowd, bearing baskets full of provisions for the Dutchman's crew. The men, however, seem to have vanished without trace into their ship. In spite of the greetings of the girls and of the hearty crew of Daland's sailing ship lying opposite, they preserve an uncanny and un-broken silence. Finally, after repeated, vain attempts ('Sie trinken nicht, sie singen nicht; in ihrem Schiffe brennt kein Licht')[15] the baffled sailor-folk make merry over food and wine and break into a dance – delightfully robust and rhythmic, and played and staged so much in Mahler's style that I should have known it for his production a mile away!

The sailors' choruses were masterly, and the little part of the steersman was sung with infectious spontaneity. But what can I say about the orchestral playing? It went with the greatest verve and vitality; it had elemental power, combined with the most tender intimacy. From the Prelude onward it literally 'reeked of sea-air', as Mahler once said of this brilliant creation of Wagner's.

Unfortunately, in the second act of this splendid performance, Mahler was greatly annoyed by an incident which led to a violent quarrel with Winkelmann[16] in the interval. Winkel-mann's personal claque (including his son) suddenly interrupted with applause at a totally insignificant place, just after Erik has made his exit. 'Here I am, trying with all my might from the very first note to lead up to the first appearance of the Dutchman, and at one stroke these wretches ruin the whole thing. They break the spell for me and the audience, and it's as if I had to begin all over again. In the indescribable rage that seized me, I was almost ready to beat up Winkelmann, who allows, not to say encourages, these scandalous goings-on. I don't expect anyone has ever led him such a dance in his life!'

Beating time

Conducting, according to Mahler, should be a continual elimination of the bar [des Taktes], so that it retreats behind the melodic and rhythmic content, like the fabric of a Gobelin under the pattern of the embroidery. On the contrary, the average plodding conductor treats every bar-line as a barrier, and scans the subdivisions of each measure indiscriminately, like a bad actor stressing the metrical feet of his lines.

In Mahler's conducting, it is often impossible to distinguish what beat he is using. His baton strokes serve only to emphasize the significant melodic and rhythmic content at any one moment. Consequently, he often glides completely over the first beat of a bar, and stresses instead the second or third beat, or wherever the principal emphasis should be placed. Of course this way of giving the beat makes quite different demands on the players from the regularly beaten 'donkey-bridges' ['Takt-Eselsbrücken'] of the average conductor. 'They have to help produce the music themselves, instead of merely following someone else thoughtlessly and relying on him,' said Mahler 'and anyone whose attention wanders is lost. What makes it even harder to play under me, and what the people complain about, is that I cannot bring myself to take the same tempi time after time. I would be bored to death if I constantly had to take a work down the same monotonous beaten track. But this has a good influence on singers and players; they simply cannot afford to be slack or lazy, but must always be on the *qui vive*.'

'To him that hath shall be given'
New Year's Eve, 1897

Mahler told me the happy news that, thanks to the efforts of Guido Adler,[17] the scores of both his still unpublished symphonies (the First and the Third) as well as the piano reductions and the orchestral parts, are to be printed by Eberle in Vienna.[18]

As a result, he is at last freed from anxiety as to the storing and preservation of these works. Furthermore, there is the prospect of their becoming known and performed, where before – quite apart from anything else militating against their acceptance – Mahler possessed only two copies (that is, original and one copy) which he did not dare let out of his hands simultaneously. Having spent years in the most arduous efforts to bring this about, and having met with nothing but bitterness and disillusionment, his desire is now being realized almost without his having to raise a finger.

'It's always like that,' said Mahler. 'To him that hath, shall be given; and from him that hath not shall be taken away even that which he hath.'

In the Director's box
30 January 1898

Yesterday's performance of *Don Giovanni* – Lilli Lehmann[19] was guest singer in the part of Donna Anna – missed disaster by a hair's breadth through the illness of Donna Elvira (Mora).[20] However, in spite of a thousand difficulties, Mahler succeeded in finding a substitute for her, in the person of a former Dresden Opera singer now living in Vienna. In spite of her own reluctance, and the resistance of the conductor[21] and the other soloists, he insisted that she should step into the breach. Thus, the performance was saved.

Nina Spiegler,[22] who had sat with Justi and Mahler in the Director's box, drew me an entertaining picture afterwards of Mahler listening, suffering and agonizing throughout the performance. Not only does he start up and practically have a fit at every wrong note, but not the slightest error in staging or action escapes him. Every other minute he jumps up from his seat, rushes to the telephone connecting his box with the stage, and Nina hears him shouting to Gaul, the scene-painter: 'What on earth is that costume that Dippel[23] (Don Ottavio) is wearing? He looks like an undertaker! That is not how a Spanish grandee looks!' During the minuet in the second act, which is played by a small group of instrumentalists on stage, Mahler again rushes to the speaking-tube: 'What is that viola-player thinking of, appearing in pince-nez? Spectacles if he must, but not pince-nez!'

And he explained to Nina: 'If I let that pass, next time they'll be coming on stage in monocles for *Fidelio*!' A moment later, the bad playing of a woodwind instrument infuriated him: 'Who is the clarinettist in the stage orchestra?' On learning the name, he telephones the stage-manager: 'He is to report to me at ten o'clock tomorrow morning in the office.' In the graveyard scene, Mahler thunders down: 'Gaul! is that meant for a stone statue? It looks like cardboard, but stone? Not on your life! And its face is shockingly painted in. Don't ever let me see anything like it again!' At the beginning of the last scene, when the onset of a storm is to lead up to the thundering collapse of the banquet-hall at the end, Mahler yells through the speaking-tube: 'The lightning's in the room, not outside! Has the electrician gone crazy?' Finally, when the infernal vapours are already rising, ill-luck must have it that Reichmann,[24] wandering around in the smoke, cannot find the spot where he is to sink down out of sight. He runs into the path of the scenery which is supposed to collapse, but which the scene-shifter now dare not let crash, for fear of injuring him! A long pause ensues, during which Richter is obliged to hold on to his last note desperately and endlessly, and the entire audience is kept in amazed suspense as to what will happen next. At this point, Mahler, who is as ignorant as anyone else of the cause of delay, roars down the speaking-tube: 'Heavens above, isn't the thing ever going to come down?' – until at last there came the final crash and collapse.

Wrong tempi: the 'Eroica'

In the evening, after the theatre, Mahler played to us – a rare thing for him to do. He showed us how the tempi are distorted in all manner of works – operas, symphonies and oratorios. He gave us the most striking examples – from Mozart and Wagner, and from *Fidelio* – of how the composer is everywhere forced into the Procrustean bed of insipid interpretation. Through this

– and, even worse, through the bad performance of singers and instrumentalists – his work is distorted out of all recognition. 'The worst of it' said Mahler 'is that this sort of rendering, because it is superficial, becomes a tradition. And then, if someone comes along and fans the nearly-extinguished spark in the work to a living flame again, he is shouted down as a heretic and an innovator. That is what happened to Richard Wagner; and wherever I have appeared as conductor – except in opera, where I am accepted and accredited – I have always been covered with shame and opprobrium.'

Of the examples which he gave us, let me mention only the beginning of the last movement of the 'Eroica', 'which is always performed wrongly':

Ex. 4

Mahler sang the passage as the bad conductors perform it, and said: 'They mistake this for the theme (after the preceding stormy opening!) and consequently take it far too quickly, instead of realizing its true meaning. Beethoven is trying it out meditatively – then playfully – he is learning to walk – he gets into his stride gradually. That's why the latter part of it – like an answer – should follow rather more quickly. Above this foundation, which serves as accompaniment throughout the whole piece, the themes sing out in all their fullness – and must by no means be rushed through casually.'

Mahler then gave us a shattering performance of the second movement. It was as if the funeral procession of the hero were passing step by step before us in all its impressiveness and tragedy.

On tempo and a feeling for Nature

'You wouldn't believe how low the musical and artistic standards of these conductors are. Mostly, they are merely concerned with hammering the beat into the players. Thus they completely miss the phrasing (which is, anyway, a closed Book

of Seven Seals for them) and totally ignore the declamation.
That is why they make such dreadful mistakes with the tempi,
because they haven't a glimmering of the lively and varied
content of the music. At least, it's easier in vocal and dramatic
music, where text and plot give one something to work on in
putting together an interpretation. But in pure orchestral music,
the door is open to stupidity and ignorance – at best, to
subjectivity.

'A mere "musician" (that is, a craftsman) is not good enough,
no matter how great his mastery of technical problems, or how
sound his instinct for the beat. What is needed is a complete
and superior *human being* – one capable of thinking and feeling
as the composer thought and felt when he wrote the work.
For instance, to understand the "Pastoral" Symphony you need
a feeling for nature which – incredibly – most people lack. From
the very first movement, "Erwachen heiterer Empfindungen
bei der Ankunft auf dem Lande" ["Awakening of cheerful
feelings upon arrival in the country"], one needs to know how
naïvely[25] Beethoven meant this picture: to know what he felt
when he breathed the fresh air, saw the sun and the open sky,
and was surrounded by woods and meadows. Then the "Szene
am Bach" ["Scene at the brook"] – nobody gets this right.
Either they take it too quickly and beat four crotchets, or they
count out the twelve quavers and then the tempo becomes far
too slow. The former mistake is more usual; this is the fault of
the joke with which Beethoven closes the movement. Rain
begins to fall, and the merrymakers run for home, naturally at
a hurried tempo which Beethoven accelerates here. This mis-
leads the muddle-headed into taking the whole movement more
quickly. In effective contrast to this ending, it should all rather
glide along as peacefully as a brook, whose even and placid
flow in the accompaniment (which must be as regular as
possible) sets the pace (Mahler sings the following):

Ex. 5

'Over this even background, there now arises the most beautiful music-making imaginable. People find it too long, even boring, because, unimaginative and insensitive as they are, they don't know what to make of it. But I swear that when you hear me do it the way it's meant to be, you won't find it a single bar too long; in fact, you'll be sorry when the last note has died away.

'Even Bülow could not get near to the spirit of the "Pastoral" – and he was miles above the usual run of conductors, if only by virtue of the high intelligence with which he accounted to himself for everything he did. But that doesn't suffice, and he lacked truly genuine, spontaneous feeling, as I once discovered to my despair on hearing him conduct this very symphony. At the time, I couldn't understand it. Later, however, I suddenly realized what was wrong. One glorious day, I was out walking with a group including Bülow's wife.[26] I remarked that her husband no doubt loved Nature above all things, and was at his best when in communion with it. "Well, you know," she replied "it's an extraordinary thing, but he has no feeling for Nature and never turns to it of his own accord."

'Then I understood that such a man could not conduct the "Pastoral" Symphony (and many other works as well!).'

Dissatisfaction

'You cannot imagine how this life as Opera Director already bores me, in spite of the varied nature of the work. It may be because the whole business is child's play to me and I have the entire Court Opera dancing on my finger-tip. So I don't feel the tiniest spark of that satisfaction which I experience in such a high degree when I can really work and compose. I feel like a buyer travelling on his own business and having to negotiate other people's at the same time – only in my case the other man's business has had to become my chief concern and there's no time left for the work that the good Lord entrusted to me.

'How distasteful I find it to live in the limelight! And how people admire you and grovel before you! I should love to tell them how miserably humble I feel, and that in my position here I have no other desire than to do my duty.'

Dealings with one's superiors

It is characteristic and highly amusing to see how little say Mahler lets his 'superiors' have in his affairs, and, how summarily he deals with them.

Plappart, the Intendant,[27] ventured to raise objections to the engagement for the first time of a very expensive singer. 'I must beg you, dear Director Mahler, to consider our finances a little and not to spend too much money on this appointment.'

'Excellency,' Mahler replied 'that is not the right attitude. An Imperial institution like the Court Opera must consider it a privilege to spend money in the best possible way. I shall, incidentally, give your request due consideration.'

Prince Liechtenstein sent for Mahler because of a 'row' with the ballet conductor. In all friendliness – for he is very fond of Mahler – he wished to impress upon him that he should avoid lending colour in this way to the reputation for intolerance and impatience that had gone before him. Mahler explained to him how necessary these storms were, in the state of indiscipline, corruption and sloppiness which prevailed at the Opera House and had been eating into it more and more deeply for decades. To restore order here was possible only by exerting the greatest severity. The understanding onlooker ought, therefore, to approve of it, and welcome every 'scandal' as a healthy sign. And so in future Prince Liechtenstein had better not send for him unless at least two scandals a week had occurred at the Opera.

The Prince understood Mahler's way of doing things much better from his half-joking, half-serious answers than from any long-winded explanations. For example, once the Prince gently warned him that perhaps he needn't always beat his head against the wall. Mahler replied, 'I do beat my head against the wall, but it's the *wall* that gets the hole in it!'

'Through such images' said Mahler 'I express myself to people most clearly. That way, I get results more easily than I might do otherwise. Recently, Prince Liechtenstein wanted to recommend to me an opera by Count Zichy,[28] with whom I had that row in Budapest, and on whose account I left. I objected that you needed only to look at the man to know that he was incompetent. Besides, I knew other works of his which were wretched things. "But is it really so impossible" hazarded Liechtenstein naïvely "that even an individual such as he might suddenly write something as good as Beethoven?" Granted, nothing is impossible; but in this case it is as likely that oranges should suddenly start growing on a horse-chestnut tree!'

'Das klagende Lied'
April 1898

'If the jury of the Conservatory, on which, among others, were Brahms, Goldmark, Hanslick and Richter, had awarded me the Beethoven Prize of 600 guilders for *Das klagende Lied*, my whole life would have taken a different course. Just then, I was working on *Rübezahl*.[29] I would not have had to go to Laibach, and might thus have escaped this whole degrading career in Opera. Instead, however, Herr Herzfeld got the first prize in composition, and Rott and I went away empty-handed. Rott became depressed, went mad, and died soon after. And I was condemned for good to this hellish life in the theatre.'[30]

Homophony and polyphony
May 1898

Mahler observed today: 'In its highest form, as in its lowest, music reverts to homophony. The master of polyphony, and of polyphony alone, is Bach. The founder and creator of modern polyphony is Beethoven. Haydn and Mozart are not yet polyphonic. Wagner is really polyphonic only in *Tristan* and *Die Meistersinger*.'

When I asked him for explanation and proof of this, he replied: 'In the *Ring* (as principal example) the themes are mostly built up in chords: various figurations grow out of these. But in true polyphony the themes run side by side quite independently, each from its own source to its own particular goal and as strongly contrasted to one another as possible, so that they are heard quite separately.'

The 1898–1899 season

After a painful operation, Mahler had spent the summer of 1898 in Vahrn, South Tyrol. The persistent pain caused by his physical condition, as well as certain unpleasant personal matters, often spoiled his mood and prevented him from properly enjoying nature and his freedom.[1]

The stage hands

Mahler had had a clash with Wlassack and Intendant Plappart because he had paid the stage hands one guilder each (a total of 90 guilders) so that they need not go home for a meal during the exceptionally long rehearsals for the *Ring*. The thrifty management found this too extravagant. Wlassack thought that the opera hands were receiving a princely salary as it was: 35 florins a month, at the most 50 with unlimited working hours! Mahler made his opinion perfectly clear to the gentlemen, giving all his reasons, and thought that he had made an impression. This time the claim was allowed. But when Mahler again promised the men their bonus, as before, it was refused. In order not to break his word to them, he paid it himself. 'In any case, God knows how often I pay the smaller items out of my own pocket without saying a word. After a long rehearsal, I always treat the children, who play the dwarfs in Nibelheim,[2] to bread and sausages and a glass of beer. That costs nine guilders every time. But I don't see why I should pay the other large and quite justifiable amounts, which have been paid for many times over by full houses; and I'm not going to!

'The working conditions of the stage hands urgently need thorough investigation and regulation, that is – improvement. But all this is too much for *one* person to look after. I used not to have time to trouble myself about these worst-paid of all my employees; I scarcely know them or anything about them. Now and again I see one of them loom up before me on the stage like a warning apparition.'[3]

Mahler becomes conductor of the Philharmonic
26 September 1898

Today, to Mahler's amazement, a delegation from the Philharmonic[4] approached him with a request that he should take over the direction of the Philharmonic concerts. Mahler could not resist the temptation of conducting concerts (the greatest wish of his life!) although it is hard to imagine how he will be able to manage it in addition to all the business of the Opera House. In fact, the evening after he had accepted he almost repented his decision, fearing that he would not be able to do justice to both tasks and that the Opera would suffer. But next morning he was beginning to view the matter more confidently. After all, as he said, he is surely equal to a little work. The opportunity is particularly valuable to him because now, with the concerts, he will have complete artistic control of the orchestra.

'Das klagende Lied'

Mahler complained to me that, with the masses of work he had to get through at the Opera, he could not get *Das klagende Lied* ready for printing.[5] 'I shall have to alter a whole passage, that is restore it to its original form from which I once changed it in Hamburg. Unfortunately, in the meantime I've lost the original version! It is the part where I use two orchestras, one of them in the distance outside the hall.[6] I knew no one would ever do *that*! In order to make performance possible, I cut out the second orchestra and gave its part to the first. When I saw the passage again, however, I immediately realized that this change had been detrimental to the work, which I must now restore to its original form – whether they play it or not!'

Performing the Beethoven quartets with orchestra

Asked about his programme for the Philharmonic concerts, Mahler replied that this year he would, so to speak, simply lay his cards on the table, indicating what he considered vital and valuable and what aims he intended to pursue. But he would definitely introduce a new type of work into the orchestral repertoire and he hoped that it would remain there. The compositions themselves would be nothing less than revelations; for he denied that anyone had really heard or understood them before. He referred to the great Beethoven quartets, for which four players were utterly inadequate. It was a bold and arbitrary idea in the first place to transfer the string quartet, which was written to be played in a room, to a concert hall. How much more so in the case of Beethoven's mighty late quartets, which were no longer conceived for four pathetic little string players, but which, in their impressive dimensions, literally *cried out* for a small string orchestra. 'As typical of them all,' Mahler continued 'I propose to choose the greatest and most difficult, the C sharp minor Quartet [op. 131]. I shall have Wagner's text reprinted,[7] and thus shall prove my point that this is the only way to play these works. Of course, the players will need a new technique and interpretation, much more sensitive than that required by the most difficult symphonies. But that will be to both their and my advantage, for only in this way shall I raise them to the highest possible level. The style for this kind of work remains to be created. Not a note of the composition must be changed. At first I'd thought of adding double-basses, but I had to give up that idea – the whole structure is so inexorable and inevitable as it now stands. You'll see, the result will be beyond one's wildest dreams!'

The Norns' rope

Mahler received a letter from Cosima Wagner in which she sprang to the defence of the Norns' rope, which Mahler, after mature consideration and repeated trial, had omitted. In his reply, he explained all the reasons for his decision, and ended with the reminder that he must reserve the right to do these things in his own way, guided by his own artistic understanding and conscience.

Schönaich,[8] who was invited with me to lunch at the Mahlers' today, wanted, as a friend of the Wagners as well as from personal conviction, to put in a word for the Norns' rope. Mahler, however, cut him short. 'Please spare me any more on this subject! You will admit that I, too, know something about it; and you can also believe that I'm not unreasonably enamoured of my own ideas – on the contrary, I abandon nineteen out of twenty of them every day. But I never saw the rope scene go off well in Bayreuth; in fact the Norns manipulated the rope so awkwardly that they actually let it drop and had to get up to recover it! Surely it proves that the thing is impossible if in Bayreuth, in spite of all the study and rehearsal devoted to it, such an accident can happen!'

Mahler let his Norns practise *with* a rope until the very last rehearsal, when he took it away from them. Then they mimed the movements of throwing and catching so convincingly that no one who did not know would guess that they had no rope. Indeed, the audience argued among themselves as to whether the Norns had used a rope or not.[9]

'I'm sure of one thing,' said Mahler 'and that is that Richard Wagner would have been much more tolerant than his descendants and worshippers; he would certainly have let me have my way if he had seen that it was the lesser of two evils.'

The first Philharmonic concert
6 November 1898

Yesterday was a great occasion: Mahler's first Philharmonic concert. For his programme, he had chosen the *Coriolan* Overture, Mozart's G minor Symphony, and the 'Eroica', and performed them for the Viennese more divinely than they can ever have dreamed possible. Yet he was depressed because, although generally admiring, the critics had found fault with his interpretation of Mozart and with various details of the 'Eroica'. Hanslick,[10] though, wrote an enthusiastic *feuilleton* about him.

Mahler remarked to me that the *Coriolan* Overture is one of the richest and most concise of Beethoven's works, and one that is grossly underestimated. The five opening chords are already an overture to the overture; they contain the whole fate of Coriolanus. 'That is why they must not be, as is always done, merely rattled through like five blows of equal force. On the contrary, they must sound like this: ◁ ▷ ascent, climax, descent and then finally complete downfall in the last two chords. In Heaven's name let the beginning of the following passage not be taken daintily and gracefully! Right after the opening chords, the semiquavers[11] in the violins should not be played in bravura style; they must sound threatening, powerful.'

Mahler also said that the piece suited him as well as if he had tried to paint his own self-portrait in it.

As the concerts continued, it was generally admitted that Mahler no longer conducted 'like a galvanized frog' as one of the gentlemen of the press had been pleased to describe him. In fact, his movements were quiet and restrained. Naturally enough! – since, for the Philharmonic concerts, he has plenty of rehearsals in which he studies every detail thoroughly with the orchestra, and so needs only a minimum of indications and gestures at the concert itself. But at the Opera, especially at the beginning, he often had to take over, without any rehearsals, productions which had been neglected and which had not been worked out to his taste. In such cases, he had to direct the players and singers with different, much more violent gestures.

It must further be reported that, on the day before the first Philharmonic concert, a scandalous article on Mahler appeared in one of the newspapers. He was attacked as the 'Jew' and 'Jewish musical dictator of Vienna', who had stopped at nothing to oust Richter[12] etc. Mahler had already been told about it by the music critic of the paper, who is a great admirer of his. He informed him that it was too late to prevent the appearance of the article, which had been accepted without his knowledge. This was the last attempt by a number of members of the opera company to attack and, if possible, overthrow Mahler, whom they hated because he demanded of them the utmost in effort and skill. Yet this attack, which did not stop at denunciation and personal libel, went off without harming Mahler; indeed, it probably benefited him – but not without preparing him for annoyance and bitterness in his new relationship with the orchestra.

The fifth Philharmonic concert
15 January 1899

Yesterday was the fifth Philharmonic concert, in which Mahler performed Beethoven's F minor Quartet, op. 95, Schumann's B flat major Symphony [No. 1], and Tchaikovsky's Overture '1812'.

The concert opened with a demonstration in favour of Mahler, provoked by a few people who hissed in opposition to the applause with which, this time, he had been received. The real reason for the demonstration, however, was an anti-Semitic campaign which had recently been direct against Mahler. Lueger,[13] the Mayor, did not want the Philharmonic's yearly benefit concert for the poor of Vienna to be conducted by the 'Jew' Mahler. Naturally, the members of the Philharmonic had refused to play under anyone but the conductor of their choice. Consequently, Mahler, who had not opened his mouth throughout the whole affair and had simply taken no notice of it, was treated to the most scurrilous attacks and insults from the anti-Semitic papers – against which, in turn, other papers took his part.

With this political background, the concert went on to afford matter for 'artistic' controversy. For everyone, critics and audience alike, was strongly opposed to Mahler's performing the Beethoven quartets with string orchestra. Taking the bull by the horns, Mahler had said to Hanslick beforehand: 'Well, I'm ready for battle today! For you'll see – all the Philistines, to a man, will rise up against this treatment of the quartets, instead of having enough natural curiosity to sit back and enjoy a different kind of performance for once.'

From the very first bars, the [F minor] quartet sounded so tempestuous that one couldn't doubt that this:

Ex. 6

could not be played by 'four miserable fiddlers' ['von vier armseligen Manderln'], as Mahler put it. Then the tender cantilenas and solo parts were played so discreetly, softly, and with such magical sounds, that a single violinist could not have rendered them more beautifully. This finally refuted the opponents' fears that this important aspect of quartet-playing would suffer from the weight of numbers.

I have never heard, nor would I have thought it possible, such powerful tone without any roughness or coarseness. Mahler commented later: 'That's because I always have the leading upper voice played loudest. Bad instrumentation or performance can often obscure the line; when the middle voices are played too loudly, it sounds crude.'

Wagner and Schumann

We were discussing how incredible it was that Richard Wagner could misjudge and condemn such wonderful works as Schumann's symphonies. 'There was perhaps some excuse for him personally,' said Mahler 'since he may have been misled by a bad, incomprehensible performance. But, with the host of his blind adherents, who are still stupid enough to smile condescendingly about Schumann, Wagner's error and violent opposition have done irreparable harm.'

Plan to perform the St Matthew Passion

Mahler said today: 'I should love some time to perform the *St Matthew Passion* in Vienna, for the benefit of the Pension Institute. I'd do it with two separate orchestras, one on the right, the other on the left. Similarly, there should be two separate choirs, as well as a third, which should actually be the congregation (the audience) and which would have to be placed somewhere else. Then there's the boys' choir, which I would put high up in the organ loft, so that their voices would seem to come from heaven. You should hear the effect when question and answer are divided like this, instead of jumbled up together, as is always the case nowadays.

'Of course, I should need a bigger room than the Musikvereinssaal:[14] a vast drill-hall such as I had in Minden, near Cassell, where I performed Mendelssohn's *St Paul* with all the choirs of the neighbouring towns. It was a joy to conduct those masses of people. Instead of a light stick, I used a real cudgel of a baton.

'The secret of success with such works is the most careful and finished rehearsing with the individual choral societies from which the choirs are recruited, *before* the collective rehearsals. I did this really zealously in Cassel and achieved brilliant results.

'Something funny happened to me on one of the rehearsal days. I arrived at the station just before the train was due to leave. I leapt into the compartment. After sitting there dreaming for an hour or so I suddenly realized that I was not moving at all, but had jumped into a disconnected coach in which I could have waited till morning for Minden to come. It was too late. There was nothing left for me to do but wire them at Minden, calling off the choir practice because I had missed the train.'

Beethoven's Seventh Symphony

Mahler told me that in his performance of Beethoven's Seventh Symphony,[15] the last movement had a dionysian effect on the audience; everybody went out as if intoxicated. 'And that's the way it has to be' he said. 'But you should have heard the power that I unleashed! And yet it didn't sound out of proportion, because the melody kept the upper hand; but, in addition, every figuration, passage and ornament came through as clearly and distinctly as possible.

'But in order to achieve this, everyone must give his all – in fact, more than that: he must go a step beyond his own capacity. And I force them to do it; for each one feels that I'll immediately pounce on him and tear him to pieces if he doesn't give me what I want. This extreme concentration of all their faculties enables them to achieve the impossible.

'People say that this Seventh is not on the same level as the others. Well, of course not, if the whole thing is just allowed to go its way like water running out of a sink! Particularly in the last movement, which sparkles with wit and gaiety and infinite fancy, there are countless changes and surprises which can be brought out only by means of the most flexible and responsive conducting: now restraining, now urging forward, now lingering at leisure.'

Mahler's Second Symphony in Vienna
9 April 1899

Mahler allowed a few of his closest friends, hidden from view, to attend the rehearsals of his Second Symphony. Yesterday, the first three movements were rehearsed; today, the fourth and fifth. At first, the orchestra's reaction was uncomprehending and baffled. Then they became more and more enthralled; and with a few exceptions, they did their best to do justice to the considerable and difficult task before them. At the eleventh hour, Mahler's previously mentioned opponents had tried to wreck the performance of the Second. Once again there appeared, in an anti-Semitic newspaper, a defamatory article. This, like the previous one, was inspired by a few slander-spreading members of the orchestra.[16] As on the day before the first Philharmonic concert, they now attempted to bring about Mahler's downfall, in the hope that what they had not pulled off against the conductor of the Philharmonic they might yet achieve against the composer. But the better element in the orchestra stood by Mahler. The others, who had protested against the performance of the symphony as a work 'that had hitherto met with failure and been hissed off the platform everywhere', finally had to hold their peace.

In a week, with not more than four rehearsals, Mahler performed the miracle of completely familiarizing the orchestra with his tremendous work – a work utterly alien to them, since they had never before played any of his music.

I have already described, in connection with his Berlin concert,[17] the intense manner in which Mahler carried on rehearsals of this kind. Again, the timpanist had a difficult part to perform; on account of this, there had to be several interruptions. In particular, he could not play as fast and as loud as required. When, at the passage where the graves burst open, Mahler called for the maximum power, he protested that the drum skin would break (the same thing had happened in Berlin). Mahler retorted that he should go ahead and break it, and didn't relax his demands by a hair's breadth – with the result that in one of the rehearsals, a drum-stick did actually break in two. Likewise, the cymbal player often did not strike hard enough. Once, Mahler scolded him severely for this. Having summoned all his strength for the cymbal-clash, the player demanded 'Is that loud enough?' Mahler cried 'Still louder!' whereupon the other clashed his cymbals with shattering force, and with an expression which seemed to say: 'The Devil himself can't do better than that!' At this, Mahler shouted: 'Bravo, that's the way! And now louder still!'

The success of the symphony at Sunday's concert was beyond all our expectations. The very fact that the great hall of the Musikverein was sold out except for a few seats showed the interest which Mahler had aroused. Loud and fairly general applause followed the first movement. The second movement, which was already familiar to part of the audience from Löwe's performance of the year before,[18] made, as usual, the most general appeal. Even the Philistines beat time to it with their worthy heads, and sanctioned its 'beautiful melodies'. But the players, particularly the cellos with their wonderful melody,[19] which Mahler wanted them to play quietly, restrainedly and without 'sentimental indulgence' ['Schmachtfetzen'], could not be held in check at the performance, so irresistibly were they carried away. The Scherzo with its gruesome humour was perhaps the most difficult for people to understand. Its ending came so unexpectedly that there was deathly silence for a moment – only then did some scattered applause break out. The greatest impression was made by 'Urlicht'. The applause here was so prolonged that Mahler even condescended to repeat it – not however, because of the applause but because he had wanted the third, fourth and fifth movements played without a break, and this way he would at least preserve the continuity of the last two.

The last movement – with its fearful opening shriek, and the cries of terror and horror of all souls; the march with which their hosts throng from all sides to the Judgement Seat; then unexpected resolution and redemption: the sublime, transcendental chorus of 'Auferstehen' – all this impressed most of the public profoundly. The rest of the audience, still un-converted, in fact probably horror-struck by the work, showed their hostility on their faces; but they no longer dared, as in earlier times, to give vent to it in hissing and audible abuse.

The concert ended, therefore, with jubilant acclaim. A storm of applause called Mahler out on to the stage again and again. It pursued him into the foyer, down the staircase, and even out into the street.

Mahler was delighted with this reception of his symphony. At table afterwards – as in the preceding days after rehearsals – he was in that exalted and enthusiastically infectious mood which the re-living of his own works puts him in more surely than anything else.

To some extent, he was dragged down from this heaven by the reviews of his symphony which appeared the following day. The critics on this occasion were hardly less uncomprehending than those of the earlier Berlin performance had been. This disillusioning contact with the 'outside world', as well as his return to the plaguing affairs of the Opera, threw Mahler into a state of wretched depression. He yearned to get away from the Opera and the bustle of the city, and to recover in solitude in the mountains.

Mahler once said, apropos of his Second: 'One mistake in the C minor Symphony is the excessively sharp (hence inartistic) contrast between the Andante, with its cheerful dance rhythm, and the first movement. It is because I originally planned both movements independently, without a thought of integrating them. Otherwise, I would at least have begun the Andante with the cello song [Gesange], and only then followed that with the present beginning. But now it's too late to recast it.'[20]

Johann Strauss

During a conversation about Johann Strauss, Mahler said to me: 'I certainly don't hold a low opinion of the waltzes; I accept them for what they are, in all their uniqueness and delightful inventiveness. But you can't call them art! They have as little to do with art as has, say, the folksong "Ach, wie ist's möglich denn", no matter how moving it is. These short-breathed melodies of successive eight-bar phrases, from which nothing develops – in which, indeed, there isn't the slightest trace of any development – cannot count as "composition" in any sense of the word. Compare them, for instance, with Schubert's *Moments Musicals*, in which the treatment, the development and content of each single bar is a work of art. Strauss is a poor down-and-outer who, in spite of all his tunes and "inspirations", can't buy himself a thing with all his wealth. He's like a man who has to live by pawning his few miserable possessions, and runs through the money straight away, while another fellow always keeps small change and banknotes in his pocket, according to his needs.'

Summer 1899

8 June–29 July

The family residence that the Mahlers had booked the previous winter – at Lausa, near Lohenstein on the Enns – was found, on arrival, to be 'required by the owner', without further explanation. A new summer residence had to be sought; which was found after ten days, in Aussee.[1]

Mahler on his Third Symphony

While we were talking about the lack of understanding of the Second Symphony shown by a certain connoisseur of music, Mahler said: 'What wouldn't they say to my Third! And what abysmal nonsense they've *already* spoken and written about it, when part of it was performed in Berlin! They didn't so much as touch the outer surface of it, or grasp even its broadest outlines. To them, the whole thing must have disintegrated into mere notes, without inner or outer connection.

'And this doesn't surprise me; for, while making the corrections at present, I myself find everything so strange that, to my amazement, I have to get used to it all over again. The Scherzo in particular, the animal piece, is at once the most scurrilous and most tragic that ever was – in the way that music alone can mystically take us from one extreme to the other in the twinkling of an eye. In this piece it is as if Nature herself were pulling faces and putting out her tongue. There is such a gruesome, Panic humour in it that one is more likely to be overcome by horror than laughter.

'Like the moment of awakening after a confused dream – or rather a gentle return to consciousness of one's own reality [Sich-seiner-selbst-bewusst-werden] – there now follows the Adagio [movement 4]. I've always wondered why the theme seemed so familiar to me; today I remembered that it's from a piece I wrote during my schooldays. The first bars were exactly the same as those in "O Mensch"; its continuation was trivial – however.'

On Löwe

In a conversation about Löwe,[2] the ballad-composer, Mahler said: 'He would understand my Humoresques,[3] for in fact, he is the precursor of this form of writing. Only, he didn't achieve the utmost in it. He settled for the piano, whereas a large-scale composition that plumbs the depths of the subject, unconditionally demands the orchestra. Nor can he quite free himself from the old style; he repeats individual stanzas, whereas I have come to recognize a perpetual evolution of the song's content – in other words, through-composition [das Durchkomponieren] – as the true principle of music. In my writing, from the very first, you won't find any more repetition from strophe to strophe; for music is governed by the law of eternal evolution, eternal development – just as the world, even in one and the same spot, is always changing, eternally fresh and new. But of course this development must be progressive, or I don't give a damn for it!'

On the mountain top
22 July

Today, we walked to the Pfeiferalm.[4] Mahler was particularly delighted because we didn't meet a soul on the way. Up there, we sat for a long time on the veranda of the alpine hut. Mahler drank in the wonderful view, and, even more deeply, the profound stillness of the place. I have forgotten now what led up to the following remarks, once he had broken the silence: 'Music must always contain a yearning, a yearning for what is beyond the things of this world. Even in my childhood, music, for me, was something mysterious that lifted me above the world; but, at that time, I encumbered it with insignificant fantasies which had nothing whatsoever to do with it.'

Later, he referred to the fateful disturbances and interruptions of his work: 'With my composing these past few summers, I've been like a swimmer who tries a few strokes to convince himself that he can still swim. Or it's like testing to see whether a spring has dried up ... mine still trickles a bit, but that's all.'

Change

Mahler said: 'In earlier years, I used to like to do unusual things in my compositions. Even in outward form, I departed from the beaten track, in the way that a young man likes to dress strikingly, whereas later on one is glad enough to conform outwardly and not to excite notice. One's inner difference from other people is great enough without that! So, at present, I'm quite happy if I can somehow only pour my content into the usual formal mould, and I avoid all innovations unless they're absolutely *necessary*. Formerly, for instance, if a piece began in D major, I would make a point of concluding it in A flat minor if possible. Now, on the contrary, I often go to a great deal of trouble to end in the key in which I began.'

In this connection, he recalled that he had ended his First Symphony in D major, and had always believed that it moved towards that key, whereas in reality the principal motive [das Hauptmotiv] modulates to A major. 'Everything would have turned out differently if I had aimed at concluding in that key.'

Composing

'Composing is like playing with bricks, continually making new buildings from the same old stones. But the stones have lain there since one's youth, which is the only time for gathering and hoarding them. They are all ready and shaped for use from that time.'

The Fourth Symphony

So it is really his Fourth Symphony that has fallen into Mahler's lap at the eleventh hour! After finishing 'Revelge',[5] he had given up working because of the many interruptions. Suddenly, there were indications that he was absorbed in a new composition. Judging from all the signs, it was no small piece, but a major work. In these circumstances, the lack of peace there and the approaching end of the holidays, were more tormenting than ever to the poor man. God knows what he succeeded in salvaging in the ten-day respite remaining to him – although one is accustomed to his achieving the impossible. In spite of all obstacles, he works whenever and wherever he can. He even composes when out walking (alone, or often even with us, when he will lag behind a little) – a thing he has never done since *Das klagende Lied*. Even so, the Aussee visitors are constantly disturbing him, and he yearns for 'Häuschen'[6] and solitude as never before. Now, we often tell one another, we really understand what the divine gift of deafness meant to Beethoven – shutting out, though at the cost of infinite anguish, the whole disturbing, distracting and futile bustle of the outside world.

Changing one's mind

Mahler has played, with Rosé, Brahms's Clarinet Quintet and clarinet sonatas (adapted for piano and violin). Previously, he didn't like them; now he thinks they are glorious. 'No wonder then,' exclaimed Mahler 'that the public talks nonsense and is incapable of judging when such a thing can happen to *us*!'[7]

An amusing anecdote

That evening (it was 30 July), in the Peterbräu at St Wolfgang,[8] we were all very merry and began telling funny stories. Finally, Mahler and Justi remembered an adventure in the Budapest City Park [das Stadtwäldchen], at the Garden Café, which rises in two splendid terraces around the Kursalon,[9] and forms the meeting-place of all the elegant society of Budapest on fine days. Mahler and Justi too had gone there for tea on this occasion, and sat chatting with their backs to the balustrade of the upper terrace. Now when he is at an inn, Mahler has the habit of wiping every plate and every piece of cutlery before using it. Even here, he proceeded to swill out a glass with water before drinking from it. Absent-mindedly, he poured the contents backwards – onto the lower terrace and a few extremely elegantly dressed ladies, who started up with cries of alarm. 'E-x-c-u-s-e m-e!' cried Mahler, who as soon as the jet of water had escaped him, realized what he had done. Horror-struck, he gazed down at the devastation caused by his watery shot. But since he was Director of the Opera House and a well-known figure in the town, whose absent-mindedness was proverbial, his offence was soon forgiven and order restored. Less than five minutes later, Mahler was preparing to pour out water for Justi, who had just asked for some. Before she could do anything about it, he was rinsing a glass for her too, and, leaning once more over the luckless lower terrace, sending down a second shower! This time there was a general outcry. Everybody jumped to their feet laughing and exclaiming; a waiter who was just approaching with a laden tray had to put it down on the spot for fear of letting it fall in helpless laughter. But it was some time before Mahler and Justi were to be seen again in the City Park.

Mahler's house on the Wörther See
[Introduction]

(*extract from a letter*)   18 August 1899[10]

Justi and I, after an unsuccessful house-hunting trip by bicycle around the lake, had just arrived in Maria-Wörth[11] quite depressed. We were already on the steamer when someone called us by name. It was Mildenburg![12] No sooner had she heard the purpose of our journey than she persuaded us to disembark and go with her to Mayernigg, where we would find what we wanted. A skilful amateur architect called Theuer was recommended to us by Frau Mildenburg. He was an independent and unusually good-hearted person, and he put his knowledge and experience at our disposal, advising us not to rent but to build, which we could do easily and cheaply with his help. Mahler was sent for by telegram. We spent three days at Schwarzenfels,[13] surrounded by the kindest hospitality. Everything was discussed thoroughly, and sites were inspected and tested from the point of view of quietness. This last was no small task, and so repeatedly led to disappointment that Mahler thought he would have to leave without settling the business. Then, at the last moment, we stumbled upon the very thing: a completely isolated wooded plot for the house by the lake and, not much higher up, a piece of truly enchanted virgin forest that could provide a secluded site for Mahler's summer-house – in short, the perfect answer to his needs. The plan of the house was immediately drawn up in the most charming style, exactly according to Mahler's instructions and requirements. Now, everything depends on whether the ground is for sale; if so, building will begin at once. Theuer, who is staying here till the end of October, will see to everything and supervise the work. So, by next summer, at least Mahler's little summer-house will be built – and perhaps he can even move into the house itself!

Schwarzenfels
12 September 1899

Mahler was here for two days, and has actually signed the contract for the purchase of land for his house and summer-house. All arrangements have been made with the builder too.

I waited for Mahler in Klagenfurt,[14] where he arrived in the morning. From there, we drove in a dog-cart to Mayernigg,[15] chatting comfortably on the way. The Opera House was doing good business in spite of Kainz, the new 'star' at the Burgtheater.[16] The cast of singers has reached a strength unknown at the Opera House before. Mahler has at last secured a mezzo-soprano of his own choice in Hilgermann,[17] who is excellent in sentimental and naïve roles. As Mignon, Kurz[18] had a positively sensational success, and in her he now has just the youthful, lyric talent that he needs.

'But the best news of all' he exclaimed 'is that I've managed to get an extension of the summer holiday at the Opera, until 15 August.'

Apart from business affairs, the two days at Schwarzenfels were spent in repeated visits to Mahler's plot. Then, for next summer, he rented the Villa Antonia, which is only twenty minutes away from the site of his summer-house.

The 1899—1900 season

Torments of creation

On the evening of my arrival in Vienna, Mahler and I went
for a walk. In the course of it he told me that he could not think
of the time in Aussee without shuddering. He remembered the
tortures that he had endured in the last days there, when he
went to his work in the mornings and found it piling up sky-
high before him – fatally ordained by the first fleeting sketches
that were all that then existed of a large-scale composition.
'Shall I be able to keep hold of it and salvage it in these few
days? How long do I have before that wretched band [Kurmusik]
starts to play?' And the very thought of it excited in him such
an emotion of physical terror that he experienced a real sensation
of dizziness. Some time before this he had climbed with Justi
and Rosé up on to the 'Sattel' [lit. 'Saddle'], from where they
hoped to get to Alt-Aussee. During the descent, the other two
went ahead of him. On the steep but not particularly difficult
path he saw them apparently step off into space for a moment.
Suddenly he, who did not know what dizziness was, was seized
with such an attack of it that his senses almost left him and he
all but sank to the ground. Justi, seeing him so deathly pale,
was terribly frightened. As soon as they learned what had caused
his attack, they turned around and went home. This same
dizziness now overwhelmed him in the face of something that
he felt might be beyond his powers; in those last few days, it
became so acute that he had to stop working altogether.
'I have never yet come to grief over working out the details
of my compositions, though when I am making my first draft
my ideas often come to a standstill. This time, however, there
was such an endless and irrepressible flow of ideas that I just
didn't know what to do with them all. And then the holidays

had to end with this ghastly discord; worse still, I am left with the dread that this fearful dizziness will attack me from now on every time I try to start work. In the end I'll have my summer-house, my peace and quiet, and everything I need for my well-being – only the creative artist won't be there!'

On the 'Pastoral'

Mahler said of the 'Pastoral' Symphony: 'Only in two places does Beethoven's subjective, individuated feeling break through; otherwise, Nature alone speaks here. There are two bars in the second movement, and four in the last, where his inner emotion overflows in passionate tenderness. Towards these most personal passages, as one might call them, the whole symphony must press forward; it must be built up as a foundation for them.'[1]

On invention

On the occasion of a Philharmonic concert (19 November 1899), Mahler commented on the symphony *Aus Italien* by Strauss, which he had conducted: 'It is only in the last movement that the delightful motif of the Italian folksong[2] offers sufficient material for the composer. On the strength of this motif, which I had not known as a song, I took Strauss for a genius when I first heard the symphony. And, indeed, it is an invention of genius. Perhaps if its originator, whom I'd like to know, had seen the light of day as a German, in the land of symphonists, he would have become a great composer.

'Let no one imagine that a really significant artistic thought ever fell into anyone's lap by chance! If anything, invention is a sign of Divine Grace. If having an idea was as easy as drawing a lucky number in a lottery, you would only have to wait long enough (betting, of course!), and something quite important would turn up by chance. But all stakes are useless here; unless Heaven has given you the lucky number in your cradle, no blind chance will ever make it yours!'

The living Beethoven

Coming from a rehearsal, Mahler related: 'Today I gave the

orchestra a regular sermon on the last movement of Beethoven's Second, and they seem to have grasped my meaning. "Just look at this passage!" I told them. "Where is the 'monumental calm' ['monumentale Ruhe'] and where is the 'impetus' ['Schwung'] that you have always been used to putting into Beethoven and often at the wrong place? Here is grace and humour; there is tenderness and restrained sentiment. But now comes a moment of passion, an unparalleled *crescendo*, and the most tremendous climax; now is the moment to change your tactics, and to sweep everything before you by the intensity, the ardour and the grandeur of your playing!" '

'Die Meistersinger'
Performance on 27 November 1899

Mahler, who is putting on a new production of *Die Meistersinger*, is as delighted with it as if he were making its acquaintance for the first time in his life. 'The fear that the work might pall if you hear it too often has fortunately proved to be quite groundless. The few years during which I have not been conducting it were enough to make it mean as much to me as ever – in fact, more! I tell you, what a piece! If the whole of German art were to disappear, it could be recognized and reconstructed from this one work. It almost makes everything else seem worthless and superfluous.'

Yesterday, after three rehearsals with orchestra and three on the stage, Mahler performed *Die Meistersinger* – for the first time without any cuts whatever. All seats were sold for this performance, which began at 6.30 and ended at 11.30 (with an interval of twenty minutes after the second act); and not one of the audience came late or left before the end.

From the first moment of the Prelude, which resounded with unheard-of power and grandeur, tenderness and inwardness, yet was full of humour as well, the attention and delight of the audience never flagged. After the Prelude, they gave vent to their feelings in stormy applause – mingled, unfortunately, with the hissing and cat-calling of a number of young fellows in the gallery, who were evidently bent on an anti-Semitic demonstration. The rest of the audience retaliated with louder and repeatedly renewed applause. Thereupon, the mischief-makers whistled even louder, so that the situation threatened to deteriorate into a battle between applause and catcalls which would have destroyed the atmosphere and the mood for the whole audience. Mahler broke it up by swiftly beginning the first act, which starts with the full strength of the orchestra. But when he met with the same reception again before the third act, where he was not about to let the delicacy of the interlude be ruined, he had no defence against the commotion. For, whenever he raised his arms to quell the uproar so that the performance could resume, the storm broke out afresh in the audience. At last, he resigned himself to letting it pass over him. He sat there with head bowed, as if it all had nothing to do with him, looking as if he were quietly waiting for an unavoidable heavy rain-shower to stop pelting down on his back.

When Mahler left the Opera House one of his youngest admirers – unknown to him – rushed towards him, bent over his hand, and, before Mahler realized what he was about, kissed it.

Invention and form

Mahler was speaking of Verdi. It had taken him a long time – in fact, till he wrote his last operas – to learn to control his overflowing abundance of ideas. He had to learn not to scatter them at random and string them together just as they came, but, rather, to hold onto them, give them logical sequence, develop them, shape them and continue them. Only this makes them what they are; and here is where music really begins.

'The opposite – an over-facile wealth of invention, whose apparent excess often merely conceals the inadequacy of its creator – is peculiar to most composers of opera. Among German opera composers, it is most conspicuous in Lortzing; but even Weber was by no means free of it. How infinitely different is the depth and perfection of the music of Beethoven and Wagner!'

Isolation

'Only through temperament' said Mahler 'can any impression be made on the public. You can experience this daily in the Opera and at concerts. It's exactly the same with my musical interpretations. What they understand, apart from that, is precious little; but my temperament – that they can grasp, and that is what carries them with me.'

He commented that the conductor Rottenberg,[3] rehearsing *Don Giovanni*, did everything very clearly and conscientiously – better than anyone else. 'But, when it comes to the true, living spirit of a work that fills my soul with its brilliant clarity and living truth – I don't find a trace of that in him. And I must once and for all learn to come to terms with this. The work of art remains a book closed with Seven Seals unless, once in a blue moon, a creative artist comes along to open it.

'But how painful it is to see these works buried alive! And how terrifying, on the other hand, is the growing isolation of which one becomes increasingly conscious! One would like best to withdraw from the world altogether, for any hope of finding understanding there is vain and idle indeed. Not only am I disgusted with the Opera, but I'd even like to get rid of the concerts. In spite of everything I would not, and could not, give up my composing. But not for other people [die Welt], who will understand it least of all – I have barred the road to them too thoroughly. No! what I create, I create for myself.'

The problem of Beethoven's symphonies

Mahler, apropos of his current study of Beethoven's C minor Symphony: 'Because of the fermatas at the beginning, I'd rather not perform it. I have lost my confidence ever since they thought, in Hamburg, that I held the pauses too long.

'Every pause, I am convinced, has to be calculated in direct relation to the basic beat: either twice or four times the length of the latter.

'What Beethoven meant by introducing a whole bar before the first[4] fermata is quite unclear to me. I wonder if he could have made a notational mistake for once? But I think that is out of the question with such a man, in whom everything is light, clarity and utmost certainty. Every slightest sign that he gives is a lamp to light our way.'

Mahler said that the first movement of this symphony must be full of power and vigour, but must also communicate a feeling of tempestuous agitation. The very beginning is a wild assault; the pauses which follow are like a giant's attempts to ward it off with his fist. 'The words which Beethoven is supposed to have said about this first movement – "Fate knocks at the door" – are, in my opinion, far from exhausting its tremendous meaning. He could more fittingly have said: "Here I am!" ["Das bin Ich!"].'

Concerning the second movement, Mahler said: 'The strongest man is also always the gentlest. You can see here – as everywhere in Beethoven – that this is natural, since the intensity of the whole human being, of his deepest insight and feeling, radiates in all directions.'

He continued: 'Beethoven's First, Second and Fourth Symphonies can still be performed by modern orchestras and conductors. All the rest, however, are quite beyond their powers. Only Richard Wagner (who can incidentally be called the discoverer of all Beethoven's symphonies) and in recent times I myself have done these works justice. And even I can manage it only by terrorizing the players; by forcing each individual to transcend his little self and rise above his own powers.

'Beethoven's symphonies present a problem that is simply insoluble for the ordinary conductor. I see it more and more clearly. Unquestionably, they need re-interpretation and re-working. The very constitution and size of the orchestra necessitates it: in Beethoven's time, the whole orchestra was not as large as the string section alone today. If, consequently, the other instruments are not brought into a balanced relationship with the strings, the effect is bound to be wrong. Wagner knew that very well; but he too had to suffer the bitterest attacks because of it.'

On the occasion of Mahler's performance of the Ninth last year in Prague, Batka[5] drew his attention to the extraordinary similarity between his comments and directions to the orchestra, during rehearsals, and Wagner's remarks on the subject as noted by his contemporaries. Batka, who had collected these statements, also jotted down Mahler's observations, and showed both to him.

Mahler remarked to me on this: 'Everywhere the same aim – and usually attained in the same way. Sometimes the same goal is sought and reached from opposite directions but never contradictory ones!'

On tradition
12 November 1899

This morning, Mahler's Second Symphony was played to him in Bocklet's[6] arrangement for eight hands. Although all the performers were highly capable – they are all enthusiastic about the work, and had heard it last year under Mahler himself – the performance was painful to him, and 'took the wind out of his sails'[7] again. The tempi were wrong, and the expression and phrasing were often so incorrect that everything dissolved into chaos. 'And that was directed and rehearsed by someone who will imagine and claim that he inherits the "tradition" straight from me! From this, you may learn the truth about every so-called "tradition": there is no such thing! Everything is left to the whim of the individual, and unless a genius awakens them to life, works of art are lost.

'Now I understand perfectly why Brahms let people play his works as they pleased. He knew that anything he told them was in vain. Bitter experience and resignation are expressed in this fact.'

Mahler on his Second Symphony

Referring to this performance of his Second, Mahler said that he had noticed something today for the first time: in the Scherzo, the most beautiful passage – the quiet theme of the middle section which forms an interlude between the surging waves of the piece[8] – occurs once and never again. At first sight, this seems an incredible waste. The pleasure of exploiting the lovely fresh motif, and repeating it in a different key or variation is, indeed, one that one would not readily forego. But that would have gone against the essence of this passage, which – like the aloe – should blossom but once.

On Brahms and Beethoven
Philharmonic concert of 3 December 1899

At the Philharmonic concert today, Mahler conducted Brahms's F major Symphony [the Third], *Die Waldtaube* [*The Wood-Dove*] by Dvořák, and Beethoven's overture *The Consecration of the House*.

Mahler is delighted with the Brahms Symphony, which was wonderfully played. Its one failing, he feels, is a lack of brilliance in the instrumental setting; but this might easily be taken care of with a few changes in the scoring. 'Also I felt the greatest desire to make a few cuts here and there, but was prevented from doing so by my inner reluctance to tamper with the work of one who was so recently alive – not to mention my fear of how the critics and public would attack me!'

Mahler declares that Brahms shunned so many useful techniques and innovations in orchestration merely out of obstinacy and opposition to Wagner. In his chamber music, such devices are by no means absent, on the contrary, he shows himself a master in their use.

'A radical improvement in the tone-quality of the violin section, giving a thrilling brilliance of tone, is achieved by letting the second violins play in unison with the first in vivid and dominating passages. Nor is this effect to be accounted for merely by the increase in numbers; it must be the effect of some acoustic law that the sound-waves encountering each other from both sides produce such a lively and brilliant tone-quality.'[9]

Later, Mahler added: 'Brahms is not concerned with breaking all bonds and rising above the grief and life of this earth to soar up into the heights of other, freer and more radiant spheres. However profoundly, however intimately and idiosyncratically he handles his material, he remains imprisoned in this world and this life, and never attains the view from the summit. Therefore, his works can never, and will never, exercise the highest, ultimate influence.'

With the Beethoven overture, said Mahler, he felt himself in his element once more – like Antaeus feeling the earth under his feet again. 'Here, I am in no doubt as to what I have to do, whereas with the others I am always apprehensive, almost tentative in my efforts to realize their intentions. With Beethoven and Wagner, however, I know exactly: this is how it is and *must* be!'

The 'Pastoral' Symphony: tempo of the second movement

In the fourth Philharmonic concert,[10] Mahler performed the 'Pastoral' as it has perhaps never been played before. His slow tempo in the second movement caused general astonishment. In his review after the concert, Hirschfeld[11] reported that this tempo of Mahler's had led him to investigate the indication 'molto moto' in the score. It turned out that there was no such thing and that the term meant precisely nothing. Probably, he thought, 'moderato' had been intended and written in the original score by Beethoven; then, later, it was somehow corrupted into the meaningless expression 'molto moto'.

Even more probable, however, is the cellist Sulzer's[12] explanation. As All° is frequently written for Allegro, Beethoven may well have written Mo^to as an abbreviation for Moderato. This was then taken for 'moto' and everywhere printed accordingly. In this way the wrong tempo could have established itself for half a century.

'It must flow on comfortably like a little brook,' said Mahler 'not "agitated" ["sehr bewegt"], which is in complete contradiction to the content. Only then does all the wonderful music-making and rejoicing [Musizieren und Jubilieren] have room to unfold in it. No one will complain that it is too long: instead, one will no more tire of listening to it than to the murmuring brook itself.'

Marie Gutheil-Schoder

Last night, Gutheil-Schoder[13] opened her engagement by appearing in *Carmen*. She is a dramatic artist of the first rank, and a 'musical genius', as Mahler describes her.

He is thrilled to have found an artist of her quality. 'It is always the way, that I encounter the highest and best achievement in *women*. Schoder and Mildenburg tower high above all the rest; they reassure one that there is still natural talent on the stage, not only affectation, grease-paint and pretence.'

On another occasion, he said of Schoder: 'There again you have the mystery of personality, in which all one's potential lies concealed. Look at this woman, unimpressive at first sight, with her average voice and its quite unsympathetic middle range! – yet every note is from the heart [ist Seele], and every expression, every movement is a revelation of the character she is trying to get inside, and whose every feature she reproduces from within as only the genius of a real creative talent is capable of doing.'

Summer 1900
Mayernigg, Villa Antonia
21 June–15 August

On 21 June, Mahler arrived at the Wörther See with Arnold Rosé. He was looking rather pale, but thankful to have escaped from Paris.[1] The same evening he was installed in his little woodland retreat [sein Waldhäuschen].[2] He insisted vehemently on breakfasting there (although Justi had hoped to persuade him out of it, because of the considerable distance and the difficulty of having everything carried up from the Villa Antonia, rain or shine).

During the first week of his stay in Mayernigg, Mahler could not immediately get down to work in the usual way. (For example, in the Steinbach *Häuschen*, ideas would often start coming to him in the first twenty-four hours.) He was quite depressed at this – in fact, desperate. He was convinced that he would no longer be able to accomplish anything, and already saw the ghastly realization of his superstitious fear that he would have the house for composing but never again be able to compose.

The trouble, of course, was the run-down physical condition in which he had come from Paris. But even more to blame, perhaps, was the nature of the work he is engaged on at present, which necessitated going back to last year's sketches of the Fourth Symphony and taking up the threads again. To get back into the work and continue it in the same vein as before, after breaking off so abruptly at the end of the holiday in Aussee, was probably the hardest thing he has ever done.

When he actually began to work (I think, but am not certain – as he preserved complete silence on the subject – that it was on his birthday [7 July]), he stayed in the summer-house from 7 a.m. till one o'clock – later, as long as eight to ten hours. This he stood better than usual, thanks to the gloriously mild climate and the delicious woodland air.

Hans Rott

Mahler was speaking about Hans Rott,[3] whose Symphony he had brought along to look through with a view to eventual performance in the Philharmonic concerts:

'What music has lost in him is immeasurable. His First Symphony, written when he was a young man of twenty, already soars to such heights of genius that it makes him – without exaggeration – the founder of the New Symphony [der neuen Symphonie] as I understand it. It is true that he has not yet fully realized his aims here. It is like someone taking a run for the longest possible throw and not quite hitting the mark. But I know what he is driving at. His innermost nature is so much akin to mine that he and I are like two fruits from the same tree, produced by the same soil, nourished by the same air. We would have had an infinite amount in common. Perhaps we two might have gone some way together towards exhausting the possibilities of this new age that was then dawning in music.'

Mahler went on to tell how Rott had composed this symphony in the Piarist monastery, where he was organist for almost negligible pay. There he had a tiny room as quiet as the grave. Mahler often went to see him in those days, and sometimes even slept in his cell. He still remembered how Rott, when he happened to be 'in pocket', used to buy a whole string of sausages [Extrawurst] to appease his hunger; this then hung on a nail in the room until it was consumed. Later, Rott unfortunately lost this post – in fact he was dismissed in a most insulting way: the monks, who were his sworn enemies, accused him of stealing and selling books out of the archives. His innocence was proved only later, when he was already out of his mind.

In addition, Rott composed highly individual songs, and often played them to his friends. Unfortunately he never wrote them down and they have disappeared with him. There was a sextet of his, too, which Mahler never heard.

On Schubert
13 July 1900

'Today,' said Mahler 'I have read through all of Schubert's chamber music. Out of twelve works, you'll find four, at most, that are any good. In the same way, perhaps eighty of his eight hundred songs are altogether beautiful – and that's certainly enough. But if only he hadn't written all those unimportant works – which would almost prompt one, no matter how enthusiastic one was about the rest, to deny his talent!

'That is because his technical skill is far from equalling his feeling and his inventive power. How easily he takes things when it comes to developing his ideas! Six sequences follow one after the other, and then comes still another one in a new key. No elaboration, no artistically finished development of his original idea! Instead, he repeats himself so much that you could cut out half the piece without doing it any harm. For each repetition is already a lie. A work of art must evolve perpetually [immer weiter entwickeln], like life. If it doesn't, hypocrisy and theatricality set in. For Schubert's melody, like Beethoven's and Wagner's, is *eternal*. That's why he shouldn't fall back on the formalism of Haydn and Mozart, which was intrinsic to the structure of their works.

'Now I understand why, as we are told, Schubert still wanted to study counterpoint even shortly before his death. He was aware of what he lacked. And I can feel for him in this, as I myself am deficient in this technique, having missed a really thorough grounding in counterpoint in my student years. Admittedly, intellect makes up for it in my case, but the expenditure of energy needed for this is out of all proportion.'

Environmental barbarity

Even in his little house, which gives him the greatest pleasure, there are many days when he is disturbed. The birds torment him with their singing, in spite of scarecrows and the firing of blank cartridges. You can hear the barking of Theuer's dogs. Sometimes the sound of a barrel-organ, or a military band on the opposite side of the lake, wafts over. The guests at the local hotel sent a band of Bohemian musicians to serenade him for an hour at their expense. He is all the more exposed to such crude attacks as the people know what elaborate arrangements he has made to ensure his undisturbed peace. This they find extraordinary, in fact crazy; and so they make him the target of their wit.

Mahler said: 'We are still surrounded on every side by such barbarity; there is no defence against it. Most people have no conception of what it means to respect a person's freedom. They are solely bent on satisfying their childish desires of the moment, such as tearing up flowers, senselessly killing or capturing animals, and the like. I am beginning to think more and more that only the deaf and the blind are fortunate, being shut out of this miserable world. I could understand a musician who destroyed his own hearing, as Democritus in supposed to have blinded himself.'

From a letter of 26 July

Mahler has returned from the Ampezzo valley,[4] completely refreshed and restored, having rushed around there like a madman, and made incredibly good use of the few days. Since then, he has been working in his little house from seven till twelve and from four till seven (after today, he will content himself with the five morning hours), so oppressed is he by the immensity of the task that he has set himself in his Fourth Symphony.

But you should see the location of his summer-house, or at least the path up to it![5] There, he is surrounded by all the miracles and all the mystery of the forest as only one who lives in it hour after hour can be. No one can imagine the feeling he has when he shuts his two wrought-iron gates behind him. The peace and security, the dionysian marvels and enchantments, far surpass even those of the little cottage on the meadow at Steinbach which he so loved. Here he works with all four windows wide open, so that he can breathe in the precious air and fragrance of the woods (whereas, in Steinbach, he could ward off the still too-penetrating sounds only by shutting himself in behind double doors and windows). Only yesterday, Mahler said again that he had never before enjoyed the happiness of the summer, and of working, as he does at present.

The mystery of art

'The effect of a work of art' said Mahler 'will always spring from its mysterious, incommensurate aspect. If you can take in a work at one glance, it has lost its magic and its power of attraction – just as the loveliest park, as soon as you know all the paths, can bore you so that you no longer want to walk in it (except perhaps to assist the operation of a dose of Karlsbad waters!)'[6]

The incomprehensibility of Nature

Mahler quoted part of a letter from a lady he knows, who was writing enthusiastically from the mountains. To her, it seems, Nature has an advantage over art in that it offers itself easily and readily; you need no commentary in order to enjoy it.

'How can people forever think' cried Mahler 'that Nature lies on the surface! Of course it does, in its most superficial aspect. But those who, in the face of Nature, are not overwhelmed with awe at its infinite mystery, its divinity (we can only sense it, not comprehend or penetrate it) – these people have not come close to it. An illustration from the Edda occurs to me: the giants, when the mightiest drinker amongst them wagers that there is no measure he cannot drain, divert the sea itself into his drinking-horn. He drinks and drinks and the horn never gets emptier – until, exhausted, he flings it down and sees the fraud. Indeed, there is no end to the infinite oceans of the world! And in every work of art, which should be a reflection [Abbild] of Nature, there must be a trace of this infinity.'

On the walk, Mahler remarked to me: 'You ask me whether they understand Beethoven today? What an idea! Because they have grown up with his works, because he is "recognized", they listen to him, play him, and perhaps even love him – but not because they are able to follow him in his flight. With their bleary eyes, they will *never* be able to look the sun in the face.'

25 July

Mahler related: 'A remarkable thing happened to me today. Compelled by the irresistible logic of a passage that I had to alter, everything that followed transformed itself so completely that suddenly, to my astonishment, I became aware that I was in a completely different world: as if you had imagined yourself to be wandering in flowery Elysian fields, but suddenly find yourself transported into the midst of the nocturnal terrors of Tartarus, with your blood running cold in your veins. In my works there are many traces and emanations of such worlds, which excite even in me a sense of horror and mystery.

'This time, too, it's the forest, with its marvels and its terrors, that dominates me and steals into my world of sound. I see it more and more: one does not compose, one *is* composed! [man komponiert nicht, man *wird* komponiert!]'

The second self

'We know' said Mahler 'that our second self is active while we sleep, that it grows and becomes and produces what the real self sought and wanted in vain. The creative artist, in particular, has countless proofs of this. But that this second self should have worked on my Fourth Symphony throughout *ten months* of winter sleep (with all the frightful nightmares of the theatre business) is unbelievable!

'For this year I find I am taking it up at a much more advanced stage than it had reached last year in Aussee, without having given it a moment's real attention in the meantime: on the contrary, I even ran away from the thought of it as I found it so unsatisfying and painful. But probably, while I was leading this meaningless life, my real self said: "This is all nonsense, I won't bother myself with it", and took refuge in the furthest corner of my soul, quite alone with its – that is, my own – higher life.'

An earlier instance that Mahler described might be mentioned here – I think it took place during his time in Leipzig. One evening, the second verse of his song 'Ringelreihn'[7] with the music to it, came to him. That same night he suddenly awoke to find the notes and words of the first and third verses so clear in his mind that he noted them down on the spot. The next morning, he found that not the least detail needed to be changed. (This was the first song that he thought worth keeping to have published later.)

Today, Mahler was stopped on the main road by a policeman: 'Where are you making for, friend?' Mahler must have struck him as a real vagabond, with his black unshaven face, open shirt (he was coatless, of course) and nondescript long trousers without braces or belt. Only when Mahler replied that he lived here did the man, on hearing his accent, appear to realize that he had made a mistake. He let Mahler go in peace, without investigation – and without locking him up.

A bet

Mahler told me that, when he was starting on his Fourth here, he made a bet with himself that he would finish it before his house was built. At first, he was in despair that the house had got so far ahead of him, but soon he had caught up with it. He is now well ahead, and nearing the end of his symphony, whereas the villa will not be ready before the end of the summer.

Conversations about the Fourth Symphony

Mahler gave us the first details about his Fourth Symphony: it is in G major, and takes forty-five minutes (that is, not longer than the first movement of his Third!).

'Actually,' he had told me before 'I only wanted to write a symphonic Humoresque,[8] and out of it came a symphony of the normal dimensions – whereas, earlier, what I imagined would be a symphony turned out, in my Second and Third, to be three times the normal length.'

To the three movements which Mahler has completed this summer, 'Das himmlische Leben' ['Heavenly Life'][9] is to be added as the Finale. He called it the tapering, topmost spire of the edifice of this Fourth Symphony.

'What I had in mind here was extraordinarily difficult to

bring off. Think of the undifferentiated blue of the sky, which
is harder to capture than any changing and contrasting shades.
This is the basic tone of the whole work. Only once does it
become overcast and uncannily awesome [spukhaft schauerlich]
– but it is not the sky itself which grows dark, for it shines
eternally blue. It is only that it seems suddenly sinister to us –
just as on the most beautiful day, in a forest flooded with sunshine, one is often overcome by a shudder of Panic dread.
The Scherzo is so mystical, confused and uncanny that it will
make your hair stand on end. But you'll soon see, in the following Adagio – where everything sorts itself out – that it wasn't
meant so seriously after all.

Mahler said that this second movement, the Scherzo, was the
only one to remind him stylistically of an earlier work of his –
the Scherzo of the Second. It offers new content in an old form.

In spite of the even tenor of the whole, the liveliest movement
of rhythm and harmony prevails – and what polyphony!
Indeed, the thousand little fragments of the picture are frequently
subject to such kaleidoscopic rearrangement that it's impossible
to recognize it again. It's as if we saw a rainbow suddenly dis-
integrate into a thousand million dancing, ever-changing drop-
lets, and its entire arc waver and dissolve. This is particularly
true of the variations in the Andante. These, Mahler said, were
the first real ones that he had written, that is, the first to be
completely transformed as he thinks variations should be. He
calls it his most beautiful Andante – in fact, the best thing he
has done so far. 'A divinely serene, yet profoundly sad melody
runs through it, that can only have you laughing and crying at
the same time.'

He also said that it bore the features of St Ursula (of whom
the fourth movement, 'Das Himmlische Leben', sings).[10] And
when I asked him whether he knew anything about the saint and
was familiar with her legend, he answered: 'No; otherwise I
should never have been able, or been in the mood, to paint such
a clear and splendid picture of her in my imagination.'

Another time, he called the Andante 'das Lächeln der heiligen
Ursula' ['St Ursula's smile'], and said that in it, his mother's face,

recalled from childhood, had hovered before his mind's eye: sad and yet laughing, as if through tears. For she, too, had suffered endlessly, but had always resolved everything in love and forgiveness.

Mahler now rejects the idea of giving the individual movements titles, as he used to do. 'I could give them the most beautiful names – but I'm not going to betray them to the idiot [Trotteln][11] listeners and pundits [Richtenden] who would promptly misunderstand and misinterpret me as foolishly as ever!'

Mahler sometimes calls this movement 'Adagio', sometimes 'Andante'. When I questioned him about this, he replied that he could just as well call it Moderato, Allegro or Presto, for it includes them all.

'Never was there a richer mixture of colours. The final dying-away is like the music of the spheres [sphärisch] – the atmosphere almost that of the Catholic Church. In this movement, as in the whole symphony,' he went on 'there is, in keeping with its subject, not a single *fortissimo*. This will no doubt surprise the gentlemen who always maintain that I use only the loudest sonorities. In fact, the trombones are absent throughout the entire Fourth Symphony.' (At the end of the Adagio he would have used some for a few bars, but did not wish to include them just for these, and so did without them.)

While Mahler was still working on the first movement, he told me that he was annoyed by two reminiscences which had slipped into it and which he had noticed too late to remove. One was from a symphony by Brahms (who had, however, taken it from Weber: 'whom, consequently, we've both robbed'); the other from a Beethoven piano concerto.[12] This movement, in spite of its freedom, was, he said, constructed with the greatest, almost pedantic adherence to the rules. Altogether, Mahler says, this work is artistically his most perfect; he feels that he has at last reached the peak of his development with it; as if he were really creating from the fullness of his powers.

Loving as he does to indulge in figurative descriptions of his music, he chatted with me about it during a bicycle ride to

Maria Saal:[13] 'The first movement begins as if it couldn't count to three, but then launches out into the full multiplication table, until at last it is reckoning dizzily in millions upon millions. He also confided in me that a kind of 'little call to muster' ['kleiner Appell'][14] (complementing the great one in the Finale of the Second) occurs in it: 'When the confusion and crowding of the troops, who started out in orderly ranks, becomes too great, a command from the captain recalls them at once to the old formation under his flag.'

Referring to the three preceding symphonies, Mahler emphasized the close connection of the Fourth with these, to which it forms a conclusion. In their content and structure, the four of them form a perfectly self-contained tetralogy [eine durchaus in sich geschlossene Tetralogie]. A particularly close relationship exists between the Third and Fourth; in fact, the latter even has themes in common with the movement of the Third called 'Was mir die Engel erzählen' ['What the angels tell me'].[15] This is so unusual and remarkable that he even has misgivings about it himself.

All three movements of the Fourth Symphony were half planned last summer in Aussee; even the variations were already there in embryo. 'You can imagine how I felt when I broke all that off and left Aussee; I was absolutely certain that I couldn't possibly ever resume the work again. (For that matter, it needed an appalling effort this summer!) I rolled up the few sketches, which no one else could possibly decipher, into a single parcel, threw them into the bottom drawer of my writing-desk, and didn't look at them any more; indeed, I couldn't even think of them without the most piercing stab of grief.'

Now that the work is as good as finished, I reminded Mahler of how he had complained, while composing it, that never before had he been so little in the creative mood. Because of this, he had been afraid that the work would suffer greatly. He admitted it, and said that yesterday was the first time that he had worked with the same great joy and spontaneity as so often in Steinbach. 'But perhaps it isn't necessary, or even desirable, for a work of art always to spring from a mood, like an eruption. There should rather be a uniform degree of skill throughout. This is true art, which is always at the disposal of its possessor, and overcomes all difficulties, even that of one's not being in good form.'

5 August

Mahler has finished the Fourth today – as always, he is not over-joyed about it: rather profoundly depressed at being deprived of the meaning it gave to his life.

Polyphony

Mahler told us at table that, on the woodland path to Klagenfurt with W.[16] (who had come to settle the repertoire [of the Opera]) he was much disturbed by a barrel-organ, whose noise seemed not to bother W. in the least. 'But when a second one began to play, W. expressed horror at the caterwauling – which now, however, was beginning to amuse me. And when, into the bargain, a military band struck up in the distance, he covered up his ears, protesting vigorously – whereas I was listening with such delight that I wouldn't move from the spot.'

When Rosé expressed surprise at this, Mahler said, 'If you like my symphonies, you must like that too!'

The following Sunday, we went on the same walk with Mahler. At the fête on the Kreuzberg, an even worse witches' sabbath was in progress. Not only were innumerable barrel-organs blaring out from merry-go-rounds, swings, shooting-galleries and puppet shows, but a military band and a men's choral society had established themselves there as well. All these groups, in the same forest clearing, were creating an incredible musical pandemonium without paying the slightest attention to each other. Mahler exclaimed: 'You hear? That's polyphony, and that's where I get it from! Even when I was quite a small child, in the woods at Iglau, this sort of thing used to move me strangely, and impressed itself upon me. For it's all the same whether heard in a din like this or in the singing of thousands of birds; in the howling of the storm, the lapping of the waves, or the crackling of the fire. Just in this way – *from quite different directions* – must the themes appear; and they must be just as different from each other in rhythm and melodic character (everything else is merely many-voiced writing, homophony in disguise). The only difference is that the artist orders and unites them all into one concordant and harmonious whole.'

The 1900–1901 season

Mildenburg

For the *Ring*, Mahler is now having Kurz[1] study the part of Sieglinde. Mildenburg, who not only sings and acts her own part incomparably but also pervades and dominates the whole work with her genius, is serving, at his request, as a kind of instructor and coach. She sings and demonstrates everything for her younger colleague just as Mahler has shown her. For she understands and is inspired by him as no artist before her. Her every expression, every gesture is so moving that Mahler himself is often greatly affected. 'I have now realized' he said 'what I had pictured in her when she came as a beginner from the Conservatory to Hamburg. Incompletely trained as she was, her musical and dramatic genius already shone through everything she did. She approached Siegmund [as Brünnhilde] with the prophecy of death so simply and nobly, singing in such tones that one's innermost being was touched as never before.'

Mahler's First Symphony[2]

Originally, Mahler had called his First Symphony 'Titan'. But he has long ago eradicated this title,[3] and all other superscriptions of his works, because he found that people misinterpreted them as indications of a programme. For instance, they connected his 'Titan' with Jean Paul's.[4] But all he had in mind was a powerfully heroic individual, his life and suffering, struggles and defeat at the hands of fate. 'The true, higher redemption comes only in the Second Symphony.'

In the first movement, we are carried away by a dionysian mood of jubilation, as yet unbroken and untroubled. With the first note, the long-sustained A in harmonics, we are in the midst of Nature: in the forest, where the sunshine of the summer day quivers and glimmers through the branches. 'The end of this movement' said Mahler 'will certainly not be under-stood by the audience;[5] it will fall flat, though I could easily have made it more effective. My hero bursts into a roar of laughter and runs away. Certainly no one will ever discover the theme which the kettledrum plays at the end![6]

'In the second movement, the young man is getting around in the world much more vigorously, sturdily and competently.' The wonderful dance-rhythm of the Trio is worthy of special notice, for, as Mahler once said, 'all music proceeds from the dance [vom Tanz geht alle Musik aus]'. 'Everyone will accuse me of plagiarism and of lacking originality because of the two opening bars, in which I lost my memory and inadvertently quoted a Bruckner symphony which is very well-known in Vienna!' (Actually, at the last moment Mahler slightly altered the opening for the performance.)[7]

Following this, there was originally a sentimentally indulgent [sentimental-schwärmerischer] movement, the love episode – which Mahler jokingly called the 'Jugend-Eselei' ['youthful folly'] of his hero. Later, he removed it.[8]

The third movement is the 'Bruder Martin' piece which was more misunderstood and scorned than all the rest of the work. Mahler recently described it this way: 'By now he (my hero) has already found a hair in the soup and it has spoiled his appetite.' He also said that even as a child he had never thought of 'Bruder Martin' as cheerful – the way it is always sung – but rather pro-foundly tragic. Even then, he could hear in it what he developed from it later. Actually, when he was composing it, the second part of this movement had occurred to him first. Only later, when he was looking for a beginning, was he continually haunted by the canon 'Bruder Martin' over the pedal-point which he needed – until at last he boldly resolved to adopt it.

Mahler composed the whole symphony in Leipzig[9] within six weeks, while constantly conducting and rehearsing. He worked from the time he got up until ten o'clock in the morning, and in the evenings when he was free. Otherwise he seized every opportunity – during a glorious March and April – of taking walks in the Rosental. He received the windfall of an unexpected holiday through the death of the Emperor:[10] ten days, of which he took the fullest advantage.

'But what meant most of all to me,' he told me once about that period 'was that I had an escape-hatch from the world! This was my relationship with the Weber family. I had come into contact with the grandson of the composer through the *Pintos*,[11] whose libretto he finished for me; and his wife's musical, radiant and aspiring nature gave my life new meaning. The enchanting children, too, were warmly and sincerely fond of me – as I of them. We were all devoted to one another.

'When I finished the first movement – it was about midnight – I ran to the Webers and played it to them both. They had to help me out at the piano, playing above and below to help supplement the first A in harmonics. We were all three so enthusiastic and blissfully happy that I don't think I have ever had a more wonderful time with my First. Then, happily charged for some time, we went walking in the Rosental.

The idea for the divinely lovely melody of the violins in the last movement[12] came to Mahler during an evening party at the Stägemanns',[13] while supper was being served. He went into the next room to write it down, and found himself in a full flood of inspiration. Ignoring the amazed and somewhat offended company, he had run out with it in the middle of the conversation. It did not worry him in the least that his behaviour was put down to 'artistic temperament'.

I told Mahler what an indescribable effect the sound of the First Symphony, and especially of the 'Bruder Martin' movement, always had on me. 'And so it *must* have' replied Mahler. 'It's because of the way I use the instruments. In the first movement, I make them completely vanish behind a shining sea of sound – as a luminous body is eclipsed by the light that streams from it. In the third movement, the instruments are quite differently disguised and masked, and appear, as it were, in strange shapes; everything must sound muted and subdued, like passing shadows. Bringing out each new entry in the canon distinctly and in a startling new coloration – so that it calls attention to itself a little – caused me a great deal of trouble in the instrumentation. Finally, I succeeded in getting the effect which you find so strangely eerie and unusual. To this day, I don't think anyone has caught on to my way of achieving it. If I want to produce a soft, subdued sound, I don't give it to an instrument which produces it easily, but rather to one which can get it only with effort and under pressure – often only by forcing itself and exceeding its natural range. I often make the basses and bassoon squeak on the highest notes, while my flute huffs and puffs down below. There's a passage like this in the fourth movement – you remember the entry of the violas?:

Ex. 7

I always enjoy this effect; I could never have produced that powerful, forced tone if I had given the passage to the cellos (the most obvious choice here).

'Although, in the first and third movements, the orchestra completely retires behind its subject-matter, in the second and fourth I took great pains to bring it to the fore as brilliantly as possible.'

About the origin of the harmonics in the first movement, Mahler told me: 'When I heard the A in all registers in Budapest,[14] it sounded far too substantial for the shimmering and glimmering of the air that I had in mind. It then occurred to me that I could have all the strings play harmonics (from the violins at the top, down to the basses, which also possess harmonics). Now I had the effect I wanted.'

About his First Symphony as a whole, Mahler also said: 'It's the most spontaneous and daringly composed of my works. Naïvely, I imagined that it would be child's play for performers and listeners, and would have such immediate appeal that I should be able to live on the profits and go on composing. How great was my surprise and disappointment when it turned out quite differently! In Budapest, where I first performed it, my friends avoided me afterwards; no one dared to mention the performance or the work to me, and I went about like a leper or an outlaw. In these circumstances, you can imagine what the reviews were like!'

Beethoven's First Symphony
17 December

In yesterday's Philharmonic concert, Mahler celebrated Beethoven's birthday [16 December] by conducting his First and Fourth Symphonies and the *Coriolan* Overture.

Of the First, he said to me on the eve of the performance that it was Haydn, raised to the highest degree of perfection. 'And that was Beethoven's good fortune! For precisely this fact gave him access to his contemporaries. They could find a link with what they already understood – whereas he himself, the later, totally individual Beethoven, would have seemed to them completely incomprehensible – in fact, quite mad. And that's what happened, too (for instance, with the B flat major Symphony [No. 4], for which they cried him down as a crackpot!)'

Mahler's Fourth Symphony
(revision)

At present,[15] Mahler is working a few hours every morning and evening at his Fourth. From the Aussee sketches, he has now laboriously reconstructed the Scherzo as he had originally planned it. At that time, it would in fact only have been developed further and become much longer, ending in a tarantella. 'Again and again' he said 'one finds that the first intention, the first conception, is the only right and feasible one.'

Mahler said that the means which he uses in this movement, and, indeed, throughout the entire Fourth Symphony, are again totally different from any that he had used before. 'The Scherzo is made of nothing but cobwebs – or, it's like one of those very delicately worked woollen shawls which fit into a nutshell, but when spread out seem never-ending – revealing the most marvellous design knitted out of strands as fine as hair.'

He is altering the violin solo of the Scherzo by having the instrument tuned a tone higher, and rewriting the part in D minor instead of E minor.[16] This makes it screeching and rough-sounding, 'as if Death were fiddling away [wie wenn der Tod aufspielt].'

He said that he must alter the part-writing in the second movement.[17] As a result of the pause between Aussee and Mayernigg, it has become too elaborate and overgrown – 'like limbs with ganglia.'

'You will hardly believe,' he said to me on another occasion,[18] 'that in the first movement, the scoring of that childishly simple and quite unselfconscious theme

Ex. 8

caused me untold trouble. It was more difficult to write than the most elaborate polyphonic passage! I'm much more accustomed to such complex interweavings, since as far back as I can remember my musical thinking was, oddly enough, never anything but polyphonic. But here I'm probably still suffering from lack of strict counterpoint, which every student who has been trained in it would use at this point with the greatest of ease.'[19]

Mahler also said of this theme: 'On its first appearance, it lies there as inconspicuously as the dewdrop on the flower before the sun shines into it. But as soon as a ray of light falls upon the meadow, it breaks up into a thousand reflections and colours in every pearl of dew, until a whole sea of light shines before us.'

On mime

Mahler observed that all actors and singers move too much, thus weakening, even destroying the significance and the true expressiveness of a gesture. He could never properly cure them of this habit, never impress them enough with the need for repose. 'Most of them quite unnecessarily emphasize by a

gesture what is already expressed in the words. If they cry
'thou' ['Du'], they point to the other person with melodramatic
movements of arm and finger; if it is a matter of the heart, they
put their hands to their heart, and so on. The ladies are always
fingering their faces till it makes you feel sick! To cure them
of this, I first make them go through a part without the use of
arms at all; only when they can convey the dramatic and
musical meaning of a role fully and vitally without supporting
gestures do I allow them to use their arms and hands. Similarly,
I first have a singer study the musical part of the role until it is
absolutely correct – perfectly timed, and precise down to the
last detail. Only when he knows it faultlessly do I allow, in fact
order him, to treat the part with artistic freedom and interpret it
from within himself. Whatever the result, he will never sing it
as sloppily and unrhythmically as someone who has not learned
the part inside out!'

Mahler persuaded the producer Stoll[20] to have the Conservatory students play every part with their arms initially tied to
their sides.

Disagreeing with a friend, who believed that it need not be
difficult for an actor who had really thought himself into his
part to find the right and natural gestures and mime on his own,
even without guidance, Mahler exclaimed: 'He won't find a
thing! His natural movements will be ludicrous and impossible
in the extreme. Unless everything is stylized, transformed into
art, which sustains and ennobles every step, every expression, it
is simply ridiculous. Everyone will recognize the actor from
head to foot as Herr Meier and nobody else. And, indeed, when
everything else in the world – cobbling not excepted[21] – has to
be learnt laboriously, why should such a difficult thing as
expressing a dramatic and musical work of art in mime be a
matter of course? No, it has to be just as thoroughly studied and
just as carefully practised as any other skill.

'Do you imagine, for example, that Mildenburg, whom you
now admire as the greatest truly classic dramatic actress, was
always so? You should have seen her as a beginner; how clumsy
and awkward she was then! Much in the same way as I drilled

her musically, I told her to study every expression and gesture of her mime and to act in front of a mirror. So that she should acquire a quiet, poised stance, I made her go out walking in the streets without umbrella and muff – nothing in her hands – with a regular and upright gait, and do exercises at home morning and evening. When she had memorized her part, I had the grand piano carried out on to the stage. There, I showed her every step, every attitude and movement, rehearsing it in the greatest detail in relation to the singing. That was how I rehearsed the Wagner roles with her, from beginning to end. Granted, I have never found anyone else – except perhaps Schoder[22] – so ready to learn as she.

'She had a particularly hard struggle to make her powerful, heavy body supple and perfectly responsive in every movement. At first, she even walked so awkwardly that she stumbled over her long dresses, and had to wear them much shorter in front in order not to fall. Only when, on Justi's advice, she started to wear long trailing gowns at home did she accustom herself to them for the stage as well.'

Ballet

Lipiner asked Mahler whether he could not produce a new, reformed kind of ballet – with deeper meaning, more plastically than balletically mimed, with nobler and more significant music, and so help this scandalously degenerated art of Terpsichore on to its feet again.

'Ballet is beyond help in its present form' replied Mahler. 'Every effort would be useless.'

'I once nursed a boy ill with scarlet fever[23] and to pass the time I invented all sorts of gruesome fairy-tales for him: about giants and monsters in the most terrifying forms, with two heads and four arms, with which they did the most frightful things. When these monsters no longer made any impression, they were given more arms than a polyp, and ten, twenty, a hundred heads – until even that did not satisfy the feverishly wandering imagination of my charge and they had to have thousands and millions. But finally, instead of the monsters, who could not be made any more grotesque, what should appear on the scene but – a normal person!

'In like manner, the imagination of all those who have had anything to do with ballet, either actively or passively, has been forced beyond all reasonable limits until it has become utterly debased. Improving it, or wanting to raise it to a higher level, is a sheer impossibility.'

On Bach
March 1901

Mahler is quite delighted with his big Bach edition,[24] which you always find him busy with when you go to his room. Recently, he said to me: 'So often, Bach reminds me of those sculptured gravestones that show the dead sleeping with folded hands above their mortal remains. This holding fast to life, even beyond our earthly existence, touches me deeply. Such monuments are inspired by the profound desire for, and belief in, a life after death. Indeed, some people are attached to that life, while they are still here on earth, even more than to their physical existence. Bach, too, presents a stonily monumental aspect – so much so that only a very few are able to call him back to life. This impression is certainly largely caused by bad performances, which don't give us the remotest idea of how Bach's music sounded when he played it on the harpsichord. Instead of the real Bach, they give us a wretched skeleton of him. The chords, are, as a rule, simply left out, as if Bach had written the figured bass without aim or purpose. But it is meant to be realized – and then what a ringing sound those surging chords produce! That is how his violin sonatas – played so ridiculously by just *one* little fiddler – should be performed, and the cantatas, too. Then, you'd be surprised how they sound!'

Mahler played for us the Bach cantata *Ich sündiger Mensch, wer wird mich erlösen?*[25] He called it a glorious work, perhaps even Bach's most glorious – one which opens up the widest perspectives. In this connection, he mentioned Bach's tremendous freedom of expression, which has probably never been equalled since, and which is founded on his incredible skill and command over all resources.

'In Bach, all the seeds of music are found, as the world is contained in God. It's the greatest polyphony that ever existed!'

Tchaikovsky's 'Pathétique'

Coming from the Berlin Philharmonic concert, Mahler was discussing Tchaikovsky's *Pathétique* with Guido Adler.[26] He called it a shallow, superficial, distressingly homophonic work – no better than salon music. Adler, who was quite satisfied with it and found its colour-effects especially delightful, protested. 'Even colouring' replied Mahler 'should not really be the sort of thing he gives us here. His is fake, sand thrown in one's eyes! If you look more closely, there is precious little there. These rising and falling arpeggios, these meaningless sequences of chords, can't disguise the fundamental lack of invention and the emptiness. If you make a coloured dot spin round an axis, it appears to be magnified into a shimmering circle. But the moment it comes to rest, it's the same old dot, which wouldn't tempt even the cat to play.'[27]

Immortal

Urged by a friend to do more about performing his works and making them more widely known, Mahler replied: 'Sooner or later, they themselves will do whatever is necessary; do you have to be there in person when you become immortal? [muss man denn dabei sein, beim Unsterblichwerden?].'

Summer 1901

The Mahler villa on the Wörther See

June–August

In the new home

Mahler arrived in Mayernigg a few days after Justi and myself, full of curiosity and anticipation about his new house.

In those few days, Justi had made so much progress with the indoor and outdoor arrangements that the house as a whole, although much still remained to be done, seemed quite habitable. Its situation between wood and lake has a magical charm which you never come to take for granted, but which you always experience afresh as completely enchanting. Two splendid, large stone terraces (an open one on the main floor, with the covered loggia underneath) offer the widest view of the lake, which smiles in at one through every window. And then, from every vantage-point, you can see the forest with its lofty fir-trees and alders. Mahler's balcony, on his attic floor, is like a high watchtower. 'It is *too* beautiful' he said. 'One can't allow oneself such things.'

And it is a fact that he feels a kind of guilt in the depths of his soul for being so privileged. That he of all people, who has no material wants – the 'barbarian', as we often called him because of his distaste for luxury and comfort and the beautiful things of life – that he should be surrounded by such splendour seems to him such an irony of fate that it often brings an involuntary smile to his lips.

Even more than with the villa itself, he is delighted with the garden and the piece of woodland, in which he has had all kinds of winding and climbing paths and charming clearings made. But dearest to all of us is the 'shore path'. This is a broad walk that has been banked and levelled between the house and the lake, where it is quite delightful to stroll out in the open air in the evening.

The discovery of a spring adjacent to Mahler's land was a great event, as the house until then had had no drinking water. Mahler at once bought the land immediately surrounding it. The spring ran out into a number of tiny channels, and he would get quite excited watching how the ice-cold, silvery stream of water would flow now more, then suddenly less, strongly.

On birdsong

Mahler is much less disturbed by the birds in his little woodland retreat than last year (when fledglings in a subsequently dis-covered nest under his roof seem to have made an atrocious din). He is actually on friendly terms with them. Recently he told me quite delightedly about a bird which, set off by the melismas of his music,[1] sang so gloriously that he was happy to listen to it, telling himself that the bird was doing better at it than he!

On another occasion, he called the birds the first composers. Listening to them again on a walk, he said to me: 'Even as a child I was struck by birdsong. I noted how it would begin with conscious singing and a definite rhythm and melody, but then would turn into inarticulate twittering – like a four-footed animal standing on two legs for a moment, but immediately falling back on all fours again.'

Beginning to create

Mahler is again complaining how difficult it is, after the long interruption, to make the forcibly dammed-up spring of creative imagination gush forth again. All the same, not three days had gone by (though he'd planned to treat himself to two weeks' relaxation for a start) before he was sitting for long periods in his summer-house. In spite of all the disturbing hammering in the house down below, he was deeply absorbed in composing. But at first we were told nothing of the subject-matter of his work.[2]

Learning and intuition

Mahler is quite delighted with an essay by Kretzschmar[3] on the performance of old music. It's written as if from his own heart, and reinforces, in scholarly and detailed fashion, truths which he himself had hit upon intuitively. For art needs only to strike the rock with its divining rod to find the spring of living water, whereas learning [die Wissenschaft] has to employ the barometer and the hygrometer – even pigs rooting for truffles! – in order to discover a little moisture.

On Schumann

Mahler said: 'Schumann is one of the greatest composers of songs, to be mentioned in the same breath with Schubert. Nobody has mastered the perfected, self-contained form of the Lied as he did; his conception always confines itself to the limits of the song, and he never demands anything that oversteps these limits. Restrained feeling, true lyricism and a profound melancholy pervade his songs, of which the dearest to me are precisely the less well-known ones which aren't forever being sung, as are those of the *Frauen-Liebe und -Leben* cycle.'

The genius of Bach

Of the Bach chorales, which are based on old and universally familiar hymns, Mahler observed: 'He was not concerned with the originality of his themes. What mattered to him was how to handle them; how to develop and transform them in a multiplicity of different ways – as the Greeks, too, repeatedly dealt with the same subjects in their tragedies and comedies, but each time in new, manifold and differentiated forms.'

He is constantly filled anew with admiration for Bach's genius, which he declares one of the greatest that ever existed. 'His polyphony is a marvel beyond belief, not only for his own, but for all times.' He was quite beside himself over the Third Motet (large Bach edition):[4] 'It's unbelievable, the extent to which the eight voices are carried through in a polyphony which he alone commands. I'm gradually learning to follow

them with the eye (they literally can't be played on the piano!).
But some day I should like to, I *must* perform this work – to the
amazement of the world!

'It's beyond words, the way I am constantly learning more and
more from Bach (really sitting at his feet like a child): for my
natural way of working is Bach-like. If only I had time to do
nothing but learn in this highest of all schools! Even I can't
visualize how much it would mean. But may my latter days,
when at last I belong to myself, be dedicated to him!'

Collecting ideas

Mahler is now beginning to note down many of the musical
ideas that come to him. He regrets that he didn't start doing it
long ago, so that later on, if the flow of invention were to
slacken, he could use and develop first one, then another of
these stored-up treasures. 'What a superhuman labour and
waste of energy it is to have to create everything you need on
the spot, without provision in advance, or any "collection"
["Sammlung"] (in the true sense of the word)! If one had been
sensible enough not to discard anything during the summer, but
had instead gathered everything in and hoarded it carefully, one
would only need to dip into it later to find just what one needed.
It was in this way that Beethoven, in later years, often took up
and used themes from times long past.

'Now at last,' he added 'the realization dawns upon me in a
new way: I would have to give up the Opera in order to be
able to work.'

Plan for an opera

Mahler told me that in Leipzig, after finishing the *Pintos* with
Weber,[5] and at the request and urging of the latter's wife, he
had wanted to write an opera of his own. He suggested the
following subject to Weber for a libretto, outlining it in detail.

A soldier on his way to the gallows is – according to medieval
custom – spared the death penalty when a girl, whose deepest
sympathy he inspires, claims him in marriage before the people
and the judges. The mourning procession turns into one of

jubilation, and everyone goes home rejoicing. But the stubborn young fellow cannot bear the shame of owing his life to the pity of a girl whom he, in turn, is beginning to love. His inner conflict becomes so intolerable that he rejects her gift of freedom and marriage, declaring that he would rather die. The last act was supposed to bring about the resolution of the matter with the girl's ardent pleading and confession of love.

Weber, however, had immediately altered this simple story. He introduced an earlier love and sweetheart of the young man, running quite counter to Mahler's intentions, and leading him very soon to abandon the whole idea. 'Der Schildwache Nachtlied'[6] was salvaged from this attempt. To it, Mahler owed his renewed acquaintance with *Des Knaben Wunderhorn*,[7] which was to become so significant for him.

Youth and maturity

Mahler says that in his youth the greatest musical masterpieces depressed him. Hearing them, he had the egotistical thought: 'You'll never be able to do anything like that!' Today, however, he has the opposite experience, and 'something less good, or weak, depresses me as deeply as if I had myself written something inadequate and bad.'

'A work whose bounds are clearly apprehended, reeks of mortality – and that's just what I can't stand in art!'

25 July

At night, a boatful of tipsy young men came to serenade Mahler with caterwauling, disturbing the peace of the house in the most coarse fashion. After they had made a horrible din, whistling, yodelling and banging their oars together, one of the crowd (no doubt duly primed) called out to the rest: 'I say, what have you got against Mahler? What harm has he done you?' Another replied furiously: 'He has written a bad symphony (the First!) and *Das klagende Lied*!' – and the uproar raged afresh.

In the morning, when Mahler happened to be standing on his balcony and looking out over the lake, the steamer came past with a crowd of girls on board. No sooner had they seen him than they raised a great cry of glee: 'It's Mahler! Three cheers for Mahler! Long live Mahler!' At this, he could not retreat quickly enough into his room; for such ovations are just as terrible to him as – caterwauling.

Alone again, however, he could not help shaking his head over the contrast, the rapid change that had occurred overnight.

Mahler on his Fifth Symphony

During these past few days, Mahler talked to me for the first time about the work he is now engaged on, his Fifth Symphony – in particular the third movement,[8] which he is writing at present. 'The movement is enormously difficult to work out because of its structure, and because of the utmost artistic skill demanded by the complex inter-relationships of all its details. The apparent confusion must, as in a Gothic cathedral, be resolved into the highest order and harmony.'

Again today (5 August) Mahler said of the same movement: 'You can't imagine how hard I am finding it, and how endless it seems because of the obstacles and problems I am faced with. They arise from the simplicity of its themes, which are built solely on the tonic and dominant. Nobody else nowadays would dare to do it. That's why the chordal progressions are so difficult, particularly in view of my principle that there should be no repetition, but only evolution. The individual parts are so hard to play that they really call for accomplished soloists. Because of my thorough knowledge of the orchestra and its instruments the boldest passages and rhythms suddenly came to me!'

He remarked that Koschat's[9] theme 'An dem blauen See' ['By the Blue Lake'] (meaning the Wörther See) had crept into the second movement. 'I'd rather it were Koschat's theme than one of Beethoven's; for Beethoven worked out his themes himself! It would be easy to pick up most of Schubert's themes, however, and develop them for the first time. In fact it wouldn't hurt them at all, for they are so totally un-developed.'

Finally, Mahler told me that the movement on which he is

working is a Scherzo which differs entirely from anything that he has written up till now. 'It is kneaded through and through till not a grain of the mixture remains unmixed and unchanged. Every note is charged with life, and the whole thing whirls around in a giddy dance.' He also compared it with a comet's tail. 'There is nothing romantic or mystical about it; it is simply the expression of incredible energy [unerhörter Kraft]. It is a human being in the full light of day, in the prime of his life. It is scored accordingly: no harp or English horn. The human voice would be absolutely out of place here. There is no need for words, everything is purely musically expressed. Furthermore, it will be a regularly constructed symphony in four movements,[10] each of which exists for itself and is self-contained, linked to the others solely by a related mood.'

Seven songs

On 10 August, Mahler played for me, in his woodland retreat, the seven songs that he has written in a fortnight (each composed one day and scored the next). Six are to poems by Rückert, and one, 'Der Tambourg'sell', is from *Des Knaben Wunderhorn*.[11]

On another occasion, he told me that the last mentioned song – almost as if according to a pre-established harmony detween notes and words – came into being as follows. It occurred to him literally between one step and the next – that is, just as he was walking out of the dining-room. He sketched it immediately in the dark ante-room, and ran with it to the spring – his favourite place, which often gives him aural inspiration. Here, he had the music completed very quickly. But now he saw that it was no symphonic theme – such as he had been after – but a song! And he thought of 'Der Tambourg'sell'. He tried to recall the words; they seemed made for the melody. When he in fact compared the tune and the text up in the summer-house, not a word was missing, not a note was needed; they fitted perfectly!

He said that he felt sorry for himself that he should have to write 'Der Tambourg'sell' and the *Kindertotenlieder*;[12] and he felt sorry for the world that would have to hear them one day, so terribly sad was their content. He said something charming about the 'Lindenzweig':[13] to him, it's filled with the kind of quiet happiness that you feel in the company of someone dear to you, and of whom you are perfectly sure, without a word needing to be exchanged. The text of 'Blicke mir nicht in die Lieder'[14] is as characteristic of Mahler as if he had written it himself. But he considers it the least important of them all, and thinks that precisely for that reason it will quickly become the most popular.

'Ich bin der Welt abhanden gekommen'[15]

Mahler had just finished his holiday work for this year, wanting to devote the last few days to relaxation, when he was suddenly seized with the urge to set the last of the Rückert poems that he had originally planned to do, but set aside in favour of the symphony. This was 'Ich bin der Welt abhanden gekommen'. He himself said that this song, with its unusually concentrated and restrained style, is brim-full with emotion but does not over-flow. He also said: 'It is my very self!'

Rubinstein's performance of the Beethoven sonatas
20 August

After supper, Mahler and I went for an hour's walk along the road to Reifnitz. We began to talk about the playing of Beethoven sonatas. Mahler said that this is particularly difficult because the sonata demands a freer, more improvisational style of performance than that suitable for orchestral works. The latter have a firm structure; they are already held together by the necessary interaction of all the various instruments. This reminded him of Rubinstein[16] as a great interpreter of Beethoven. There was only one movement, the finale of the E flat major Concerto ['The Emperor'], which Rubinstein (like everybody else) played too delicately for Mahler's taste: merely graceful, instead of being stormy and vigorous as it absolutely must be.

He called Rubinstein a 'man of the Steppes' [eine 'Steppennatur'] by which he meant to indicate the elemental force, the boundless power and the lack of cultivation – in the sense of nature, which needs no cultivation – of that magnificent artist.

The 1901–1902 season

'All dynamic markings exaggerated'

During an evening at Mahler's, with Walter[1] and the Lipiners, the conversation turned to problems of musical performance. Mahler said: 'I realize more and more that people respond too violently to dynamic markings: the *forte* is too *forte*, the *piano* is too *piano*, the *crescendi*, *diminuendi* and *accelerandi* are too violent, the *largo* too slow, the *presto* too fast.

'How much simpler and more moderate my conducting has become than it used to be! When you see how they exaggerate and distort all your own indications, then you begin to realize what the others have to put up with.

'One would almost be tempted to write in no tempi and no expression marks, and leave it to the performer to understand and articulate the music in his own way.'

Bruno Walter

Mahler really enjoys Bruno Walter. The first opera he conducted was *Aida*,[2] and Mahler, who was listening to the performance in his box, was so delighted with it that he declared that from now on he could let Walter conduct in his place with complete confidence, and turn everything important over to him. Listening to somebody else conduct, he usually experiences so many musical discomforts that he becomes practically 'seasick'. But in this case you could see from his expressions and gestures – as from his frequent enthusiastic exclamations – that he was completely in agreement with what was going on.

The critics, however, did not like Walter at all. These gentlemen were already furious with him because they had found out that Mahler had summoned him here and thought highly of him. They also tried to make out that he imitated Mahler's movements and copied his outward mannerisms.[3]

'Die drei Pintos'

A new production of *Die drei Pintos*[4] is being prepared in Frankfurt, and Mahler has been recalling the time when the work first came into existence. Weber had told him about his grandfather's sketches, which he had already shown to many capable musicians, without finding anyone who dared think it possible to salvage anything from those rough hints – let alone transform them into a whole. He begged Mahler to take the sketches home with him and see if he could succeed in raising the sunken treasure.

For days on end, Mahler had the sketches lying on his piano, immersing himself in them. But he could not break the spell that bound them. Then – it was on a brilliant afternoon, and Weber's pages were streaked with coloured shafts of sunlight – the complete structure of one number came to him. He ran straight to the Webers and played it to them, to their great delight. From that moment on, one number after another came to him until in about a week all of the material had been worked out and completed. Having set about the work in the most faithful and conscientious fashion, respecting every note of Weber's and developing it in the way it seemed to suggest, Mahler would have much preferred to publish his completed version together with the original sketches (which are in Weber's possession) and then have it performed as such. But Weber and Stägemann (the director of the Leipzig Opera) were united in their insistence that it should be turned into a full-scale opera. Weber wanted to write the text, and Mahler was to add the necessary music. So that is how the *Pintos* came into being.

'You'd be surprised' said Mahler 'to see how little was actually composed by Weber: not much more than a few wonderful themes, not a note of the orchestration. So I had to write by far the greater part of the work. And, hesitant as I was at first in completing the sketches, I grew all the bolder as the work progressed.* I let myself be carried away by the subject and by my own inspiration, and forgot to worry about whether

Weber would have done it that way. In the end, I simply let myself go and composed as I felt inclined; I became more and more "Mahlerish", until finally, when I drafted and worked out the new section, every single note was my own. (Even in the text, I did a lot without asking my librettist or signing my name to it.) And it is precisely these new numbers which were most highly praised by critics and public afterwards, and which were considered "pure Weber"!'[5]

Mahler says that his scoring of the *Pintos* is rather clumsy, as he lacked experience and skill at the time. Later, when he conducted the work in Prague, he toned down the orchestration considerably. He wrote down the modifications and alterations that he made at that time, and sent them to the publisher with the request that they should be added as an appendix to the whole edition. But this was never done, and Mahler did not even receive back his manuscript, which he had sent away without making a copy.[6]

Mahler's Fourth Symphony
Reading rehearsal, 12 October 1901

Today, Mahler led the Philharmonic in a reading rehearsal of his Fourth, which is to be played here this winter, as also in Munich and Berlin. He simply wanted to play the work through from the proofs of the score in order to hear, before it was actually printed, whether there were any mistakes; but even more, he wanted to find out whether everything had turned out as he had imagined it. The reading, however, promptly became an intensive rehearsal from the first bar onwards – all the more so as the considerable originality and difficulty of the conception presented particular problems, even for this brilliant and well-drilled orchestra.

In the initial reaction to Mahler's work by the orchestral players here (and elsewhere), there could again be sensed – no matter how well they did their part – a certain inner resistance. Judging from their manner and the expressions on their faces, he fancied that he was surrounded by ill-wishers and enemies, rather than admirers and friends. 'And it is on this miserable rubbish-heap' he complained in despair 'that I have to make a blossoming world arise!'

In the reading, the beautiful *cantabile* themes (first in the violins, later in the cellos) were overdone, and played too loudly for his taste – whereas the final dithyrambic soaring of the same melodies could not get powerful and exuberant enough. He warned us beforehand that the audience would find the opening theme too old-fashioned and simple-minded. Playing it to us the evening before on the piano, he pointed out that it was followed by six others (making seven in all) which are elaborated in the development. Such a work, he said, *must* contain an abundance of germ-motifs which are then developed organically and richly – otherwise, it does not deserve the name of symphony. 'There must be something cosmic about it; it must be as inexhaustible as the world and life, if it is not to belie its name. And it must be organically *all of a piece* – nothing extraneous; no seams and patches to break it up.'

Concerning the mood of the first three movements, he added: 'They breathe the serenity of a higher world, one unfamiliar to us, which has something awe-inspiring and frightening about it. In the last movement ("Das himmlische Leben") the child – who, though in a chrysalis-state, nevertheless already belongs to this higher world – explains what it all means.' In the Scherzo, at the rehearsal, the solo violin passage still did not sound sharp enough for him, even though the instrument had been tuned a step higher. Therefore, he decided to give it to the viola, which the leader [Arnold Rosé] also plays.

At the very beginning of the Adagio, the strings, especially the cellos, emphasized the *crescendi* and *diminuendi* too strongly; so he had the expression-marks removed.

'Instrumentation' said Mahler 'is not there for the sake of sound-effects, but to bring out clearly what one has to say.' In the variations of the Fourth, one passage seemed to him obscured by too many notes. To remedy this, he cut out some sustained notes that padded out but were not essential to the harmony – which is created by the intertwining of the individual lines whose delicate tracery is like that of a miniature painting.

Mahler said that he had learnt a great deal about orchestration from Verdi, who had blazed quite new trails in it.

Finally, he showed me in the score that, when he wants a passage played somewhat more slowly, he does not mark it *ritardando* (which the orchestra would immediately exaggerate) but 'do not hurry' ['nicht eilen']. Conversely, when he wants an *accelerando* he writes 'do not drag' ['nicht schleppen']. 'That's how you have to treat musicians – with cunning!'

Hidden octaves
21 October 1901

Mahler, having come home from a rehearsal at ten o'clock after a hard day's work, was working after supper, as usual, at the correction of his Fourth. Unexpectedly, he came upon a faulty progression.[7] He was furious that such a thing should have happened to him. 'Every time I heard it, I was upset by its commonplace sound, without knowing why. When you find a thing like that in your score, it's as if someone of noble birth were suddenly to discover a swineherd in his family tree!'

He and Walter discussed the frequency of such hidden octaves in other masters: Bach, Schumann, etc. 'Beethoven is the only one' said Mahler 'that I have not caught out. But the others have the excuse of having written a great deal. When you write only one work a year, this just shouldn't happen!'

Humour

'There's a lot of laughter in my Fourth – at the beginning of the second movement!' exclaimed Mahler.

In answer to a question of mine, he called Beethoven the father and true founder of humour [in music]. 'What humour there is in his C major Symphony [No. 1] and the "Pastoral"! People misunderstood this; in fact, they held it against him so strongly that precisely *these* works had the hardest struggle to be accepted. Haydn and Mozart certainly manage wit and gaiety, but not yet humour.'

'Trompeter von Säckingen'

Recalling old times, Mahler told how, in Prague, in sheer despair at having to conduct the ghastly *Trompeter von Säckingen*[8] so often, he once eliminated the leitmotiv from the whole opera as a joke. From then on, the work was played that way without anyone noticing the difference. (Everything is, of course, equally important or unimportant in such trash.) The manager did once say that it struck him oddly, as if something were missing; but he never did discover what it was!

'For that matter, this wretched pot-boiler is such that one could just as well remove all the woodwind and brass, even all the strings really, without anyone being the wiser! For all the instruments – brass, woodwind, strings and percussion – always play exactly the same thing.'

'Dalibor' and the three greatest German opera composers

After a performance of *Dalibor*,[9] Mahler said: 'You can't imagine how annoyed I was again today by the imperfection of this work, the work of so highly gifted an artist. He was defeated by his lack of technique and his Czech nationality (which hampered him even more effectively, and deprived him of the culture of the rest of Europe). For this partially enchanting opera is never performed anywhere except in Vienna, and even my own revision can't do more than merely keep it in the repertory. It's far from popular or well-attended, which means that I can afford to give it only once a year. And when I'm conducting it I'm practically beside myself; there is a lot more that I should like to cut and re-orchestrate, even re-compose – so unskilfully is it written, in spite of its many beautiful passages.

'There are really not more than three perfect German opera composers: Mozart, whose sureness of aim in all that he did is unparalleled, Wagner – and you'll be surprised at the third!' 'Weber?' I asked. 'No! His *Oberon* and *Euryanthe* can't be counted among the perfect works. He worked in an opera house[10] – which grated on his nerves, paralyzed him and carried him off before his time; who knows what and how much he might have written otherwise! The third, in my opinion, is Lortzing. His *Zar*[11] and *Wildschütz*[12] reveal him, in text, plot and music, to be the greatest operatic talent next to Mozart and Wagner.

'That's not to speak of Beethoven and his unique *Fidelio*, which is *hors concours*. For wherever he reached out his hand, the greatest art arose!'

'The Tales of Hoffmann'

Yesterday and today,[13] dress rehearsals of *The Tales of Hoffmann*, which Mahler is preparing with three casts because he considers it a box-office draw, à la *Cavalleria* and *Pagliacci*. 'But with this,' he said 'I earn the money to put on greater things: new productions of Wagner and Mozart, in cycles comprising *all* their works!'

The Tales of Hoffman has been under a cloud ever since the terrible fire at the Ringtheater.[14] The work was not given again until this autumn, when, in its performance at the Theater an der Wien, it proved its power of attraction again. Mahler has now produced it with the whole apparatus available to him at the Opera. He has added so much of his own – revising text, plot, and music – that, if not entirely Hoffmann, at least a great deal of the romantic, grotesque and demonic character of the original inspiration came over.

From the very beginning, its success, with all three casts, was enormous. Throughout the winter the work drew full houses – almost to the despair of Mahler, who could no longer bear to hear and see it.[15]

Liszt's 'Heilige Elisabeth'

On the Empress's name-day, Liszt's *Heilige Elisabeth*[16] was performed. Mahler so loves this work that he never misses hearing it. 'This work *demands* to be realized on the stage' he told me. 'The music alone would be nothing – it's much too softly sentimental and melting, nothing but atmosphere – and yet, the most wonderful atmosphere that you can imagine. You can really say that it's a genuinely Aryan work.'[17]

Mahler had just received a refusal from a Hamburg orchestral player whom he had wanted to engage for the Opera. Annoyed, he exlaimed: 'If an old man doesn't want to leave the place where he has lived for a long time, or give up his friends there and be transplanted, it's understandable and excusable. But if a young man doesn't do everything possible to learn and grow, and develop himself when opportunity offers – if, indeed, he isn't prepared to go to the ends of the earth in order to do it – then he deserves to have done to him what the ancient Jews did to a slave who, at the end of his period of slavery, could take his freedom but did not want it. As a mark of eternal, self-chosen bondage, a wooden stake was driven through his ear, signifying that he was nailed fast to the portals of the house.'

Mahler's Fourth Symphony in Munich

On 20 November,[18] Mahler travelled to Munich for the performance of his Fourth, and we – his closest friends and relations – all went with him. He was unhappy about the orchestra there. In order to get anything but the crudest possible performance of the Symphony out of them, it was necessary to work like a sculptor, from the first blows of his chisel on the unhewn block of stone to the completion of the statue. The inadequacy of the players was all the more noticeable because of the subtlety and difficulty of all the instrumental parts – compared with the '*al fresco* style' (as Mahler calls it) of the Second Symphony, which they has mastered more easily a year ago.[19] Worse still, as bad luck would have it, the only brilliant player, the first cellist, was called away on the day of the performance because of the death of his father. 'In Budapest,' exclaimed Mahler 'when the news of my mother's death reached me, I was too conscientious to walk out on the *Lohengrin* performance which I was supposed to conduct that evening. Instead, I buried my grief inside me, and didn't tell anyone about the blow which had struck me.'[20]

Commenting on the individual movements, he said: 'The first begins characteristically enough, with the bells of the Fool's Cap [mit der Schellenkappe]. Will they find out, I wonder, that the third movement consists of variations – and the second, too?'

In the first movement, the audience was initially surprised by the apparently excessive simplicity of the themes (as they had expected something 'outrageous' from Mahler). But then, in the development section, they were filled with consternation when they realized how little they could follow. The conclusion, after the transition to the recapitulation [nach dem Rückgang] (of which Mahler himself said: 'They won't discover just how artful it is until later!'), only partially stilled the mounting opposition, which had asserted itself in the outbreaks of hissing against the loud applause. The public was completely alienated by the second movement, of which it could make nothing at all. Here, the hissing became so loud that even Mahler's large youthful following in Munich, which showed its warm support of him by packing the standing-room in the parterre of the overcrowded hall, was unable to drown out the opposition by clapping. The last movement received the longest and least-disputed applause; but Mahler refused to appear for a long time, continually pushing the singer forward instead – finally acknowledging the applause more angrily than affably.[21]

He was particularly depressed by the fact that, among the musicians of Munich, only Weingartner[22] took a positive attitude towards the work and uttered anything like an intelligent or approving comment. On the contrary, after the dress rehearsal several of them had come up to Mahler to tell him that they did not yet understand his Fourth, but would try their best to do so at the concert. But when none of them turned up after the concert, Mahler had good grounds for thinking and saying that even his former followers of last year had deserted him on account of the Fourth.

The general reaction was expressed most clearly and sharply the next day, in practically all the papers. Almost without exception, they reproached Mahler for having thoroughly disappointed their expectations of a work comparable to the C minor Symphony [No. 2] which they had heard the previous year (and which they had not reviewed at all favourably at that time!). Thus, what Mahler had foretold now happened: they used the Second as a stick to beat the Fourth to death with. Once again they all claimed that he lacked inventiveness and originality. Unanimously, they clamoured for verbal explanations of the meaning and content of the work. 'They are already so corrupted by programme music' exclaimed Mahler 'that they are no longer capable of understanding a work simply as a piece of music! This disastrously mistaken attitude stems from Liszt and Berlioz. They, at least, were talented, and gained new means of expression in this way. But now that we have these means at hand, who needs the crutches any more?'

Performance in Frankfurt

I asked our friend Frau Mankiewicz,[23] who had attended the performance of this same symphony in Frankfurt,[24] what kind of reception it had had. She replied that she could not and would not tell even me, let alone Mahler, what it had been like (it was so bad!). All I could get out of her was that the public thought it a practical joke; that he was trying to mystify them!

Performance in Berlin

In the middle of December,[25] Mahler went to the performance in Berlin, where he conducted all the rehearsals, as well as the concert, with the Strauss Orchestra.[26] Fortunately, he was well satisfied with these players. The reception was warmer and more understanding than in Munich, though there was still some opposition. The greatest impression was made by the Adagio; but this time, the last movement, usually brilliantly successful, was less well received – possibly because the singer[27] was not equal to it. Richard Strauss, who felt closer to the work at each successive rehearsal, was finally quite swept off his feet by it, especially by the third movement. He declared that he could never write such an Adagio. They met afterwards at a rather large gathering, and he told Mahler that he had learnt a tremendous amount from him. 'I have studied your Second Symphony particularly thoroughly, and have appropriated a good deal from it for my own use.' As a sign of his high esteem, Strauss later sent him the scores of all his works.

But the Berlin critics, to a man, fell hysterically upon Mahler and his work, heaping their filthy abuse, mockery and scorn upon him with less restraint than ever before. This embittered him profoundly.

Performance in Vienna

On 12 January 1902, Mahler conducted his Fourth at the Philharmonic concert in Vienna, in an admirable performance.

Its reception was about the same as that in Munich, if not worse (if that were possible), because of the conservative audience that attends these concerts. From the very beginning the most uncomprehending and hostile remarks were heard; it even seemed as if people had come only in order to make fun of the work. They even laughed out loud, showing their disapproval in their looks and behaviour. Afterwards they stood about in groups chattering. I heard some say: 'It starts just as if he were out to play a carnival joke on the public'. Others were disappointed that there had not been more hissing. A few callow youths found it 'ghastly', and not music at all.

Mahler, who was used to worse fiascos, seemed depressed by this one. He said to Walter: 'They don't really know *what* to do with this one: which end should they start gobbling it up from?'

Walter, however, when I was with him and his wife afterwards, said: 'Why is it that even the best of them apply only *their* yardstick, consider only *their* verdict, refusing to understand that the sun does not revolve around the earth, but the earth around the sun!'[28]

Editor's Afterword to the first edition

It hardly seems necessary to say more about the author of the foregoing journal. The sort of person she was is clearly betrayed in the particular way in which she relates what was, after all, primarily personal experience. But for those whose gaze is directed only towards the exalted and eternal, and whose nature it is to have nothing to do with the mundane, empirical side of life, outward appearances are so insignificant as to be scarcely worth noting. Unperturbed by convention or the attitudes prevailing around here, the author in fact lived her life in her own way. She came of a respectable bourgeois Viennese family. Through ceaseless striving, and through association with people in whom she sensed greater depths, she acquired that knowledge and outlook which raised her far above the general run. She concentrated especially on her development as a musician. As a member of the Soldat–Röger Quartet, she made concert tours not only through Austria and Germany, but also, on several occasions, in other countries. Her real calling, however, was to convey to others the intellectual and spiritual values which she had gained from the greatest amongst those with whom she came in contact. She was particularly concerned to convey these ideals to the younger generation, for whose benefit she always strove zealously.[1]

We owe this book to a similar urge. The great power naturally radiated by a being of genius in his daily life was not in this case to fade away in evanescent sparks. Instead, it was to be preserved for posterity – in so far as this can be done through the written word – that it might kindle new flames.

Anyone who therefore approaches the work with a coldly critical eye, or rummages through it for Mahler quotations, is doing it an injustice. The book was experienced by the author and demands to be experienced anew by the reader. One need not have a very keen ear to notice that Mahler's remarks have not been recorded and played back by a phonograph, but by a living, devoted soul.

In editing these recollections, most of which had not been prepared for publication by the author, my principal aim has been to retain their personal and subjective quality. In making a selection from this considerable body of material, which could not possibly be published in its entirety,[2] I hope that I have succeeded in choosing what is of the greatest general interest. As far as possible, the content has been limited to those sections dealing with Mahler and his opinions; characteristic peculiarities of the style that do not obscure the sense have not been tampered with. Of these two aims, the former I felt I owed to Mahler and the reader; the latter, to the author.

Finally, I must express my appreciation here to a young friend of the author for several valuable suggestions.

The Editor [J. Killian]

Bibliography

List of Abbreviations used in the Notes

AMM   Alma Mahler: *Gustav Mahler: Memories and letters*, ed. Donald Mitchell, 3rd ed, London, 1973.

BWM   Bruno Walter: *Gustav Mahler*, trans. James Galston (with a biographical essay by Ernst Křenek), Vienna House edn, New York, 1973.

BWT   Bruno Walter: *Theme and Variations*, London, 1947.

DMW   Donald Mitchell: *Gustav Mahler, the Wunderhorn Years*, London, 1975.

FPM   Ferdinand Pfohl: *Gustav Mahler: Eindrücke und Erinnerungen aus den Hamberger Jahren*, ed. Knud Martner, Hamburg, 1973.

FWB   Felix Weingartner: *Buffets and Rewards*, London, 1937.

GDM   *Grove's Dictionary of Music and Musicians*, third edn, London, 1927.

HLG   Henry-Louis de La Grange: *Mahler*, vol. I, London, 1974.

KBS   Kurt Blaukopf: *Mahler: A Documentary Study*, London, 1976.

NGS   Friedrich Nietzsche: *The Gay Science*, trans. and commentary by Walter Kaufmann, New York, 1974

WMG   William J. McGrath: *Dionysian Art and Populist Politics in Austria*, New Haven and London, 1974.

WWR   Arthur Schopenhauer: *The World as Will and Representation*, (2 vols), trans. E. J. F. Payne, Dover edn, New York, 1966.

NOTES

Introduction to the German edition
p. 20

1. In 1902 she married Arnold Rosé who was leader of the Philharmonic and Court Opera Orchestra throughout Mahler's time in Vienna.
2. '*des ewigen Abschieds*': Stefan refers, of course, to the final movement of *Das Lied von der Erde*, 'Der Abschied'.
3. *The Portraits of Gustav Mahler*, Leipzig, 1922. Roller (1864–1935) had been brought into the Vienna Opera by Mahler as a stage designer in 1903.
4. A collection of them was published the following year (*Gustav Mahler: Briefe, 1879–1911*, ed. Alma Mahler, Berlin-Vienna-Leipzig, 1924). They are now available in English: *Selected Letters of Gustav Mahler*, ed. Knud Martner, London, 1979.

p. 21

5. Stefan (1879–1943) was an important early supporter of Mahler. Following his *Gustav Mahlers Erbe* (Munich, 1908) and *Gustav Mahler: Ein Bild in Widmungen* (Munich, 1910), his revised *Gustav Mahler: eine Studie über Persönlichkeit und Werk* (Munich, 1920) is one of the most valuable of the early biographies of the composer.

Early history of my friendship with Gustav Mahler
p. 23

1. Natalie graduated from the Conservatory in 1872, but apparently continued to use its facilities while her sister was a student. Mahler was there from 1875–8. (See *Geschichte der K. K. Gesellschaft der Musikfreunde in Wien*, by Richard von Perger and Robert Hirschfeld, Vienna, 1912, vol. I, p. 332.)
2. The violinist Joseph Hellmesberger (1829–93) was Director of the Vienna Conservatory from 1851 until his death. His son, the composer and conductor of the same name (1855–1907), was to succeed Mahler as conductor of the Philharmonic Concerts in Vienna in 1902.
3. It is known that Mahler won prizes for piano *quintet* movements

in July 1876 (a first movement) and July 1878 (a scherzo). (See HLG, p. 706.) For a full discussion of Mahler's early works see the new edition of *Gustav Mahler: the Early Years* by Donald Mitchell (London, 1980).

4. The Bohemian writer Richard von Kralik (strictly, Richard Kralik von Meyerswalden) had joined the circle of young aesthetes surrounding the poet Siegfried Lipiner (see below, p. 71 n. 41) at about the same time as Mahler, in 1878. With Mahler and Lipiner he founded a somewhat short-lived, Wagnerian-romantic 'Saga Society' in 1881. It would appear to have been at a meeting of the Saga Society that this incident took place (see WMG, p. 101ff).

p. 24

5. October 1888 to March 1891.
6. Leopoldine Mahler, subsequently Quittner (1863–89).
7. Born in 1873, Otto Mahler committed suicide in 1895.
8. The archaeologist Friedrich Löhr (1859–1924).

PART 1: *Mahler abroad*

Visit to Budapest

p. 28

1. The incident occurred in October 1890. Mahler's letter, declining the challenge to duel, was published in the *Pester Lloyd* (see HLG, pp. 217–18).

Steinbach am Attersee, July and August 1893

p. 29

1. *Die drei Pintos*, the opera realized by Mahler from Weber's sketches and first produced at Leipzig in January 1888 (see below, p. 176ff). The Andante of the Second Symphony was completed on 26 July 1893.

p. 30

2. '*Wahrheit und Dichtung*'. Mahler was almost certainly alluding here to the title of Goethe's autobiography, *Dichtung und Wahrheit*.

p. 31

3. It is clear from the following that Mahler refers to the finale. Donald Mitchell surely correctly identifies this transition as that preceding fig. 34 (see DMW, p. 210ff).

p. 32

4. Literally 'fish-sermon' – referring to Mahler's song (from Arnim and Brentano's *Des Knaben Wunderhorn*) 'Des Antonius von Padua Fischpredigt' ('St Anthony of Padua's sermon to the fishes'), of which the Scherzo of the Second Symphony is an expanded orchestral version.

5. In Arnim and Brentano's anthology, the poem is entitled 'Verspätung'. Mahler set a slightly abridged version of it, as 'Das irdische Leben', sometime between April 1892 and the summer of 1893 (see DMW, pp. 140–1).

6. Mahler's title for the *Wunderhorn* poem 'Der Himmel hängt voll Geigen', his 1892 setting of which was subsequently to become the finale of the Fourth Symphony.

p. 33

7. Born in the Bohemian village of Kalischt (now Kališt), Mahler spent the main formative years of his childhood in nearby Iglau (Jihlava) in Moravia – now part of Czechoslovakia.

8. Literally 'dancing rhymes'. As 'Rheinlegendchen' ('Rhine-tale'), Mahler's setting of the *Wunderhorn* poem 'Rheinischer Bundesring' was written in August 1893, and is throughout in a lilting waltz-tempo.

9. One of Mahler's nine earlier *Wunderhorn* settings for voice and piano, published in 1892 as vols. II and III of the *Lieder und Gesänge*, and thought to have been written between 1887 and 1891.

10. Mahler's friendship with Baron Karl von Weber (grandson of the composer) and his wife Marion, during his period in Leipzig (1886–8), developed largely as a result of *Die drei Pintos* (see p. 29 note 1 and p. 176ff). His fondness for the Webers' three children was matched only by his love for their mother, with whom, it would appear, he on one occasion planned to run off (see HLG, pp. 172–3). The implication is that 'Um schlimme Kinder artig zu machen' was one of the songs written 'for Frau Weber's children'.

p. 34

11. Prior to the Hamburg performance of the First Symphony in October 1893, the only significant performances that he had had were of three *Lieder* in Prague in 1886 and in Budapest in 1889, the first performance of the First Symphony in Budapest in 1889,

and of two orchestral *Wunderhorn* songs ('Der Schildwache Nachtlied' and 'Verlorne Müh') in Berlin in 1892.

12. Mahler was first conductor of the Hamburg City Opera from 1891 until 1897.

13. Presumably the Hamburg cycle of May 1892 is referred to, although Mahler had conducted another in London during June and July, in the Wagner season organized by Sir Augustus Harris.

p. 35

14. Mahler was Music and Choral Director at the Cassel Theatre from 1883 until 1885. A similar incident is related by Ferdinand Pfohl of Mahler's period in Hamburg (see FPM, p. 34).

p. 36

15. His sensitivity to noise can be matched only by that of the philosopher Schopenhauer, from whose *Die Welt als Wille und Vorstellung* Mahler later liked to quote on the subject (see AMM p. 47).

16. The disturbing effect upon the king of the mill's noise had been outweighed by its value to the miller as a rightful source of livelihood.

p. 37

17. Mahler's feelings about Brahms changed radically, however, (and more than once) during the course of his life. In a letter to his wife of 1904, Mahler was to call him 'a puny little dwarf with a rather narrow chest' (AMM, p. 239).

18. Born in 1824, Bruckner was in fact sixty-nine in 1893. He died in 1896.

19. The novelist Jean Paul, whose real name was Johann Paul Friedrich Richter (1763–1825), was an important precursor of the Romantic movement in German literature, and a favourite writer of Mahler's. Although Mahler claimed that the original title of his First Symphony – 'Titan' – had nothing to do with Jean Paul's novel of the same name, the subtitle of the first part of the Symphony in the original programme (*Aus den Tagen der Jugend, Blumen-, Frucht- und Dornstücke*) alludes directly to that of another novel by Jean Paul, *Siebenkäs*, or, to give it its full title, *Blumen-, Frucht- und Dornenstücke oder Ehestand, Tod und Hochzeit des Armenadvokaten F. St. Siebenkäs*.

Steinbach am Attersee, summer 1895

p. 40

1. Natalie's journal did not cover the summer of 1894, since she was not invited – on Mahler's specific request to his sister Justine – to join them in Steinbach that year. Mahler did not, he said, wish to be 'placed under surveillance' in that way (see HLG, p. 303). Her devoted interest must indeed have become oppressive at times, but posterity must be grateful for the fact that Mahler lifted his ban in subsequent summers.

2. On 5 June.

3. To the suggestion, made at a banquet, that if Columbus had not discovered America, someone else would have done so, the famous explorer responded by challenging any member of the company to make an egg stand on its end. He finally demonstrated how to do it, by tapping one end of the egg enough to indent the shell and so make it stable – the moral being that others might do such a simple thing, but he had had to show them the way. Mahler invoked this trick on more than one occasion (see e.g. AMM, p. 240) when speaking of novel ideas.

4. *The Youth's Magic Horn* – Arnim and Brentano's famous collection of 'old German songs', dedicated to Goethe and published in two volumes, in 1806 and 1808.

5. Zarathustra's 'Roundelay' – the so-called 'Mitternachtslied' ('Midnight Song') from *Also sprach Zarathustra*.

6. 'Der Sommer zieht ein'. In the following list of titles, as in all subsequent plans, the formula reads 'Der Sommer marschiert ein'.

p. 41

7. As 'Was mir das Kind erzählt', the title 'What the child tells me' was eventually attached to the *Wunderhorn* song 'Das himmlische Leben', which would therefore have formed the finale of the Third Symphony. It was discarded, however, only to be resurrected later as the finale of the Fourth. The titles of the other six movements, although omitted from the published score, are basically as they are to be found in Mahler's 1896 fair copy of the Third Symphony – now in the Pierpont Morgan Library, New York (property of Robert O. Lehmann). Movement 4 – the Nietzsche setting – was eventually simply called 'What Man tells me'; movement 5, 'What the angels tell me'.

8. Literally 'my joyful knowledge', although Mahler clearly alludes here to the title of Nietzsche's work *Die fröhliche Wissenschaft* – usually translated into English as *The Gay Science* (see Introduction by Walter Kaufmann to NGS, pp. 4–7).

Visit to Hamburg, January 1896

p. 42

1. *Songs of a Wayfarer*, composed in 1884 and 1885 for voice and piano, and first orchestrated, according to Donald Mitchell, between 1891 and 1893 (see DMW, p. 111 and preceding). It is probable that Natalie found Mahler simply revising and polishing the orchestration for the Berlin first performance of the cycle on 16 March 1896.
2. *Sic.* In fact the first complete performance of the Second Symphony had taken place in Berlin, under Mahler, on 13 December 1895.
3. Natalie Bauer-Lechner was the viola-player of a ladies' quartet founded and led by Marie Soldat-Röger, a pupil of Joachim. The other members of the quartet were Elly Tinger-Baileti (second violin), and Lucy Herbert-Campbell (cello).
4. On 20 November 1889.
5. The Hamburg performance of the revised First Symphony took place on 27 October 1893. The earlier performance of the Second Symphony referred to was that of the first three movements only, by the Berlin Philharmonic under Mahler, on 4 March 1895. The rest of the concert had been conducted by Richard Strauss.

p. 43

6. Bruno Walter (1876–1962), as Bruno Schlesinger, had been appointed *Korrepetitor* at the Hamburg City Theatre, where Mahler was first conductor, in 1894. Mahler's interest in his talented younger colleague formed the basis of a friendship that was to last until his death in 1911.
7. Dr Hermann Behn (1859–1927) was a wealthy Hamburg lawyer, whose musical interests and talents (he had studied composition under Bruckner) were themselves considerable. An important friend of Mahler's, he was partly responsible for financing the Berlin first performance of the Second Symphony.

p. 44

8. Mahler in fact provided some interesting explanations of the work in subsequent years – e.g. the Dresden 'programme' of 1901 (see AMM, pp. 213–14).

p. 45

9. Mahler was himself a dedicated, even notorious 'editor' of the works of Beethoven and other composers (usually with respect to orchestration). The subject is returned to in these recollections. The concert that prompted these comments took place on 24 January and was conducted by Richard Barth.

In Hamburg again, mid-February 1896

p. 47

1. It is of Hans Rott's mother that Mahler would appear to have related this anecdote to his wife in later years (see AMM, p. 107). The present version is the correct one.

2. Although he had been on terms of quite close friendship with Bruckner, Mahler in fact never studied under him in any formal way. Rudolf Krzyzanowski (1862–1911) was one of Mahler's inner circle of student friends and appears to have collaborated with him on the piano-duet version of Bruckner's Third Symphony, which the composer had entrusted to Mahler, under whose name it was published in 1880.

p. 48

3. The reference is enigmatic. Probably Bruckner is referring to his Ninth which remained unfinished at his death.

Mahler concert in Berlin, 16 March 1896

p. 49

1. Comprising the first movement of the Second Symphony (as 'Todtenfeier' still), the *Lieder eines fahrenden Gesellen* (first performance) and the First Symphony.

2. One must assume that Natalie is referring primarily to the First Symphony here.

p. 50

3. See p. 42 and note 1.

p. 51

4. Many of whom (according to a note by J. Killian in the original German edition) had in fact been given complimentary tickets.

5. The familiar German title of the students' round, better known

elsewhere (and in the major key) as 'Frère Jacques'. The third movement of the First Symphony is largely based upon it.

6. Nikisch (1855–1922) was at this time conductor of the Gewandhaus
Concerts in Leipzig. While technically Nikisch's junior colleague
at the Leipzig Stadttheater (1886–8), Mahler considered him a
serious rival and occasionally treated him, it must be said, with
both suspicion and scorn. Nikisch appears to have borne no grudge,
however, and the promise mentioned here eventually materialized
with his inclusion of the second movement (the 'Blumenstück') of
the Third Symphony in a Berlin concert of 9 November 1896
(Berlin Philharmonic), and again in a Leipzig Gewandhaus concert
of 21 January 1897. The planned performance of part of the Second
Symphony in fact took place at a Lisztverein concert in Leipzig on
14 December 1896 under Mahler's own direction. This orchestra
was less good than that of the Gewandhaus, however, and the performance of the first and second movements of the symphony was
not a success.

7. Hermann Wolff (1845–1902). Based in Berlin, he had organised the
16 March concert referred to above.

Easter visit to Hamburg, April 1896

p. 52

1. Subsequently 'Was mir die Blumen auf der Wiese erzählen' ('What
the flowers in the meadow tell me'). Mahler seems to have drafted,
but not fully orchestrated, all the movements of the Third Symphony but the first (to be completed in the summer of 1896), in
the summer of 1895. The final fair copy of the 'flowers' minuet is
dated 'Hamburg, 11 April '96'.

p. 53

2. The dramatic cantata *Das klagende Lied* (*The Plaintive Song*) had
been completed in October 1880, when Mahler was nineteen years
old. The vegetarianism referred to was the direct result of his ardent
'Wagnerism' at that time. He had, in 1877, joined the Vienna
Wagner Society, many of whose members took the Master's
admonitions on this and other matters extremely seriously.

3. See p. 29 note 1; also p. 33 note 10. The first movement of the
Second Symphony had been called 'Todtendfeier' ('Funeral Rites')
when originally drafted in 1888.

Steinbach am Attersee, summer 1896

p. 55

1. According to Killian's original note here, Mahler had left Vienna for Steinbach on 11 June. Natalie had followed two days later.

2. Weyregg is about 5 kilometres north of Steinbach, on the eastern shore of the Attersee. Natalie had presumably crossed by steamer from Attersee itself.

3. De La Grange (HLG, p. 888 note 3) has located the relevant couplet:

   So geht es im Schnützelputz-Häusel
   Da singen und tanzen die Mäusel

   (That's how it is in the Schnützelputz-Häusel,
   The little mice sing and dance)

4. Mahler had had the little structure built for the summer of 1894, on the lake edge of the grassy peninsula that extends some way behind the *Gasthof*. Although the peninsula is now a camping and caravan site, the general situation is little altered. The fact, however, that the inn bears a large commemorative tablet in Mahler's honour barely mitigates the incorporation of part of the 'Schnützelputz-Häusel' into a larger structure that now contains toilet facilities for the campers.

5. See p. 43 note 7.

p. 56

6. The initial problem over 'getting going' this summer presaged similar experiences in the working summers of later years. It might be observed that on this occasion it was largely a result of the forgotten sketches, which did not arrive until 20 June. The sketch-draft of the movement was in fact completed in little over a week when finally they did arrive (see below, p. 60).

p. 57

7. i.e. the *Gasthof* where Mahler and his party stayed (see above, p. 55 note 4).

8. Hermann Grädener (1844–1929), composer and teacher of harmony at the Vienna Conservatory.

9. Theodor Billroth (1829–94), the important Viennese physician (Professor of Surgery at the University of Vienna) – a notable amateur of music and friend of Brahms.

10. The first movement of a piano quartet in A minor (1877–8) does in fact survive. It is conceivable that it might be the work referred to here. (See HLG, pp. 721–2 and *Gustav Mahler: the Early Years*, London, 1980 – the last mentioned includes the most up-to-date information on the early works.)

11. For a conjectural catalogue of Mahler's youthful works, pieced together from such statements as this, see HLG, p. 704ff. Mahler is thought to have worked at *Die Argonauten* (*The Argonauts*) during 1879 and 1880. Although no record of a prize remains, a sonata for violin and piano was performed by Mahler and a student friend, Richard Schraml, in his home town of Iglau in July 1876. It appears to have been known subsequently to a number of Mahler's friends, but such of it as *was* written down (presumably at least the violin part) is now lost.

p. 58

12. Perhaps these three movements formed part of the manuscript collection, supposedly of 'four unknown early Mahler symphonies', examined in the library of the Weber family in Dresden by Max von Schillings and Willem Mengelberg in the 1930s. The library was destroyed in 1944, before their claim was fully investigated (see HLG, pp. 718–19).

13. Unterach is situated on the south-west tip of the Attersee, about 16 kilometres from Steinbach and just beyond the small resort of Burgau, whose inn is referred to here as 'the Burgau'.

14. To fully understand Mahler's notion of 'faithful performance', would be to find in no way contradictory the ideas expressed here concerning musical *content* and those concerning the need to revise the orchestration of a work where he felt that its content was obscured by the composer's inadequate technical command of his medium of expression. (See also below, p. 63 etc.)

p. 59

15. Mahler refers to the second stanza of Hölderlin's poem 'The Rhine' ('Der Rhein') – a fact that Natalie Bauer-Lechner's text seems once to have made clear (see Appendix 1). The relevant lines of the Hölderin are as follows (the musing poet is struck by the beauty of the Alps in the midday sun, but is duly vouchsafed a vision of the river, personified as a 'youth', struggling to rise from bondage beneath them):

Im kältesten Abgrund hört
Ich um Erlösung jammern
Den Jüngling, es hörten ihn, wie er tobt',
Und die Mutter Erd anklagt'
Und den Donnerer der ihn gezeuget,
Erbarmend die Eltern, doch
Die Sterblichen flohn von dem Ort,
Denn furchtbar war, da lichtloser
In den Fesseln sich wältzte,
Das Rasen des Halbgotts.

16. Having first considered the attributes of the two deities more or less interchangeable for his purposes, in elaborating the inner programme of this movement, Mahler later came to see an important distinction between the Bacchic (with which he associated Pan) and the Dionysian. The movement was eventually sub-titled 'Bachuszug' ('Bacchic Procession'), the introduction (originally conceived as a separate movement) being independently entitled 'Pan erwacht' ('Pan awakes').

17. A somewhat misleading statement. Apart from the enigmatic, 'programmatic' links detailed by Mahler in the following lines, there are significant reminiscences of actual first movement material in both the Nietzsche setting and the Finale. Surviving sketches do nevertheless indicate that other 'interrelationships', involving material from the subsequently discarded *Das himmlische Leben*, were eventually shelved. Only the fifth, 'Morning Bells' movement still bears an undisguised reference to the music of that song.

p. 60

18. See p. 41 and p. 59 note 16. The numbering suggests that Mahler may still have been thinking of the first movement as clearly divided into two at this time.

p. 61

19. While indeed essentially a military-band instrument, the E flat (tenor) *Flügelhorn* – or *Althorn* – entered the symphony orchestra in the nineteenth century as a useful alternative for the two upper Wagner tubas in the *Ring* cycle. It should be noted that in the 1896 fair copy of the movement and in the first published edition, Mahler clearly scores the posthorn solo in the third movement for

Flügelhorn. The instrument was not called for in later editions, which specify a 'posthorn in B♭'.

p. 62

20. A reference to Goethe's *Faust*, Part 1, line 480ff.

p. 63

21. The part-division was adopted in the final version, not so this title of course.

22. In fact Mahler was eventually satisfied with four trumpets, eight horns and five clarinets.

p. 64

23. On the occasion of the final Philharmonic subscription concert in Hamburg, 11 March 1895. One of the features of this particular performance, for which Mahler had 'revised' Beethoven's orchestration according to the principles outlined here, was the positioning of a group of wind instruments off-stage in the *alla marcia* section of the Finale, prior to the entry of the tenor (see HLG, p. 323, and below, p. 69ff).

24. The fourth movement was for long entitled 'What night tells me' (see above, p. 41 note 7).

25. The concluding Adagio, entitled 'What love tells me' (Was mir die Liebe erzählt) in the final manuscript. Apparently 'Das himmlische Leben' – as 'What the child tells me' – had already been discarded by this time (4 July 1896). (See above, p. 41 note 7.)

26. Max Marschalk (1863–1940), composer and music critic. He was an important correspondent of Mahler's.

p. 65

27. Bad Ischl, the well-known health resort (by road about 20 kilometres from Weissenbach on the Attersee) latterly favoured by Brahms, whom Mahler took trouble to visit on the first day of this trip (11 June). It was in fact the last time that Mahler met Brahms, who died in April 1897.

p. 66

28. Mahler had returned to Steinbach on 16 June, after the trip mentioned on p. 65.

29. On the north-west shore of the Attersee, some 20 kilometres from

Steinbach! 'Die Stunde' can mean either 'hour' or 'lesson'; Natalie possibly had a violin pupil there.

p. 67

30. An annoyingly vague description. Of eleven consecutively numbered pages of sketches found amongst Natalie Bauer-Lechner's papers (now in the Library of Stanford University, California) along with this dedicatory wrapper, those numbered 1–4 (the sides of a double sheet) seem to be the ones most likely referred to in the inscription. The first side, dated '1893 Steinbach' (possibly in Natalie's hand) bears a sketch of some of the main components of the Third's subsequent first-movement march material. The other three sides bear sketches of Second Symphony material, mainly for the second movement (which is known to have been completed in 1893). This single page must represent the 'seed' that Mahler speaks of. The remaining seven pages, although certainly including further first-movement sketches, begin with a draft of the opening of the Third's *second* movement, prominently entitled 'Was das Kind erzählt' and dated 1895 in the same hand as before. Whether these too were given to Natalie on this, or a subsequent occasion, is not clear.

31. See below, p. 71 note 41.

32. So successful was Mahler in his dovetailing that, without clear manuscript evidence, the point at which the 'introduction' gives way to the 'first movement' is impossible to identify in the final version. Sketches in the Austrian National Library, Vienna, do however suggest that the passage eight bars before fig. 18 underwent some lengthening and alteration before it reached its final form. Could this be the section referred to?

33. Killian's original editorial note here reads: 'The day is no longer ascertainable, since several pages are cut out at this point. The following events took place after Mahler's return from Bayreuth, where he had gone with Justi on 6 August.'

34. Bruno Walter states (BWM, p. 136) that, when he first got to know him in Hamburg (1894–6), Mahler was 'quite under the influence of Schopenhauer'. The idea expressed here can perhaps only be fully understood with reference to *Die Welt als Wille und Vorstellung*, where Schopenhauer associates the stilling of the individuated will within the self (whereby the true nature of the world can be clearly perceived) with 'the highest good and the state of the gods'

(WWR, vol. I, p. 196). Schopenhauer himself uses the 'Ixion's wheel' image on more than one occasion ('. . . without peace and calm true well-being is absolutely impossible. Thus, the subject of willing is constantly lying on the revolving wheel of Ixion.' WWR, ibid.).

p. 69

35. See p. 33 note 7. Mahler somewhat exaggerated the poverty of his parents' home in Kalischt. Concerning this and the following remarks about his parents, see HLG, p. 7ff.
36. 'Here is Rhodes, and here you dance!'
37. The popular title (since Bülow had been their conductor until 1893) of the Hamburg Philharmonic subscription concerts. Mahler was not invited to conduct a second series. While he had gained considerable respect as an opera conductor, his innovations in the concert hall (see e.g. p. 64 note 23) were not generally appreciated.

p. 70

38. Bernard Pollini (previously Pohl; 1838–97), lessee and somewhat despotic director of the Hamburg Stadttheater.
39. 13 December 1895 (see above, p. 42ff).

p. 71

40. On the first stage of the journey to visit Siegfried Lipiner and his wife in Berchtesgaden (see below, p. 71ff).
41. Remembered in Germany largely for his translations of the Polish poet Mickiewicz, Siegfried Lipiner (1856–1911) was himself a dramatic poet of highly individual character, whose *Prometheus Unbound* (written when he was seventeen) had considerably impressed Nietzsche. In his day, however, his reputation seems to have depended upon his personal fascination as a 'bon viveur' and skilled improviser of philosophical rhapsodies, inspired by a painting or other current topic, with which he would entertain an illustrious circle of acquaintances in Vienna. Mahler and his friends Nina and Albert Spiegler (see below, p. 110 note 22) were for long dominant members of this circle, which included Fritz Löhr, the politician Engelbert Pernerstorfer and, somewhat later, Bruno Walter. The *Christus* referred to was planned, but never completed, as an epic trilogy with a preludial drama entitled *Adam*.
42. Lipiner's wife.

Reunion in Hamburg, September to October 1896

p. 73

1. The manuscript is dated 17 October 1896.

p. 74

2. While he literally longed to move southwards, towards Vienna, the Nietzschean ring of this witticism could well have been intentional. Natalie reveals above (p. 73) that Mahler was reading Nietzsche at this time, more or less while completing the fair copy of the not un-Nietzschean first movement of the Third Symphony – one of whose central sections is headed in the manuscript 'Der Südsturm!' ('Southern Storm!'). Nietzsche frequently extols southern lightness and charm as opposed to Germanic, northern heaviness.

3. Ignaz Brüll (1846–1907), the Austrian composer, was in fact a fairly long-standing acquaintance of Mahler's, having a house at Unterach on the Attersee. During the summer, Mahler and his friends would often join the broad circle of Viennese artists and intellectuals that Brüll entertained there. His one-act opera *Gloria* was staged (unsuccessfully) in Hamburg for the first time on 15 October 1896, along with Emil Hartmann's *Runenzauber*. Natalie must have thought that both operas were by Brüll.

4. Karl Goldmark (1830–1915). His opera *Das Heimchen am Herd*, based on Dickens's *The Cricket on the Hearth*, was given its first performance on 26 October.

5. Otto Weidig (as Knud Martner believes the name to have been spelled) was also a member of the opera orchestra in Hamburg.

p. 75

6. It is interesting, not least in relation to Mahler's possible Nietzschean sympathies (see above, p. 74 note 2 – *Carmen* was the central work of the 'southern' spirit that Nietzsche extolled as a necessary antidote to Wagner), that the Czech composer Joseph Bohuslav Förster requested a score of *Die Meistersinger*, in order to study its orchestration, at this time, but was instead given *Carmen* by Mahler, who considered it a better example (see HLG, p. 382).

7. An idea surely derived from Goethe's *The Metamorphosis of Plants* (botanical treatise, 1790; expository poem of the same name, 1798).

8. On Mahler's invitation, Bruno Walter had spent part of the summer of 1896 at Steinbach. Walter describes the visit in BWM (pp. 22–9).

p. 76

9. Possibly an exaggeration on Natalie's part, unless the visit to Berkhan's, referred to below, had in fact taken place earlier in 1896, perhaps in February. (See HLG, p. 899 note 40.)

10. Wilhelm Berkhan, a Hamburg industrialist, was Mahler's benefactor on more than one occasion.

p. 77

11. The full score of the Second Symphony was published by Hofmeister in 1897. The Third Symphony was published by Weinberger in 1902, following its first complete performance at Crefeld in June that year.

Trial concert in Munich, 24 March 1897

p. 78

1. In fact *one* concert, on 24 March, preceded by a public rehearsal in the normal way. The programme comprised the overture to *Die Meistersinger*, movements 2 and 3 of Berlioz's *Symphonie fantastique* and Beethoven's Fifth Symphony (see HLG, pp. 404–5). Mahler was seeking appointment as conductor of the Kaim orchestra (founded by the philologist and literary historian Franz Kaim in 1893). The position went to Felix Weingartner.

2. Mahler had been in Moscow from the 12th to the 15th of March, on which date he had conducted the eighth concert of the Imperial Russian Music Society (including Beethoven's Fifth once more and Wagner's *Siegfried Idyll*).

3. Wagner must be meant here (see above, p. 78 note 1).

The call to Vienna, 1 May 1897

p. 80

1. Mahler's contract (initially he was appointed as *Kapellmeister* only) was ratified on 16 April 1897. It was to commence on 1 June although Mahler in fact began work at the Court Opera on 27 April 1897 – his first task being to go to Venice for the world première of Leoncavallo's *La Bohème* (which Jahn wanted to produce during the next season).

2. Although ailing (he was going blind) and clearly overdue for retirement, Wilhelm Jahn (1835–1900) was still technically Director of the Hofoper when Mahler took up his duties. Felix Mottl

(1856–1911), who had been chief conductor at Bayreuth since 1886, was General Music Director at the Grand Ducal Opera in Karlsruhe. He was in fact a serious rival for the post. Ernst von Schuch (1846–1914) was Director of the Dresden Theatre, where he remained until his death.

3. Having left Vienna on 28 March, Mahler had arrived back on 1 April, after conducting a highly successful Philharmonic Concert in Budapest (again including Beethoven's Fifth Symphony).

Mahler's personality and appearance
p. 82

1. The figure in the children's cautionary picture-book, who would not look after his hair or finger-nails.

PART II: Mahler in Vienna

The opera season, May to summer 1897
p. 90

1. A note attributed to Natalie Bauer-Lechner in the original edition, suggests that the writer of this letter, received by Mahler the day after the performance, 'was possibly an older member of the orchestra'.

p. 91

2. 'See, see, how strange a marvel' – Act I, scene 3 (the arrival of Lohengrin).
3. 'In the forest's distant solitude' (Ortrud) – Act II, scene 2.
4. 'O heaven, shield her from danger' – Act II, scene 5.
5. 'You heroes . . .' – Act II, scene 5.
6. 'The sounds of revelry now forsaken' – Act III, scene 1 (from the Bridal Chorus).

p. 92

7. (1843–1916). The famous German conductor, who had been a protégé of Wagner's, was still attached to the Vienna Opera, although concert tours took up an increasing amount of his time. Twenty years his junior, Mahler had anticipated problems in the collaboration, but seems largely to have avoided them by treating Richter with due deference and tact. Richter finally relinquished his post at the Opera in 1900.

p. 93

8. The jargon word 'punktieren' is in fact used by Mahler here to imply 'engage a guest singer' – its literal meaning being to dot, punctuate or stipple.

9. The Prater is an extensive recreational park between the Danube and the Danube Canal, to the east of the city centre. The Sophien-brücke was renamed the Rotundenbrücke in the 1920s, and is the bridge that leads from the Third District of Vienna into the centre of the Prater.

10. 5 June 1897.

11. The word used is 'Furor' – indicating a passionate emotional in-volvement of the kind that might be expected to excite a 'furore' in others.

p. 94

12. Marie Wilt (1833–91), the operatic soprano, famous for her 'bravura' singing.

13. Scheduled for 26 May, the performance of *Die Walküre* had finally been cancelled as the result of a cast indisposition (Mahler himself had risen from his sickbed to conduct the rehearsals). The per-formance of *Die Zauberflöte* took place on 29 May.

Summer 1897

p. 96

1. Jahn (see above, p. 80 note 2) had a villa at Trofaiach in northern Styria. He received Mahler there – with great, even unexpected warmth – on 29 May. Mahler later felt that Jahn was not fully aware that he was about to be retired. Mahler was officially appointed deputy conductor on 13 July 1897.

2. Now Dobbiaco. It was here that Mahler was in fact to spend the last three summers of his life (1908, 1909 and 1910).

The 'Ring' Cycle, August 1897

p. 98

1. '*Anschwellen des Tons in der Mitte des Bogens*': Natalie's parenthetical explanation of *portamento* is not, of course, what is generally under-stood by the word nowadays (i.e. sliding from one note to another with a more or less perceptible *glissando*). Mahler clearly used the

word in this context to refer to the way the note is 'held', in the literal sense of *portamento*.

p. 99

2. Sophie Sedlmair (1857–1939).
3. Arnold Rosé (1863–1946), subsequently Mahler's brother-in-law (see p. 20 note 1).

p. 100

4. M. de La Grange notes that the musicians' salaries ranged from 660 to 900 guilders per year, with additional 'activity pay', ranging between 120 and 200 guilders, according to the amount of playing-time put in (see HLG, p. 909 note 29). It was common for orchestral musicians to supplement their income by giving private instrumental lessons. (A guilder was worth about 1s 8d in the old British currency – the 2s piece, or florin, being the nearest coin equivalent; 10p in modern British currency.)

p. 101

5. Such cuts, particularly that of the entire Norns' scene at the beginning of *Götterdämmerung*, were still quite common at this time.
6. First performed in 1868 in Prague, the work was not a success, in spite of the heroic and nationalistic sentiments which were later to endear it to the Czech people. The première of Mahler's production was on 4 October.

p. 103

7. *Tsar and Carpenter* (1837), a comic opera by the largely self-taught Berlin composer Albert Lortzing (1803–51).

p. 104

8. The first performance of the revival of *Zar und Zimmermann* (see also p. 103) had been on 11 September. The first performance of the new *Magic Flute* took place on 16 October.

p. 105

9. The Orpheus of legend was able to tame wild animals with his lyre. Arion, about to be put to death at sea, had requested leave to play briefly before dying. On finishing, he threw himself into the sea and was carried to the shore by dolphins who had been charmed by his music.

10. The usual bowdlerized version runs: 'Sie kommt, lasst uns bei
    Seite gehn, / Damit wir, was sie mache, sehn.' ('She comes, let's
    stand aside / To see what she will do.') It is sung by the Three Boys
    as they watch over Pamina in Act II. De La Grange (see HLG, p. 912
    note 18) observes that the phrase 'auf die Seite geh'n' is in fact a
    German euphemism for relieving oneself.

11. Eduard Wlassack, a banker and high court official, was Director
    of the Chancellery of the Opera, but remained generally one of the
    most active of the senior officers of the administration. He had been
    centrally involved in the machinations in support of Mahler's
    nomination for the post of Director.

p. 107

12. The practice of hiring a claque was long established for major
    operatic singers; Mahler never altogether eradicated it.

13. The original edition bore a note attributed to Natalie Bauer-
    Lechner here: 'Entrance to the auditorium was forbidden to late-
    comers. It primarily applied during the overture in all operas, but
    with Wagner was extended to the prelude and the first act, where
    they ran together. The same applied to all subsequent acts.'

14. Prince Rudolf Liechtenstein, the Lord Chamberlain, under whose
    jurisdiction fell the administration of both the Hofoper and the
    Burgtheater (although Mahler's official dealings were generally
    with his assistant and future successor, Prince Alfred Montenuovo,
    the court official specifically responsible for the administration of
    the Opera).

p. 108

15. 'They're not drinking, they're not singing; no light burns in their
    ship.'

16. Hermann Winkelmann (1849–1912), the dramatic tenor who had
    created the role of Parsifal at Bayreuth in 1882.

p. 109

17. Five years older than Mahler, Adler came from the same part of
    Moravia (he too was brought up in Iglau). The two met in the
    late 1870s, when both were members of the Wagner Society in
    Vienna, and remained close friends. Adler, who was to be an
    important advocate of Mahler's, became a well-known musi-

cologist and in 1898 succeeded Hanslick as Professor of the History of Music in the University of Vienna. He published a study of Mahler in 1916.

18. A note attributed to Natalie Bauer-Lechner in the original edition explains: 'In addition, Adler secured a contribution of 3000 guilders towards the cost of printing, from the Society for the Promotion of German Science, Art and Literature in Bohemia [Gesellschaft zur Förderung deutscher Wissenschaft, Kunst und Literatur in Böhmen].'

p. 110

19. (1848–1929). The famous soprano, who had taken part in the first Bayreuth Festival in 1876 and was to become artistic director of the Salzburg Festival in 1905. In 1906 she invited Mahler to conduct *Le Nozze di Figaro* there.

20. Fanny Mora[n-Olden] (1855–1905).

21. Hans Richter – as we later learn (see p. 92 note 7).

22. The Spieglers were in Mahler's closest inner circle of friends throughout his time in Vienna (see also p. 71 note 41). Nina Spiegler was to be described by Bruno Walter as the 'heart' of the circle: a 'sufferer from physical ailments and ethereally delicate' (see BWT, p. 164). When the circle met for dinner at the Restaurant Hartmann after an opera performance, she would see to it that a bunch of violets was placed beside Mahler's plate.

23. Andreas Dippel (1866–1932).

p. 111

24. The baritone Theodor Reichmann (1849–1903), who had created the role of Amfortas in *Parsifal*.

p. 113

25. 'Naiv' – surely to be taken in Schiller's sense of the naive (*On Naive and Sentimental Poetry*): as indicative of a sense of oneness with Nature.

p. 114

26. Having finally become divorced, in 1870, from Cosima, later Cosima Wagner, Hans von Bülow had married, in 1882, Marie Schanzer – the daughter of a director of the War Ministry in Vienna. Bülow had become acquainted with her as an actress at Meiningen.

p. 115

27. Baron August von Plappart was largely concerned with the technical and financial aspects of the Opera's administration. His post was that of an intermediary between Prince Montenuovo (see p. 107 note 14) and the Opera staff. Mahler considered himself responsible only to Montenuovo.

28. Count Géza Zichy (1849–1924), a Hungarian aristocrat and well-known one-armed piano virtuoso, had been appointed Intendant of the National Theatre and Opera in Budapest in January 1891. His overbearing manner was indeed largely responsible for Mahler's departure from that institution in the same year.

p. 116

29. Mahler's own libretto for this planned opera, dating from 1879–80, has survived. No music remains, and the opera was never completed. Rübezahl is the mountain-spirit of an East German legend (see HLG, p. 712ff).

30. This account is not accurate. According to de La Grange (HLG, pp. 79–82) *Das klagende Lied* (see p. 53 note 2) was submitted to the jury in December 1881, when the prize went to Robert Fuchs. Rott had apparently intended to submit two scores in 1880, but had gone mad before the prizes were awarded. The possibly decisive failure for Rott had been in a composition contest of 1878. Mahler was conductor at the provincial theatre of Laibach (now Ljubljana) for the season September 1881 to April 1882. The Herzfeld referred to was Viktor von Herzfeld (1850–1920), subsequently a music critic in Budapest, where, in spite of friendly relations with Mahler, he was to write a highly unfavourable review of the latter's First Symphony.

The 1898–1899 season

p. 117

1. The operation had been for haemorrhoids, a recurrent complaint of Mahler's. The information included in this prefatory note would appear to have been gleaned by Killian from a section of Natalie's journal that has, according to de La Grange, been 'carefully censored by outside hands' (HLG, p. 480). Although Mahler later denied any but physical distress at this time, the 'painful personal matters' could conceivably refer to his feelings about the revelation of a romance between his sister Justine and his *Konzertmeister*,

Arnold Rosé (see also p. 20 note 1), who spent that summer in Vahrn with them. In addition, Mahler's younger sister Emma (1875–1933), had married the cellist Eduard Rosé, brother of the above, on 2 June, prior to leaving for the United States with him.

2. *Das Rheingold*, scenes 3 and 4.
3. As a note for 1 April 1900 indicates, Mahler later 'got an increase in pay for all workers, in the face of the most determined opposition from the management.' [Note by J. Killian.]

p. 118

4. In terms of personnel the same orchestra that played for the Opera, the Vienna Philharmonic was (and remains) a self-governing body that elected its own conductors.
5. It was finally published in 1901/2 by Joseph Weinberger.
6. 'Hochzeitsstück' ('Wedding Piece'), four bars before fig. 47.

p. 119

7. It is unclear precisely which Wagner text Mahler might have referred to here. His ideas about the general inadequacy of Beethoven's instrumentation (see above, pp. 63–4) relate most clearly to Wagner's essay 'Zum Vortrag der neunten Symphonie Beethovens' ('The Rendering of Beethoven's Ninth Symphony') of 1873. The quartet performed orchestrally on 15 January 1899 was in fact that in F minor, op. 95 (see below, p. 122).
8. Gustav Schönaich was an influential Viennese music critic.

p. 120

9. It should be noted that the Norns' scene was receiving its first staging in Vienna in this September 1898 *Ring* cycle under Mahler.
10. Dr Eduard Hanslick (1825–1904), the eminent critic and musical aesthetician whose approbation, even support, Mahler had won against many odds. (Hanslick was regarded as something of an 'establishment' figure, whose conservative principles had led him inevitably to side with Brahms in the Brahms–Wagner controversy.)

p. 121

11. '*Sechzehntel*': in fact the violin figuration immediately after the initial chords is in quavers (*Achtel*). This must have been a slip on Mahler's part.
12. See p. 92 note 7.

p. 122

13. Karl Lueger had been Mayor of Vienna since 1895, and was to remain in office until the First World War. His anti-Semitic and somewhat theatrical style earned him the admiration of the young Hitler.

p. 124

14. The Music Society Hall, facing the northern perimeter of the Karlsplatz.
15. In the eighth and final Philharmonic concert of the series, 26 February 1899.

p. 125

16. The ringleaders, according to de La Grange, were two cellists named Kretschmann and Sulzer (HLG, p. 505).
17. See above, p. 42ff.

p. 126

18. 3 March 1898; the Kaim orchestra under Ferdinand Löwe. Mahler had not been present.
19. Presumably a reference to the prominent counter-melody given to half the cellos, seven bars after fig. 5. In fairness to the players, the marking is *molto espressivo* here!

p. 127

20. Killian added a note here, to the effect that 'In Mahler's original draft (found amongst the author's papers) the Andante is actually marked as the fourth movement'. The present whereabouts of this 'original draft' is not known. Interestingly, an apparently early pencil sketch for the movement exists in which the cello counter-melody referred to above (see p. 126 note 19) has been subsequently inked in by Mahler beneath the main theme at the outset. There are other indications that this opening caused Mahler much thought (see DMW, p. 274 note 52).

Summer 1899, 8 June to 29 July

p. 129

1. The Villa Seri, situated in fact some way above the small town of Bad Aussee, a Styrian health resort to the south-east of Bad Ischl.

p. 130

2. Dr Karl G. Löwe (1796–1869), known best for the ballads to which Mahler refers: miniature narrative pieces, whose dramatic realism and motivic technique have been considered anticipatory of certain aspects of Wagnerian music-drama.

3. *Humoresken* – a generic title that Mahler liked to give to his *Wunderhorn* songs. Some were in fact first performed under it (see HLG, plates 45 and 47). The Fourth Symphony was initially entitled 'Humoreske'.

4. Literally the 'piper's *Alm*'. An *Alm* is a clear, sloping stretch of mountainside pasture.

p. 131

5. The *Wunderhorn* song, dated July 1899. Mahler was rather proud of the fact that it was sketched while sitting in an outside privy (see HLG, pp. 522–3).

p. 132

6. Literally 'little house'; a reference to Mahler's Steinbach summer-house (see above p. 55).

7. See also above, p. 37 (and note 18).

8. Natalie had accompanied Arnold Rosé, Justine and Mahler to Bad Ischl, where the latter was to visit Prince Liechtenstein (see p. 107 note 14). They subsequently met Siegfried Lipiner, who accompanied them to St Wolfgang on the Wolfgangsee, whence Mahler was to return to Vienna two days later (see HLG, pp. 526–7).

9. The equivalent of a spa pump-room.

p. 133

10. Mahler had been back at the Opera since 1 August, but the unfortunate experiences of that summer had made it clear that a new and more reliable holiday retreat was required for following years. Natalie and Justi had been detailed to carry out the search for a suitable residence.

11. A small village on the southern shore of the Wörther See.

12. The Wagnerian soprano Anna von Mildenburg (1872–1947), who came from this part of Austria. As his protégé in Hamburg, she had literally been 'created' by Mahler, who brought her to Vienna in 1898, where she was to establish herself as one of the great stars of his reign there. Their protracted love-affair was already waning,

particularly on Mahler's side, by this time. By virtue of her temperament and highly theatrical personality, however, 'die Mildenburg' was to cause Mahler many problems during subsequent years, particularly following his marriage to Alma Schindler in 1902.

13. The Schlössl Schwarzenfels was a *Frühstückspension* (a bed-and-breakfast boarding-house), occupying a commanding position on the shore of the Wörther See, somewhat to the east of the spot where Mahler's villa was subsequently to be built.

p. 134

14. The provincial capital of Carinthia, situated just inland of the easternmost tip of the Wörther See.

15. Maiernigg (as it is now spelled) is situated a few kilometres around the south-eastern shore of the Wörther See, west of Klagenfurt. The Mahler villa is in fact in the locality just beyond Maiernigg, now known as Seekirn.

16. The famous home of traditional drama, opposite the Rathauspark, on the Ringstrasse. Joseph Kainz is the actor referred to.

17. The mezzo-soprano Laura Hilgermann (1869–1937) had been engaged by Mahler that year. She had sung for him previously in Budapest.

18. Selma Kurz (1877–1933), later to become a famous coloratura soprano.

The 1899–1900 season

p. 136

1. Once again it might be suggested that Mahler's ideas are best understood in terms of the philosophical ideas of Schopenhauer, who held that it was the role of the artist ultimately to sink his awareness of himself as an individual in a broad sympathetic awareness of the world, or Nature, in all its apparent diversity. Herein the 'will-freed' state in which the 'Ixion's wheel' is stilled (see p. 67 note 34). Mahler was in no sense simply a Schopenhauerian, however, and his regard precisely for the moments of *individuated* 'inner emotion' in these movements is highly significant.

2. The tune 'Funiculi funicula' Strauss had in fact mistakenly thought to be a genuine Neapolitan folk-song. Its composer was Luigi Denza (1846–1922), who became Professor of Singing at the Royal Academy of Music in London in 1898.

p. 139

3. Dr Ludwig Rottenberg (1864–1932), the pianist and conductor, who was *Kapellmeister* at the Frankfurt Opera.
4. Clearly a mistake. The first fermata is indicated above a single minim. It is the *second* fermata that is mysteriously notated

p. 141

5. Dr Richard Batka (1868–1922), Prague critic and co-founder of the *New Musical Review* in 1896; a particular adherent of Richard Strauss.
6. Heinrich von Bocklet, whose arrangement of Mahler's Second Symphony was published by Universal Edition in 1914, was the son of the violinist and pianist Karl Maria von Bocklet (1801–81).
7. The original reads: 'ihm, wie er sich ausdrückte, einige "Seifensieder aufgesteckt" habe.' Literally rendered, this would be: '. . .and had, as he put it, set "a few soapmakers" on to him again.' The idiom, whose origin is obscure, has no direct parallel in English.
8. The passage referred to is that between figs 40 and 43.

p. 142

9. In accordance with general nineteenth-century practice, Mahler would normally have had the first violins on his left and the seconds on his right along the front of the platform, rather than grouped together on the left in the modern way.

p. 143

10. 17 December 1899. The concert also included the Brahms Violin Concerto, played by Marie Soldat-Röger – of whose string quartet Natalie Bauer-Lechner was a member.
11. Dr Robert Hirschfeld (1858–1914), critic and musical aesthetician.
12. Presumably the same Joseph Sulzer that would appear to have been at the centre of the anti-Mahler campaign the previous April (see above, p. 125 note 16).

p. 144

13. (1874–1935). She had sung at the Weimar Opera under Richard Strauss prior to moving to Vienna in 1900, where she was to achieve many successes – not least in contemporary works (Elektra was one of her famous roles; she also sang in the first performance

of Schoenberg's Second String Quartet). The *Carmen* performance referred to was on 26 May 1900.

Summer 1900, Mayernigg, Villa Antonia

p. 145

1. Mahler had taken the Vienna Philharmonic to the World Exhibition in June. The orchestra had given four concerts there.
2. See below, p. 148.

p. 146

3. A close student friend of Mahler's and a pupil of Bruckner's, Rott (b. 1859) had succumbed to madness in 1880, his condition exacerbated by poverty, the lack of recognition, and even outright discouragement on the part of Brahms. He died of tuberculosis in a psychiatric hospital in June 1884. A number of his compositions, including one complete symphony and three movements of another, have survived in the Nationalbibliothek in Vienna (see HLG, p. 845 note 29).

p. 148

4. He had been on a solitary walking and cycling tour there from 15 to 19 July.
5. Of thick stone walls, the Maiernigg retreat was a much more spacious and substantial affair than the Steinbach *Häuschen*. It can still be reached only by climbing a steep woodland path – between tall trees and often quite thick undergrowth – that leads upwards, away from the lake, from the road behind the villa (not yet built in 1900, of course). The interior consists simply of a square room with centrally placed, shuttered windows on three sides and a large door in the fourth (this must be the fourth 'window' referred to below). A small, lockable safe-cupboard is inset in one wall. The building is surrounded by a modest terrace walk, slightly raised above the forest floor, whose shape is still more or less preserved by vestigial rockery. Natalie's 'wrought-iron gates' might suggest that this once supported a low surrounding fence.

p. 149

6. The alkaline sulphur springs of Karlsbad (now Karlovy Vary in Czechoslovakia) were famous for their efficacy in treating digestive disorders.

p. 150

7. Entitled 'Hans und Grethe' in vol. I of Mahler's *Lieder und Gesänge*, it also exists in a manuscript version entitled 'Maitanz im Grünen'. The text of this song, which is musically related to the Scherzo of the First Symphony, begins with the nursery-rhyme formula, 'Ringel, ringel Reih'n!' (more or less an equivalent of the English 'Ring-a-ring-o'-roses'). It should be noted that the song was, in fact, written in 1880, before Mahler went to Leipzig.

p. 151

8. See p. 130 note 3.
9. See p. 32 note 6, and p. 41 note 7.

p. 152

10. The text of the song includes the lines:

> Elftausend Jungfrauen zu tanzen sich trauen!
> Sankt Ursula selbst dazu lacht!

> (Eleven thousand maidens join in a dance!
> St Ursula herself has to laugh!)

St Ursula is known to legend as a virgin martyr who, with ten companions, was slaughtered for her faith by the Huns at Cologne. Later versions of the story turned the eleven maidens into eleven thousand.

p. 153

11. The Hamburg critic Ferdinand Pfohl relates that this word was a favourite colloquial expletive of Mahler's – uttered in a great variety of tones and in response to a wide variety of human follies, not least those of critics with whom he disagreed (see FPM, p. 15).
12. The first movement of the Fourth Symphony is fascinatingly allusive throughout, and it is difficult to pin-point precisely the passages that Mahler might have referred to. Donald Mitchell, however, has isolated a portion of ballet music from Weber's *Oberon* (Act II) which bears a clear resemblance to the first two bars (flutes) following fig. 13 in the Mahler movement (see DMW, pp. 296-7).

p. 154

13. Some seven or eight kilometres north-east of Klagenfurt, the location of a famous cathedral church.

14. The section between bars 221 (fig. 17) and 233 is clearly what is referred to here. The trumpet motive that was to open the 'Trauermarsch' of the Fifth Symphony is heard here for the first time. The passage in the Second Symphony designated by Mahler 'Der grosse Appell' (and so marked in one manuscript source) begins at fig. 29 in the finale. The word 'Appell' means roll-call, or muster in the military sense which, in a consideration of the Fourth Symphony, would clearly have to take precedence over the explicitly apocalyptic sense in which the word was understood in the context of the earlier work.

p. 154

15. Originally called 'Was mir die Morgenglocken erzählen' ('What the morning bells tell me'), this *Wunderhorn* setting forms the fifth movement of the Third Symphony. The relationship is between it and the song finale – 'Das himmlische Leben' – of the Fourth (cf. Fourth Symphony, finale: bars 36–9 and bar 55ff, and Third Symphony, movement 5: eight bars before fig. 6ff and fig. 5ff). Mahler had, of course, once planned to use the song as the finale of the Third Symphony.

p. 155

16. Identified by de La Grange as Hubert Wondra, the nephew of the previous director, Jahn. He was chorus director at the Opera and was described by Alfred Roller as a 'guardian of "tradition"' (KBD, p. 237). Bruno Walter, while identifying him as Karl Wondra, echoes this description (BWT, p. 172). It might be added that while Mahler seems to have felt no special antipathy towards him, de La Grange describes Wondra as 'secretly one of his most dangerous enemies' (HLG, p. 911 note 49).

The 1900–1901 season

p. 157

1. See p. 134 note 18.
2. Compare this section with Natalie Bauer-Lechner's letter to Ludwig Karpath of 16 November 1900. See Appendix II and Plate 4.
3. Described as a 'Symphonic Poem in two parts' at its Budapest première (1889), the First Symphony was performed in Hamburg

in 1893 as ' "Titan", a tone-poem in symphonic form'. When performed in Berlin in 1896, the work was simply 'Symphony in D for large orchestra'. The title was never reintroduced. Note, however, that Mahler still referred to the hero of the work as a 'struggling Titan' at the time of this 1896 performance (see above, p. 50)

4. A novel (1800–3). (See above, p. 37 note 19, and DMW, p. 225ff.)

p. 158

5. The First Symphony was to be performed in Vienna on 19 November 1900. The audience indeed neither understood nor liked it on that occasion.

6. I assume Mahler meant that he doubted if anyone would recognize the thematic origin of the jocular D–A reiteration which the timpani interpolate in the final tutti. These are, of course, the opening notes of the first subject of the exposition.

7. The first two bars of the main theme of the Trio (in a slow waltz-tempo) bear a clear resemblance to those of the second theme of the Scherzo of Bruckner's Third Symphony (bars 61 and 62), of which Mahler had produced a piano-duet version in 1878, the year after the work's first performance in Vienna (see p. 47 note 2). The nature of the 'slight alteration' made on this occasion is not known.

8. The movement referred to, discarded along with the 'Titan' title by the time of the 1896 performance in Berlin, was a romantically wistful Andante entitled 'Blumine'. It had in fact come between the first movement and the Scherzo (not after the latter, as stated here).

9. Mahler conducted at the Leipzig Stadttheater from 1886 until 1888 (see p. 51 note 6). The work was in fact probably first sketched in 1885, the Scherzo possibly even earlier (see HLG, p. 746).

p. 159

10. Emperor Wilhelm I had died on 9 March 1888.

11. See above, p. 33 note 10.

12. At fig. 16.

13. Max Stägemann (1843–1905) was Director of the Leipzig Stadttheater.

p. 160

14. Prior to the first performance on 20 November 1889. It is clear

from this that the first A had not in fact been 'in harmonics' when he first played the work over to the Webers (see p. 159).

p. 161
15. End of December, 1900. [Note by J. Killian.]

p. 162
16. If the soloist is to tune his strings a whole tone higher than usual, the part must clearly be notated in the key a whole tone below that of the other instruments. This passage is interesting, however, in that the final version of the movement is in C minor, the *scordatura* fiddle part being written in B flat minor. Is Natalie mistaken here, or did Mahler originally conceive the Scherzo in E minor? Mahler might have come to feel that the romantic 'point' of a scherzo in E minor and a finale in E major was a little too obvious.
17. In the final version, the Scherzo *is* the second movement, of course. Natalie's apparent distinguishing between Scherzo and second movement might indicate confusion on her part rather than uncertainty as to their final order in Mahler's own mind. It is impossible to tell from the reference which of the two movements is referred to here.
18. Beginning of January 1901. [Note by J. Killian.]
19. The extent to which Mahler actually avoided formal training in counterpoint was to become a somewhat contentious issue (see HLG, pp. 38–9). It might be pointed out that Mahler is not alone among major composers who have questioned their grasp of 'strict counterpoint' in mid-career (see also above, p. 147).

p. 163
20. August Stoll, Chief Stage Director at the Opera; he also taught at the Conservatory. He is amusingly described by Bruno Walter as one of those long-established members of the Opera administration who 'represented the persevering and untouchable spirit of a former epoch, until the only power superior to them, Time, put an end to their activities.' (BWT, p. 172.)
21. Surely inspired by *Die Meistersinger*, Mahler was fond of alluding to Hans Sachs's trade whenever he wanted a humorous example of a lowly occupation.

p. 164

22. Marie Gutheil-Schoder (see p. 144 note 13).

23. Almost certainly one of his own younger brothers. Although he
did not die of scarlet fever, it is known that Mahler spent long
hours at the bedside of his favourite brother Ernst, prior to the
latter's death in 1875. Mahler was fourteen at the time (see HLG,
pp. 11 and 26).

p. 165

24. The Bach Gesellschaft edition must be referred to here, although
whether Mahler had in fact acquired all sixty volumes must be
open to doubt. The last of these had been published in 1900,
at which time the Society had been dissolved. In its place a
New Bach Society (Neue Bach Gesellschaft) came into being
under Hermann Kretzschmar as President, its object being the
popularisation and publication of practicable performing versions
of Bach's music. Along with names like Felix Weingartner and
Ferrucio Busoni, Mahler's appears on its list of *Ausschussmitglieder*
(committee or board-members). In view of the Society's aims,
the volumes of the original Gesellschaft edition may well have been
presented to the new 'ex-officio' members (GDM, vol. 1, p. 187).
Mahler's place on the Neue Gesellschaft board ('advisory council'
might be a better term – he was not on the central, governing
committee) perhaps came about as a logical sequel to his election
to the board of Guido Adler's *Denkmäler der Tonkunst in Österreich*
(*Monuments of Austrian Music*) in 1898 (see HLG, p. 465).

25. As Donald Mitchell has pointed out, this must be Cantata 48
(Church Cantatas vol. v in the Bach Gesellschaft edition), whose
correct title should read: *Ich elender Mensch, wer wird mich erlösen?*
(*Who will redeem me, pitiful creature that I am?*). *Sündig* means
'sinful'. (See DMW, p. 349.)

p. 166

26. According to de La Grange, this conversation took place on
18 April 1901 (see HLG, p. 938 note 25). The concert might well
have been under Nikisch, who, along with his duties in Leipzig,
was principal conductor of the Berlin Philharmonic from 1897
until his death in 1922. That the work was in his repertoire at this
time is attested to by Bruno Walter's recollection of an 'over-

powering rendering' of it under Nikisch in Berlin, prior to his (Walter's) removal to Vienna in 1901 (BWT, p. 140).

27. Mahler had had similarly unkind things to say about *Eugene Onegin* in 1892, which he had conducted in the presence of Tchaikovsky in Hamburg. By the composer himself (who had been greatly pleased with the performance) Mahler was more favourably impressed, however (see HLG, p. 248). He was in some way to make up for his excessively harsh opinion of Tchaikovsky at that time, and in respect of this performance of the Sixth Symphony, by giving himself over with some enthusiasm to the preparation of *The Queen of Spades* in Vienna, in December 1902 (see AMM, p. 50).

Summer 1901, the Mahler villa on the Wörther See

p. 168

1. Mahler had a piano in his retreat, on which he must clearly have been trying out some of his ideas (see AMM, p. 45).
2. Cf. the beginning of the previous summer (above, pp. 145–6).

p. 169

3. Dr A. F. Hermann Kretzschmar (1848–1924), the famous musicologist, who had been Professor of Music at Leipzig University since 1887. (Thomas Mann was to give his name to the organist and lecturer on music who plays a crucial role in the earlier part of his novel *Dr Faustus*.) (See also p. 165 note 24.) The essay referred to could well have been the 'Bemerkungen über den Vartrag alter Musik', published in the '*Jahrbuch der Musikbibliothek Peters*, VII (1900).
4. Again the *Bach Gesellschaft* edition is referred to (see above, p. 165 note 24). The 'Third Motet' is otherwise identified by de La Grange as BWV 227 (HLG, index p. 965).

p. 170

5. Baron Karl von Weber, the composer's grandson (see above, p. 33 note 10).

p. 171

6. 'The Sentinel's Night-Song'. The voice and piano version of this setting of a *Wunderhorn* poem (of the same name as the song) is in fact dated 28 January 1892, and Donald Mitchell has expressed

doubt that it was actually conceived in 1888, which is what the foregoing passage here would seem to suggest (see DMW, p. 259 note 33). In the song the fatalistic musings of a sentinel on night-duty are interrupted by the (imagined?) reassurances of his faithful loved-one, but to no avail. It is certainly difficult to see quite how the song could have stemmed from the opera-plan. Perhaps the latter had been suggested to Mahler by the *Wunderhorn* poem, which he would only later set in its original form.

7. See above, p. 40 note 4.

p. 172

8. The Scherzo in the final version. What follows seems to confirm that it was this movement that Mahler was working on.

9. Thomas Koschat (1843–1914) was a native Carinthian, having been born near Klagenfurt. Of his compositions, the hundred or more 'Carinthian' quartets for men's voices achieved some considerable popularity. His *Liederspiel, Am Wörthersee*, had recently been given at the Vienna Opera (see HLG, p. 941 note 59). The song referred to is not, alas, to be found in the (incomplete) collection of the composer's works held in the British Museum, and other attempts to unearth it have so far proved fruitless.

p. 173

10. The Fifth Symphony was ultimately to be cast in five-movement form. The foregoing seems to suggest that the Scherzo was already conceived as the third movement, but without manuscript evidence it is impossible to say which of the other movements was yet to be added to the envisaged scheme – unless Mahler was thinking of the first two movements as essentially a unit (which in many respects they are). The matter is further complicated by the fact that the final version is presented as a three-part structure (Part I: movements 1 and 2 – Part II: movement 3 (Scherzo) – Part III: Adagietto and Rondo-Finale).

11. The subsequent reference to the late completion of 'Ich bin der Welt abhanden gekommen' that summer, brings the total to eight, of course. From what follows, and from certain other sources (see e.g. DMW, p. 439, addenda to p. 35), it is possible to be fairly sure that these included all but one ('Liebst du um Schönheit' [see AMM, p. 60]) of the five independent Rückert settings, and three of the *Kindertotenlieder* – almost certainly the first three in order of the

five later grouped under the title (see HLG, p. 709). The manuscript of these seven songs would appear to have been presented to Natalie Bauer-Lechner by Mahler (see DMW, p. 35). The title of the remaining *Wunderhorn* song is usually given in the form 'Der Tamboursg'sell' ('The Drummer-Boy').

12. Usually translated as *Songs on the Death of Children*. Mahler eventually set five of the 428 poems that were directly inspired by the deaths of two of Rückert's own children (see also previous note).

p. 174

13. 'Lime-branch' – a reference to the independent Rückert song whose text plays upon the words 'lind' ('soft', 'gentle') and 'Linde' ('lime' or 'linden'). Its full title is 'Ich atmet' einen linden Duft' ('I breathed a gentle scent').

14. 'Do not look at my songs' – another of the independent Rückert settings composed this summer. The poet begs not to be disturbed at his work until it is finished.

15. 'I have become lost to the world' – possibly the finest of the five independent Rückert settings that were to be grouped with the *Wunderhorn* songs 'Revelge' and 'Der Tamboursg'sell', after Mahler's death, under the title *Sieben Lieder aus letzter Zeit*.

16. Anton Rubinstein (1829–94), the famous Russian pianist and composer. Mahler had first heard him as a student, when Rubinstein had given a complete cycle of the Beethoven piano sonatas in Vienna. He was to meet him later in Leipzig and again in Hamburg.

The 1900–1902 season

p. 175

1. Bruno Walter (see p. 43 note 6) had been offered a conducting post at the Opera by Mahler in 1898, but had at that time felt that 'it was necessary to become firmly rooted within myself before exposing myself again to the powerful influence of Mahler' (BWT, p. 125). The offer had been repeated at the end of 1900, at which time Walter had decided to accept.

2. 27 September 1901.

3. It was Mahler's view that his own opponents were simply using Walter as a means of attacking him in a way that would not instantly mobilize his supporters. The campaign against him caused Walter considerable distress (see BWT, p. 172ff).

p. 176

4. See above, p. 29 note 1 and p. 33 note 10.

p. 177

5. Mahler omits to mention here that while only seven of the twenty-one musical numbers are based on Weber's sketches for the opera, most of the remaining numbers were derived from lesser known works of the composer. Only the entr'acte, between Acts I and II, and the finale (nos 20 and 21) are known to have been entirely composed by Mahler, using themes from Weber's sketches. (A useful checklist of the work's musical sources is provided in the notes, pp. 28–9, of the 1976 RCA recording of the work under Gary Bertini.)

6. The work had been published by C. F. Kahnt, Leipzig 1888 (see KBD, pp. 179–80).

p. 179

7. From what follows, we learn that this refers to 'hidden octaves' in a harmonic progression. According to the rules of conventional harmony, the parallel motion of two parts at the distance of an octave or a perfect fifth is forbidden.

p. 180

8. *The Trumpeter of Säckingen* (1884), a popular but rather commonplace opera by Viktor E. Nessler (1841–90). Its source was a well-known romantic narrative-poem by J. V. Scheffel. Mahler himself had been required to write incidental music for a series of tableaux based on it in 1884, while he was at Kassel.

9. See also above p. 101ff (and p. 101 note 6). The performance was on 5 November 1901.

10. Having been *Kapellmeister* at the National Theatre in Prague from 1813, Weber (1786–1826) had been appointed conductor at the Royal Opera in Dresden in 1817. It was there that he created both *Der Freischütz* and *Euryanthe*. *Oberon* was written for England, and first performed at Covent Garden in 1826, some eight weeks before the composer's death.

p. 181

11. *Zar und Zimmermann* (see p. 103 note 7).

12. *Wildschütz* (literally *Wild Shot*) was based on a comedy by Kotzebue and first performed in 1842.

13. 9 and 10 November 1901. [Note by J. Killian.]
14. The fire at the Ringtheater in Vienna, in which more than 400 people lost their lives, broke out during a performance of *The Tales of Hoffmann* (8 December 1881). [Note by J. Killian.]
15. Mahler had by this time met the young Alma Schindler, who was later to become his wife. Natalie Bauer-Lechner's chronicle, its days already numbered, can henceforth be supplemented with Frau Mahler's own later memoirs. (Here see AMM, pp. 5 and 15, for example; also the letters of 4 and 5 December, pp. 205–6).
16. *Die Legende von der heiligen Elisabeth* (*The Legend of St Elisabeth*), a concert-oratorio (1865) that was in fact staged in a number of places with considerable success. The performance referred to took place on 19 November 1901.
17. '*ein echt arisches Werk*': intervening history has given this statement by Mahler the Jew (although he had become a convert to Roman Catholicism in 1897) an unfortunate ring. It would be difficult to say quite what he meant by it.

p. 182

18. The original German edition has the date as 26 November, but this must have been the result of a mis-reading of the manuscript. The performance itself in fact took place on 25 November 1901 (see HLG, pp. 645 and 647).
19. Mahler had conducted the Second Symphony at the inaugural concert of the Hugo Wolf Verein on 20 October 1900.
20. According to de La Grange, a telegram informing Mahler that his mother's condition was 'very grave' had reached him prior to a *Lohengrin* performance on 9 October 1889. Frau Mahler had in fact died two days later, on 11 October (see HLG, p. 201).

p. 183

21. For a further and elaborate account of this first performance, the reader is referred to the report by William Ritter that is quoted by de La Grange (see HLG, p. 648ff).
22. Felix Weingartner (1863–1942), who was to be Mahler's successor at the Vienna Opera, was at this time conductor of the Kaim concerts in Munich (see above, p. 78 note 1). He had, on Mahler's request, allowed the latter to conduct the first performance of the Fourth there, prior to its being taken on tour by the Kaim

Orchestra (subsequently under Weingartner himself, of course). Weingartner was to state in his memoirs that he considered this particular work of Mahler's 'the best thing he has done' (FWB, p. 255). There was inevitably a measure of rivalry between the two men, however, and while Mahler succeeded in persuading Weingartner not to include a Brahms symphony in the same concert, his request that another vocal work should not precede it was not heeded. Before the Fourth, Weingartner conducted a performance of his own *Wallfahrt nach Kevlaar* (*Pilgrimage to Kevlaar*) for contralto soloist and orchestra (see HLG, p. 647 and p. 943 note 34). In true nineteenth-century style, the concert, which had opened with a Mozart symphony, concluded with a group of Lieder (Weingartner at the piano) and Beethoven's *Egmont* overture (see HLG, p. 944 note 39).

p. 184

23. Henriette Manckiewicz – a semi-invalid Viennese embroidery artist whom Mahler had come to know at the beginning of 1900. She was subsequently to become a friend of Natalie Bauer-Lechner, who appears to have copied out part of the *Mahleriana* for her benefit (see HLG, p. 565 and p. 931 note 9).

24. 28 November, under Weingartner (see above, p. 183 note 22). This was the second concert of the Kaim Orchestra's tour, which had started in Nuremburg on 26 November. As far as the reception of the Fourth Symphony was concerned, the whole tour was to be a complete failure.

25. The concert took place on 16 December at the Opera House where Strauss was conductor.

26. The Tonkünstler Orchestra. Mahler only conducted his own symphony; the rest of the programme was conducted by Strauss (see HLG, p. 659).

27. Thila Plaitchinger, a Berlin opera-singer. Mahler had initially hoped that the Czech soprano Emmy Destinn would sing in the work (see HLG, p. 658).

p. 185

28. The narrative of Natalie Bauer-Lechner's *Mahleriana* ceased in January 1902. This edited version, from which all revelations of a more personal nature were omitted (along with much else) inevitably fails to quote the actual final lines of the manuscript.

According to M. de La Grange, they run as follows: 'Mahler became engaged to Alma Schindler six weeks ago. If I were to discuss this event, I would find myself in the position of a doctor obliged to treat, unto life or death, the person he loved most in the world. May the outcome of this rest with the Supreme and Eternal Master!' (HLG, p. 699.)

Editor's Afterword to the German edition

p. 186
1. The original edition bore a note here referring readers who wished to know more about Natalie Bauer-Lechner to her *Fragmente: Gelerntes und Gelebtes* of 1907. (See editorial Foreword to the present volume.)

p. 187
2. It is very much to be hoped that the plans of the present owner of the manuscript (M. Henry-Louis de La Grange) to make the complete text available will in fact be realized at some future date (see Foreword).

Appendix I

Newly translated material from the extracts from Natalie Bauer-Lechner's journal published in Der Merker *(anonymously) in 1913 (III, 5, 1913 – pp. 184–8) and the* Musikblätter des Anbruch *(II, 7–8 April 1920 – pp. 306–9) in 1920. The following passages appear to have been omitted from the foregoing text when it was compiled and edited by J. Killian in 1923 (see Foreword, pp. 11–12). Except where specifically indicated, the material is taken from the* Der Merker *extracts.*

p. 29   *. . . the* Pintos *there* – it was the most fruitful period of my life [es war meine fruchtbarste Zeit].

       . . . in a full, broad stream rather in Schubertian fashion; . . .

       . . . is to amount to anything.

       Of course, God alone knows whether my movement will turn out to be as good as I believe it to be at the moment. While I was working on it, with everything coming straight from the heart, it showed every sign of turning into something altogether new and much improved – although I admittedly fell back again to being dissatisfied afterwards, and was stricken with agonies [und mich packt der Katzenjammer darüber] to think that I might still not have succeeded in the way that I had hoped.

p. 30   *. . . I have written into them,* in my own blood [mit meinem Herzblut], *everything that I have experienced . . .*

p. 34   *. . . my performances* – involving all the musicians under me (this is the difficult part); they detest me as a result – *in the minutest detail,* . . .

p. 35   *. . . And that in itself is enough.* Yet even if no one else had any use for what I do, I would still not be able to see my responsibilities in any other light; I would have to do it for myself – would want to carry out my duty as I saw it, to the full extent of my powers. I hope that it will always be the same, and I will never become careless and indifferent in the way that I see happening with most of my *Kapellmeister* colleagues, even the famous ones (including our K. [Rudolf Krzyzanowski?], who is otherwise such a splendid fellow).

p. 37 *... in the territory of someone else's mind!* As to the thoughts of a Voltaire (Frederick the Great's guest) that might thus have been put paid to, or the extent to which all humanity might have suffered as a result, the story remains silent.

p. 43 *... must succumb* – and *his death.*

p. 44 *. . . present life.* It is the day of the Last Judgement [des jüngsten Gerichts] . . .

p. 45 *... of a 'sustained melodic line'* [des 'Festhalten der melodischen Linie'], which he had sorely missed with N [ikisch?].

... Wagner was later to do (or as I still take pains to), *nor was he ...*

p. 46 *... the use of these clarinets.* Others are also happily introducing them, and boasting about it – naturally keeping quiet about the fact that they learned the technique from me.' [From the *Anbruch* extracts.]

p. 51 *The following complete anecdote also appears in the* Der Merker *extracts:*

March 1896

On the day of his Berlin concert, Mahler was on his way over the railway viaduct that crosses the Spree from the Schöneberg Bank when he encountered a man staggering along beneath a heavy bundle. This he was carrying on his shoulders, but had had to rest on the wall to keep himself from falling. Mahler thought that he must be drunk, as he was also talking aloud to himself; and as he approached he heard the words: 'God will go on helping'. They were muttered to himself, he saw, by an old man of horribly wasted countenance and wretched appearance. He looked to be on the verge of fainting from weakness, and could go no further – trying to keep himself and his burden upright against the wall of the viaduct. Mahler took the bundle from him, and supported him – learning from the poor man, as he began to regain his strength a little, that he had been ill in hospital for some months and had now been discharged as fit; but as he had neither shelter nor money he would have to go on the streets. For the hospital is unable to take care of convalescence for its discharged patients. He was now going with his few belongings in search of somewhere to stay, and of some employment (even when he could hardly feel physically capable of it) by which he might sustain the life that had been preserved for him.

Mahler, terribly shaken by the sight and the story of the unfortunate man (who presented the saddest contrast to the Sunday solemnities; to the bustle and throng of people), did for him and gave him what he could on the spur of the moment. He was deeply moved and altogether grief-stricken about it, however, and took it so much to heart that he arrived home in a state of complete distraction, lay down upon the sofa and began to weep bitterly – he whom I had never seen weep – and sought consolation like a child in my deepest sympathy.

p. 52   *Inserted before 'You can't imagine . . .'*
. . . I remarked upon the graphic clarity of his score, the compelling logic of the part-writing and its most precisely delineated expressive effects. To this Mahler said: 'That comes of the fact that I have written not a single note that is not absolutely true [wahr].' Concerning the piece itself, he then went on to say: . . .

. . . *and graceful as can be*, unaffected by any gravitational pull from the depths [ohne Schwere nach unten in der Tiefe], *like the flowers . . .*

p. 54   *Omitted introductory sentence:*
Mahler in very depressed mood over the limited success and continuing repercussions of his last Berlin concert. '*You'll see . . .*

. . . *contact with me.* Because even the First, in which I have presented myself to them, has none of those elements which would once have ensured comprehension. . . .

. . . *personal style*, different as it is from all others, *that there is . . .*

. . . *the earlier works.* In connection with this, I have not written a great deal, and nothing small-scale (with the exception of the few songs) – only a few, admittedly enormous, works at great intervals: my First and Second Symphonies, which at every turn avoid what people are accustomed to and are used to hearing. Even Beethoven started out with a

Mozartian style, and Wagner relied on Meyerbeer's operas; but I unfortunately search in vain for things which share a common ground with mine.

All communication between composer and listener depends upon a convention. The latter justifies this or that motive or musical symbol, or (as one might otherwise put it) supplies the expressive vehicle for this or that thought or particular mood [geistigen Inhalt]. Everyone relies heavily upon Wagner in this way at the moment; but Beethoven can also serve us, and, to a greater or lesser extent, each of the others has contributed his particular and now generally accepted way of expressing what he wants to say. *People have not yet accepted* . . .

p. 54   *In the* Der Merker *extracts, a short, self-contained passage follows at this point:*

After the play-through of a particularly feeble and empty work.

'When I see' said Mahler 'all that the poor devil had wanted to put into it, and also what it means to him, then I become really horribly depressed about such self-deception, and ask myself whether it is possible that the same thing might have happened to me, and that I have imagined myself to have expressed things in my compositions that are in fact empty and meaningless to others.'

p. 59   . . . *trembles and vibrates.* I hear it in my inner ear, but how to find the right notes for it?

. . . *rigid Nature* (as in Hölderlin's 'Rhein').

. . . *inorganic matter*, that is thrown over the conclusion of the introduction.

p. 68   *The* Anbruch *extracts include the following section at this point:*

Composition and orchestration
16 July

Today Mahler accompanied a performance of his songs. He praised the woman's singing, but found it not sufficiently simple [schlicht]: 'Unfortunately,' he said 'in all the feeling she put into it she wanted only to advertise herself and her own little ego.'

A musician who had been present told Mahler that he should orchestrate the *Gesänge*. 'A master of Mahler's standing' he thought 'could orchestrate one of them in two hours.'

Mahler's reply to the musician, who went about his own orchestration in a childishly pianistic fashion, was wilfully paradoxical: 'Composing is quicker than orchestrating –and in a such a change of medium the whole thing would in fact have to be reworked! It is never enough simply to orchestrate a piano accompaniment which hasn't been orchestrally conceived. In the same way, the translation of poetry from a foreign language only works where a free rendering, rather than a precise, word-for-word equivalent, is given.'

In connection with this, he went on: 'Composition requires the most strenuous self-criticism. No single attractive idea should be allowed to spoil the overall proportions, the general structure and development etc. Everything should have its integral place in an organic conception of the whole and be in due proportion to the rest.'

p. 96   ... *the last movement of his Second Symphony.* But he is also compulsively attentive to the rushing sound of a waterfall, to bells or the melodic creaking of a door.
[from the *Anbruch* extracts.]

p. 176   *Alternative version, possibly a précis of the foregoing paragraphs:*

Mahler told me how he came to bring out Weber's *Pintos* in Leipzig. 'Having been interested in it by Weber, the composer's grandson, we at first simply wanted to look through the work in the Leipzig archive. My imagination was so taken by the fragments, however, that I immersed myself more deeply in them and began to continue various unfinished passages in my mind, until I became resolved to tackle the completion seriously. I then devoted myself to becoming steeped in the spirit of Weber, in order to work the material out in a style conforming as faithfully and modestly as possible to Weber's own. But the deeper I became involved in it, the more bold did I become. *I let myself . . .*'

Appendix II

Letter from Natalie Bauer-Lechner to Ludwig Karpath, 16 November 1900. Transcription and translation (by permission of Mr Knud Martner, Copenhagen).

The letter has been included here as an example of Natalie Bauer-Lechner's writing (if admittedly done in some haste) which we can be sure has been edited by no hand other than her own. The subject-matter itself is important, however, in that it includes some highly interesting commentary on the third and fourth movements of the First Symphony – material that does not appear in the section of the foregoing text (see p. 157ff.) that would otherwise appear to derive almost directly from parts of this letter. The corrections and insertions in the original (see Plate 4) could well be taken as an indication that it was seen from the start as a rough draft of material that had been mentally ear-marked for the *Mahleriana*. This would explain the personal 'need' for the letter mentioned by the author in its final lines. The postscript, which was written at the head of the letter, might have been added when it was subsequently returned to Ludwig Karpath (music critic of the *Neues Wiener Tagblatt*). It should be recalled that the performance of the First Symphony in Vienna was to take place on 18 November.

WIEN, III. SALESIANERGASSE 23.   D. 16/XI 1900

Sehr geehrter Herr Karpath; nur ein paar Andeutungen über Mahler's I^{te}, die [ich] seinen Worten entnehme; da zu allem Ausführlicher'n leider mir ganz die Zeit gebricht, die [ich] unmenschl[ich], v[on] Früh bis Ab[end] gehetzt, in diesen Tagen bes[onders] verbringe! (Sonst hätte [ich] *gleich* zu einem ausgiebigern Plaudern darüber Ihre freundliche Einladung beim Schopf gepackt. –)

'Titan' hatte M. diese I^{te} ursprungl[ich] genannt; hat es aber, wie alle Titel & Überschriften von seinen Werken längst gestrichen, die ihm als Schein eines Programms (– das *er hasst* und als 'unkünstlerisch' & 'antimusikalisch' in der Musik völlig verdammt & *nie* solcherart geschaffen hat –) missdeut[et] & auf's Platteste, unverstehendste ausgelegt wurden. So brachten sie ihm auch diesen 'Titan' mit dem

236

Jean Paul'schen gleichnamigen Werk in Verbindung, an das er dabei
nicht dachte, sondern einfach bei *seinem* 'Titanen', einen heldenhaft
kraftvollen Menschen im Sinn hatte: sein Leben & Leiden, sein
Ringen & Unterliegen gegen das Geschick (: 'wozu die wahre &
höhere Auflösung & Erlösung erst die II^te bringt.')Die I^te ist noch
ganz vom Standpunkte des unbewehrten (– wehrlos allem Ansturm
preisgegeben –) unmittelbarst erlebenden und erleidenden *jungen*
Menschen aus geschrieben.

Im I^ten Satz reisst uns seine dionysische Jubelstimmung[,] die noch in
nichts gebrochene & getrübte, mit sich fort. (Wobei es übrigens
auch *gar nicht* nöthig ist an den Titan, den jungen Feuergeist, in dem
sich diese Welt so nachspiegelt, zu denken[,] betont M. immer.) – Mit
dem ersten Tone (: dem langausgehaltenen, durch alle Lagen und
Instrumente durchgehenden Flageolette-A), sind wir mitten in der
Natur: im Walde, wo das Sonnenlicht des sommerlichen Mittags
durch alle Zweige zittert und flimmert. – (: & hat man je eine solche
Naturstimmung, die Natur *selbst* sich tönend offenbaren, wie im
Laufe dieses Satzes[,] vernommen? – – die mit ihrem Leuchten &
zauberhaften Leben, aber auch mit der ganzen unheimlichen Mystik
uns anpackt.) 'Den Schluss dieses Satzes werden sie gewiss nicht
capieren', sagte mir Gustav, 'den abfallen wird, während ich ihn viel
wirksamer leicht hätte machen können: (mein Held) schlägt eine
Lache auf & läuft weg. Das Thema, wels. [welches] die *Pauke* zuletzt
hat, finden sie gewiss nicht heraus!' –

'Im II^ten Satz treibt sich der Jüngling schon lebenstüchtiger & kräftig-
männlicher in der Welt herum' (: aber auch dieses Scherzo & Trio ist –
wie *Alles* bei Mahler & wie er es durchaus *wünscht* – nur *rein musikalisch*
zu geniessen und [zu] erfassen.) Der wundervolle *Tanz-Rhythmus* des
Trios ([']von dem alle Musik ausgeht', dem Tanz näml[ich], wie G.
auch einmal sagte) sei Ihrer Aufmerksamkeit empfohlen. 'Da werden
sie Alle, wegen der 2 Anfang Tacte, bei denen mich das Gedächtnis
einen Augenblick im Stiche liess & und die an Bruckner's (?-Sym-
phonie) erinnern[,] als 'Dieb' & unoriginellen Menschen über mich
herfallen, passt auf', rief neu[lich] Gustav. –

Hieran schloss sich früher ein sentimental-schwärmerischer Satz[,] den
er scherzhaft auch die 'Jugend-Eselei' nannte & den M. leider entfernte.

Als III^ter folgt jetzt der Bruder-Martin-Satz (der, glaub' ich[,] zu
den geistvollsten[,] kühnsten Inventionen gehört, wie sie nur das
geborene Genie haben kann! Nat[ürlich] haben sie den G. am meisten

missverstanden & geschmäht.) G. sagte neul[ich] davon zu mir: [']Jetzt hat er (mein Held) schon ein Haar in der Suppe gefunden & und die Mahlzeit ist ihm verdorben!'

Äusserlich mögen Sie sich den Vorgang etwa hier so vorstellen: An unserm Helden zieht ein Leichenbegängnis vorbei & das ganze Elend, der ganze Jammer der Welt, mit ihren schneidenden Contrasten & der grässlichen Ironie[,] fasst ihn dabei an. Der Trauermarsch des Bruder Martin (auf's genialste dazu herbeigezogen gastaltet & umarbeitet – wodurch er erst zudem *wird* –) hat man sich von einer elenden Musikkapelle, wie sie bei solchen Leichen spielt, dumpf abgespielt zu denken. Dazwischen tönt die ganze Roheit[,] Lustigkeit & Banalität der Welt in den Klängen, irgend einer sich dreinmisch-enden, 'böhmischen-Musikanten-Musik' hin*ein*. Dabei die furchtbar schmerzliche Betrachtung & Klage unseres Helden. Es ist in seiner Ironie & schneidenden Schärfe das Erschutterndste, was man je vernommen hat, meiner Meinung nach! Bes[onders], wo wir nach dem wundervollen Zwischensatz den Zug nach dem Begräbnis an uns vorbei zurückkommen sehen & wo die Leichenmusik die übliche (einem hier durch Mark und Bein gehende) 'lustige Weise' anstimmt.

Mit einem entsetzlichen Aufschrei beginnt der letzte Satz, in dem wir nun unseren Heros, völlig preisgegeben, mit allem Leid dieser Welt im furchtbarsten Kampfe seh[e]n[.] Im[m]er wieder bekommt er eins (– & das sieghafte Motiv mit ihm –) auf den Kopf von dem Schicksal wenn er sich drüber zu erheben & seiner Herr zu werden scheint, & erst im Tode, nachdem er *sich selbst besiegt hat* (& der wundervolle Anklang an seine erste Jugend, mit den Themen des I[ten] Satzes wieder auftaucht) erringt er den Sieg (: herrlicher Siegeschoral!)[.]

So – dies die äusserlichsten Andeutungen, lieber Herr Karpath, die [ich] in wahnsinniger Hetz herschmiere. Heut[e] Ab[end][,] wo wir uns bei Mahler's sehen, werde [ich] Ihnen noch manches *Wichtigste*, hoff' ich, sagen können. *Den Brief* erbitte [ich] aber *vielmals* mir *dann* zurückzubringen, da ich ihn *für mich selbst* noch nöthig habe (& das *weiss ich*[,] werden Sie mir erfüllen, nicht wahr?) erst dann ihn Ihnen, sollten Sie ihn wollen, zurückgeben.

V[on] Herzen

I[hre] N[atalie] B[auer]

(P.S. Die Bitte v[on] diesen Zeilen & ihrem Inhalt *keinerlei* Gebrauch zu machen, sagte [ich] Ihnen in Eile neulich schon!)

Dear Herr Karpath; just a few points about Mahler's First, based on his own words; I simply haven't the time for anything more detailed, being *in*humanly occupied from morn till night these days! (Otherwise I would immediately have seized upon your kind invitation to come and talk about it in more depth with you.)

Mahler originally called this First 'Titan'; but has long abandoned that, as he has all titles and superscriptions to his works. Such things he felt were misunderstood and altogether uncomprehendingly interpreted in the tritest way as indications of a programme (something *he hates* and thoroughly condemns in music as 'inartistic' and 'anti-musical', never having composed in such a fashion). In this way, they took him to be associating this 'Titan' with Jean Paul's work of the same name, which he was not thinking of – rather having in mind simply his own particular Titan, a mighty and heroic being; his life and sufferings, his wrestling and defeat at the hands of Fate ('the real, higher release and redemption from which only the Second effects.') The First is still altogether written from the standpoint of the unarmed (open, defenceless to all attack), most directly experiencing and suffering *young* man.

In the first movement we are swept along by his mood of dionysian affirmation, which so far nothing has broken or troubled (in which – Mahler always emphasizes – it is in no way necessary to be thinking of the Titan himself, the fiery young spirit in whom the world is thus mirrored). With the first note (the long sustained harmonic A in all registers and instruments), we are in the midst of Nature: in the forest, where the summer midday sunshine shivers and glitters between all the branches – (and has one ever known such an experience of Nature; Nature revealing her very self in sound, as we hear in the course of this movement? – which strikes us with its radiance and enchanting life, as also the altogether eerie sense of the mystery of things). 'They certainly won't grasp the ending of this movement,' Gustav said to me 'which will fall flat, although I could have made it much more straightforward in its effect: (my hero) bursts out laughing and runs away. The theme that the timpani have at the end will surely not be spotted!'

In the second movement the young fellow is already getting on in the world more ably, having become stronger and more 'manly' (but this Scherzo and Trio – as *everything* with Mahler, and as he has always *wanted* it – is only to be taken and enjoyed as *pure music*). The wonderful *dance-rhythm* of the Trio ('from which all music proceeds', the Dance that is, as G. also once put it) has to be commended to your attention. 'On account of the two opening bars, in which my memory let me down for a moment – they recall Bruckner's (? Symphony) – they will all go for me as a "thief" and a man of no originality, it's certain' Gustav recently exclaimed.

At this point there once followed a sentimentally indulgent movement, which he also jokingly called the 'Youthful Folly', and which he was unfortunately to omit.

The 'Bruder Martin' movement now comes as the third (and is, I believe, one of the cleverest and most daring inventions, of the sort that only come to the born genius! Of course, they have misunderstood and abused G. most of all on account of it). Telling me about it recently, G. said: 'He (my hero) has already found a hair in his soup, and the meal is ruined for him!'

You might also picture what happens in it in some such way as this: Our hero watches a funeral procession draw past him, and all the misery, the sum of the world's sorrow, possesses him with its sharp contrasts and hideous irony. The 'Bruder Martin' funeral march (extended and recast in the most brilliant way here – in the course of which, moreover, it *comes into being* for the first time) one has to think of as being mechanically sight-read by a miserable group of musicians of the sort that plays at such funerals. This is periodically interrupted by all the crudity, frivolity and banality in the world, with the sounds of some sort of motley 'bohemian players' band. And thereby the terrible and painful thoughts, the lamentation of our hero. With its irony and cutting edge it is, to my way of thinking, the most staggering thing one has ever heard! Particularly the point, following the wonderful middle section, where we see the procession returning past us after the burial, and where the funeral-players intone the customary 'merry tune' (here it cuts straight through one).

A horrifying scream opens the final movement, in which we now see our hero altogether abandoned, with all the sorrows of this world, to the most terrible of battles. Again and again he gets knocked on the head (and the triumph-motive with him) by Fate whenever he appears to pull himself out of it and become its master. Only in death, after he *has overcome himself* (and the wonderful reminiscence of his earliest youth has brought back with it the themes of the first movement) does he achieve the victory (– magnificent victory-chorale!).

So – here are the most basic points, dear Herr Karpath, scribbled down in a mad rush. This evening, when we see each other at Mahler's, I hope I shall be able to tell you much more of what is *most important*. However, I *sincerely* beg you to bring the letter back to me then, as I still have need of it for *my own purposes* (I *know* you will do that for me, won't you?). Then I will give it back to you, should you want it.

Sincerely,

Yours N.B.

(P.S. In haste, I once again ask you not to make any use of these lines and their contents!)

Index

Material in the Notes – to be found between pages 190 and 231 – is indexed according to the original page and note-number to which the material refers; e.g. *166n.26*, or, in cases where more than one note to a page is referred to, *42nn.2&5*.

Adler, Guido, 109, *109nn.17&18*, *165n.24*, 166
Anti-Semitism: in Schwerin, 51
    in Vienna, 103, 121, 122, 125, 137–8
Arion, legend of, 105, *105n.9*
Arnim, Achim von, see *Knaben Wunderhorn, Des*
Attersee, Upper Austria (lake), 15, *55n.2*, 66, *74n.3*
Attersee (village), 15, 66, *66n.29*
Aussee, see *Bad Aussee*

Bach, Johann Sebastian, 116, 165–6
    165nn.24&25, 169–70
    Cantata No.48 (*Ich elender Mensch*), 165, *165n.25*
    chorales, 169
    St Matthew Passion, 123
    Third Motet (BWV 227), 169–70, *169n.4*
Bad Aussee (Styria), 129, *129n.1*, 132, 135
Bad Ischl (Upper Austria), 65, *65n.27*, *129n.1*
Bauer-Lechner, Natalie, 9–11, 12–13, and *passim*
    Erinnerungen an Gustav Mahler, 9
    Fragmente, 9, 12, *186n.1*
    Mahleriana, 9, 10, 12, *185n.28*, *187n.2*, 226, 231
Batka, Dr Richard, 141, *141n.5*
Bayreuth (the Wagner Festspielhaus),

67n.33, *80n.2*, 104, *108n.16*, *110n.9*, 120
Beethoven, Ludwig van, 29–30, 38, 45, *45n.9*, 50, 66, 78–9, 84, 116, 119, *119n.7*, 132, 136–7, 138, 147, 149, 161, 172, 179, 181, 228–9
    Fidelio, 111, 181
    Coriolan overture, 120–1, 161
    The Consecration of the House overture, 142–3
    Piano Concerto No.5, 174
    piano sonatas, 174
    String Quartet in C sharp minor, op.131, 119
    String Quartet in F minor, op.95, *119n.7*, 122–3
    symphonies, general, 139–41;
    Symphony No.1, 161, 179;
    Symphony No.2, 137; Symphony No.3 ('Eroica'), 111–12, 120; Symphony No.4, 161;
    Symphony No.5, 78, 139–40, *139n.4*; Symphony No.6 ('Pastoral'), 44–5, 113–14, 136, 143, 179; Symphony No.7, 124–5; Symphony No.8, 73–4;
    Symphony No.9, 30, 63–4, *64n.23*, 70
Beethoven Prize (Vienna), 116, *116n.30*
Behn, Dr Hermann, 43, *43n.7*, 55, 77
Berchtesgaden, 67, 71, *71n.40*
Berkhan, Wilhelm, 76–7, *76nn.9&10*

Berlin, *51n.7, 166n.26*, 227–8
 performances of **M.**'s works in,
 34n.11, 42–3, *42nn.2&5, 43n.7*,
 49–51, 54, 127, *157n.3*, 184–5,
 184nn.25–7, 228
Berlioz, Hector, 61, 78, *78n.1*, 184
Billroth, Theodor, 57, *57n.9*
Bizet, Georges: *Carmen*, 75, *75n.6*,
 144, *144n.13*
Blaukopf, Kurt, *155n.16*, 189
Bocklet, Heinrich and Karl Maria
 von, 141, *141n.6*
Brahms, Johannes, 37, *37n.17, 57n.9*,
 65n.27, 116, *120n.10*, 141, 142–3,
 146n.3, 153, *183n.22*
 Symphony No.3, 142–3
Brentano, Clemens, see *Knaben
 Wunderhorn, Des*
Bruckner, Anton, 37, *37n.18*, 47–8,
 47n.2, 48n.3, 146n.3, 158, *158n.7*
 Symphony No.3, *47n.2, 158n.7*
'Bruder Martin', 51, *51n.5*, 158, 235;
 see also Mahler, Gustav, works:
 Symphony No.1, movement 3
Brüll, Ignaz, 74, *74n.3*
Budapest, 10, 24, *80n.3*, 132–3
 first performance of Symphony
 No.1 in, *34n.11*, 42, *116n.30*, 42,
 116n.30, 157n.3, 160–1
 M.'s life in, 27–8, *28n.1*, 83, 132–3,
 182
 Royal Opera, 10, 24, 27–8, *115n.28*
Bülow, Hans von, 69, *69n.37*, 92,
 114, *114n.26*
Bülow, Marie von, 114, *114n.26*
Busoni, Ferrucio Benvenuto, *165n.24*

Cassel (Kassel), **M.** as conductor in,
 35, *35n.14, 180n.8*
Cervantes Saavedra, Miguel de:
 Don Quixote, 85
Claque, the, 106–7, *107n.12*, 108–9
Columbus's Egg, 40, *40 n.3*

Denza, Luigi, *136n.2*
Der Merker (periodical), 12, 226
Destinn, Emmy, *184n.27*
Dippel, Andreas, 110, *110 n.23*
Dresden, *44n.8, 58n.12, 80n.2, 180n.10*
Dvořàk, Antonin: *Die Waldtaube*,
 142

Eckermann, J.P., 19
Edda the Elder, 149

Frankfurt, *139n.3*, 176, 184
Franz Joseph, Emperor, 107
Frederick the Great, 36, *36n.16*, 227
Fuchs, Robert, *116n.30*

Goethe, Johann Wolfgang von, 19,
 30 n.2, 73, *75n.7*
 Faust, 62, *62n.20*
 The Metamorphosis of Plants, *75n.7*
 Wilhelm Meister, 24
Goldmark, Karl, 74, *74n.4*, 116
Gombrich, Professor E. H., 10
Gombrich-Hock, Professor Leonie,
 10
Grädener, Hermann, 57, *57n.8*
Guilder (*Gulden*), *100 n.4*
Gutheil-Schoder, Marie, 144, *144n.13*

Hamburg, **M.**'s life in, 43, *43nn.6&7*,
 44, 47, 55, *64n.23, 67n.34*, 69–70,
 69n.37, 73–4, 76–7, *76n.10*,
 153n.11, 174n.16
 M.'s Symphony No.1 performed
 in, *34n.11, 42n.5, 157n.3*
Hamburg Stadttheater, 34–5,
 34nn.12&13, 35n.14, 70, *70n.38*,
 73, 74, *74n.5, 133n.12, 166n.27*
Hanslick, Dr Eduard, *109n.17*, 116,
 120, *120 n.10*, 122
Harris, Sir Augustus, *34n.13*
Hartmann, Emil, *74n.3*
Haydn, Joseph, 66, 116, 147, 179

Hellmesberger, Joseph (father and son), 23, *23n.2*

Herzfeld, Viktor von, 116, *116n.30*

Hilgermann, Laura, 134, *134n.17*

Hirschfeld, Dr Robert, 143, *143n.11*

Hölderlin, Friedrich, 38, *59n.15*, 229

Iglau (Jihlava), *33n.7*, *57n.11*, *109n.17*

Jahn, Willhelm, *80nn.1&2*, 96, *96n.1*, *155n.16*

Jews, the, *see under* Mahler, Gustav, on Jews, *and* anti-Semitism

Joachim, Joseph, 10, *42n.3*

Kaim, Franz, *78n.1*

Kaim Orchestra, 78–9, *78n.1*, *126n.18*, *183n.22*, *184n.24*

Kainz, Joseph, 134, *134n.16*

Kalischt (Kališt), *33n.7*, 69, *69n.35*

Karpath, Ludwig, 231, 234–6

Kaufmann, Walter, *41n.8*

Killian, J., 10–12, *67n.33*, *117nn.1&3*, *127n.20*, 226

Klagenfurt, 16, 134, *134n.14&15*, *154n.13*, 155

Knaben Wunderhorn, Des (eds Arnim and Brentano), *32nn.4–6*, *33n.8*, 40, *40n.4*, 55, *55n.3*, 58, 73, *152n.10*, 171, *171n.6*, 173

Koschat, Thomas, 172, *172n.9*

Kralik, Richard von, 23, *23n.4*

Kretzschmar, Dr A. F. Hermann, *165n.24*, 169, *169n.3*

Krzyzanowski Rudolf, 47, *47n.2*

Kurz, Selma, 134, *134n.18*

La Grange, Henry-Louis de, 10, 11; *see also* Notes, *passim*

Laibach (Ljubljana), **M.** as conductor in, 116, *116n.30*

Lehmann, Lilli, 110, *110 n.19*

Leipzig, 24, *29n.1*, *33n.10*, *51n.6*, 150, *150n.7*, 158–9, *158n.9*, *159n.13*,

16 6*n.26*, *169n.3*, *174n.16*, 176–7 230

Leoncavallo, Ruggiero: *I Pagliacci*, 181

La Bohème, 80 n.1

Liechtenstein, Prince Rudolf, 107, *107n.14*, 115–16, *132n.8*

Lipiner, Clementine, 71–2, 175

Lipiner, Siegfried, *23n.4*, 71–2, *71nn.40&41*, *110n.22*, *132n.8*, 164. 175

Liszt, Franz, 30, 37–8, 78, 184

Die Legende von der Heiligen Elizabeth, 181, *181n.16*

Löhr, Friedrich (Fritz), 24, *24n.8*, *71n.41*

London, **M.** conducts in, *34n.13*

Lortzing, Albert, *103n.7*, 138, 181

Wildschütz, 181, *181n.12*

Zar und Zimmermann, 103, *103n.7*, *104n.8*, 181

Löwe, Ferdinand, 126, *126n.18*

Löwe, Dr Karl G., 130, *130 n.2*

Lueger, Karl, 122, *122n.13*

Mahler, Emma (subsequently Rosé), 57, 96, *117n.1*

Mahler, Ernst, *164n.23*

Mahler, Gustav

absent-mindedness, 81–2, 124, 132–3

on Adagio movements, 67

appearance, 81–5

on art, 37, 38, 50, 58, 62, 68, 96–7, 128, 136, 147, 149, 154–5, 169, 171; irony in, 96

on ballet, 164–5

on birdsong, 168

on the clarinet in E flat, 46, 61, 227

childhood, recollections of, 33, 69, 85, 152–3, 155, 158, 168

on composition, 29, 30–1, 32, 33–4, 38–9, 40, 52, 53–4, 58, 60, 61, 65–6, 67, 71, 75, 76, 81, 130–2,

Mahler, Gustav—*continued*
135–6, 138, 139, 150, 154–6, 158–
60, 161–2, 170, 172–3, 178–9,
229, 230; the mystical in, 30–1,
53, 56, 61–2, 65–6, 136, 149–51; of
songs, 32, 33, 50, 58, 138, 169, 173
as conductor, 34–6, 49–50, 58, 63,
69–71, 73, 78–9, 83–4, 89–95,
98–104, 106, 107, 109, 111–14,
118, 120–1, 122–7, 136–8, 139–
41, 142–3, 175
on counterpoint, 147, 162, *162n.19*
on creativity, 30–2, 38–9, 53–4,
62–3, 65, 76, 139, 154–5, 168, 170
daily routine while composing, 64,
73, 145, 148–9
on dance, 158, 234–5
editing other composer's music, 45,
45n.9, *58n.14*, 63–4, *64n.23*,
101–2, 119, *119n.7*, 122–3, 140,
142, 180
on the *Flügelhorn*, 61, *61n.19*
on genius, 30, 38
on God, 44, 48, 53, 76, 166
on Jews, 76, 182
on metronome-markings, 46
on military-band music, 46, 61
on modernism, 68
on music, general, 62, 129, 130,
158; history of, and progress in,
29–30, 38, 45, 63–4, 66, 75, 147,
179
on opera, 27, 32, 34, 100, 103–4,
114–15, 116, 127, 138–9, 170–1;
great composers of, 180–1;
plans to compose, *116n.29*, 170–1,
171n.6
as opera producer, 93, 101–2,
104–6, 107–9, 110–11, 119–20,
157, 162–4, 181
on orchestration, 34, 45–6, 52, 61,
63–4, 68, 75, *75n.6*, 92, 119,
122–3, 140, 142, 159–60, 162,
177, 178–9, 229–30

on orchestral players, 35–6, 49, 73,
78, 89, 92, 93–4, 99–100, 109,
121, 124–6, 140, 177–9, 226
on performance and interpretation,
44–6, 58, 78–9, 90, 92–3, 93–5,
98, 102, 108–9, 111–14, 120–1,
123–5, 136, 137, 139–41, 143–4,
162–3, 165, 174, 175, 179, 229
on programme-music, 184
on polyphony, 116, 155–6, 162,
166, 169
sensitivity to noise, 36, *36n.15*,
56–7, 96, 135, 147–9, 168
on singers, 73, 93–4, 99, 105, 108–9
on the symphony, 30, 40, 66, 67,
146, 178
on titles of works, 30, 153, 157, 234
on vegetarianism, 53, *53n.2*
on women, 144
Mahler, Gustav, works
Bohemian music in, 35, 235
dionysian mood in, 59, *59n.16*, 157,
234
Drei Pintos, Die (opera after Weber),
29, *29n.1*, 53, 159, 170, 176–7,
177nn.5&6, 230
early and unfinished works, 23,
23n.3, *57nn.10&11*, *58n.12*, 116,
116n.29; *Die Argonauten*, 57,
57n.11; Piano Quartet, *57n.10*;
Piano Quintet movements,
23n.3; Piano Suite, 23, *23n.3*;
Rübezahl, 116, *116n.29*; symphonies, 23, *23n.3*, 58, *58n.11*;
Violin Sonata, 57, *57n.11*
Humoresques (*Humoresken*), 130,
130n.3, 151
humour in, 32–3, 40, 41, 60, 129,
158, 179, 234
Kindertotenlieder, 173, *173n.11&12*
Klagende Lied, Das, *53n.2*, 54, 116,
116n.30, 118, *118nn5&6*, 171
Lieder eines fahrenden Gesellen, 42,
42n.1, *49n.1*, 50

Mahler, Gustav, works—*continued*
Lieder und Gesänge, *33n.9*, 229;
'Hans und Grethe', 150–1,
150n.7; 'Um schlimme Kinder
artig zu machen', 33, *33n.10*
Lied von der Erde, Das, 20, *20n.2*
Rückert settings (other than *Kindertotenlieder*), 173–4, *173n.11&12*;
'Blicke mir nicht in die Lieder',
174, *174n.14*; 'Ich atmet einen
Linden Duft', 173–4, *173–4n.13*;
'Ich bin der Welt abhanden
gekommen', *173n.11*, 174,
174n.15; 'Liebst du um Schönheit', *173n.11*
Songs from *Des Knaben Wunderhorn*, general, *22n.11*, 130,
130n.3; 'Des Antonius von
Padua Fischpredigt', 32–3,
32n.4; 'Das Himmlische Leben'
(*see also* Symphony No.4, movement 4), 32, *32n.6*, *41n.7*,
59n.17, *64n.25*, 151–2, *152n.10*,
154n.15, 178; 'Das Irdische
Leben', 32, *32n.5*; 'Lob des
hohen Verstandes', 58; 'Revelge', 131, *131n.5*, *174n.15*;
'Rheinlegendchen', 33–4, *33n.8*;
'Der Schildwache Nachtlied',
34n.11, 171, *171n.6*; 'Der
Tambourg'sell', 173, *173n.11*,
174n.15; 'Verlorne Müh', *34n.11*
Symphony No.1, *34n.11*, *37n.19*,
40, 42, *42nn.4&5*, 49–50, *49n.1*,
53, 68, 96, 109, *116n.30*, 131,
157–61, *157n.2*, *158nn.5&9*, 171,
228, 231, 234–5; 'Blumine',
158, *158n.8*, 235; movement 1,
54, 157–8, *158n.6*, 159, 160, 234;
movement 2, *150n.7*, 158,
158n.7, 234; movement 3, 51,
51n.5, 158, 159–60, 235; movement 4, 31, *31n.3*, 159, 160, 235
Symphony No.2, 20, 30–1, 40,
42–4, *42nn.2&5*, *43n.7*, *44n.8*, 51,
53, 61, 62, 63, 67, *67n.30*, 69–71,
76–7, *77n.11*, 125–7, *126n.18*,
141, 151, 157, 182, *182n.19*,
183–4, 194–5, 228; movement 1,
43, *49n.1*, 53, *53n.3*, 127; movement 2, 12, 29, 43, *67n.30*, 126,
126n.19, 127, *127n.20*, 226;
movement 3 (Scherzo), 30, 31,
32, *32n.4*, 43–4, 126, 141–2,
141n.8, 152; movement 4
('Urlicht'), 44, 126; movement
5, 43, 44, 67, 126–7, *154n.14*
Symphony No.3, 20, 40–1, *41n.7*,
46, 52–3, *52n.1*, *55n.6*, 58–67,
59n.17, 109–10, 129–30, 151, 154;
Christ, in a discussion of, 62;
and 'Das Himmlische Leben',
41n.7, *59n.17*, *64n.25*, *154n.15*;
introduction and movement 1,
40–1, *40n.6*, *52n.1*, 55–6, *56n.6*,
59, *59n.16&17*, 60, 61–4, 66–7,
67nn.30&32, 73, *74n.2*, 75–6, 229;
movement 2, *51n.6*, 52–3, *52n.1*,
67n.30, 228; movement 3, 59,
61n.19, 129; movement 4, *41n.7*,
46, *59n.17*, 60, 64, *64n.24*, 129–
30; movement 5, *41n.7*, *59n.17*,
60, 154, *154n.15*; movement 6,
59, *59n.17*, 60, 64, *64n.25*, 67;
Pan, in relation to, 59, *59n.16*,
60, 63, 129; posthorn used in,
61n.19
Symphony No.4, *130n.3*, 131, 135,
145, 148, 150–5, 161–2, 177–9,
182–5, *183nn.21&22*, *184n.2*;
movement 1, 153–4, 162, 178,
182–3; movement 2, 152, 161–2,
162nn.16&17, 178, 179, 183;
movement 3, 152–3, *162n.17*,
178, 184; movement 4 (*see also*
Songs from *Des Knaben Wunderhorn*, 'Das Himmlische Leben'),
32n.6, *41n.7*, 151–2, *154n.15*, 178,

Mahler, Gustav, works—*continued*
183, 184; *see also* Ursula, St
Symphony No.5, *154n.14*, 172–3,
172n.8, 173n.10
Symphony No.8, 20
Mahler, Justine, *see* Rosé, Justine
Mahler, Leopoldine (subsequently
Quittner), 24, *24n.6*
Mahler, Otto, 24, *24n.7*, 37
Mahler's parents, 69, 85
mother, 69, 152–3, 182, *182n.20*;
father, 60, 85
Mahler-Werfel, Alma Maria (*née*
Schindler), 9, 11, 20, *20n.4*,
133n.12, 181n.15, 185n.28
Maiernigg, *see* Mayernigg
Mankiewicz, Henriette, 184, *184n.23*
Mann, Thomas, *169n.3*
Maria-Wörth (Carinthia), 16, 133,
133n.11
Marschalk, Max, 64, *64n.26*
Mascagni, Pietro: *Cavalleria Rusti-
cana*, 181
Mayernigg (Maiernigg) M.'s house at,
16, 133–4, *134n.15*, 145, 147–9,
148n.5, 151, 167–8, *168n.1*,
171–2, 173
Mendelssohn, Felix: *St Paul*, 124
Mengelberg, Willem, *58n.12*
Meyerbeer, Giacomo, 229
Mickiewicz, Adam, *71n.41*
Mildenburg, Anna von, 13, 106, 133,
133n.12, 157, 163–4
Mitchell, Donald, 10, 11, *31n.3*,
42n.1, 153n.12, 165n.25, 176n.6
Montenuovo, Prince Alfred, *107n.14*,
115n.27
Mora[n-Olden], Fanny, 110, *110n.20*
Moscow, M. conducts in, 78, *78n.2*
Mottl, Felix, 80, *80n.2*
Mozart, Wolfgang Amadeus, 30, 66,
92, 105, 111, 116, 120, 147, 179,
180–1, 229
Don Giovanni, 110–11, 139

Symphony No.40, 30, 120
The Magic Flute, 92, 94–5, *94n.13*,
104–6, *104n.8*
Munich, 78–9, 93, 182–4
Musikblätter des Anbruch (periodical),
12, 226

Nature, 59, 62, 71, 96–7, 113–14,
113n.29, 129, 136, *136n.1*, 149,
157, 174, 234
Nessler, Viktor E., *180n.8*
Der Trompeter von Säkkingen, 180,
180n.8
Newlin, Dika, 11
Nietzsche, Friedrich, 40, *59n.17*,
71n.41, 73, *74n.2, 75n.6*
Also sprach Zarathustria, *40n.5*
Die fröhliche Wissenschaft, *41n.8*
Nikisch, Arthur, 51, *51n.6, 166n.26*

Offenbach, Jaques: *The Tales of Hoff-
mann*, 181, *181n.14*
Opera, *see* Mahler, Gustav, on opera
Orpheus, legend of, 105, *105n.9*

Pan, *see* Mahler, Gustav: works,
Symphony No.3
Paris, M. conducts in, 145, *145n.1*
Paul, Jean, *see* Richter, 'Jean Paul'
Pfohl, Ferdinand, 9, *35n.14, 153n.11*
Pichler family, the, 23
Plaitchinger, Thila, *184n.27*
Plappart, Baron August von, 115,
115n.27, 117
Pollini, Bernhard, 70, *70n.38*
Prague, *34n.11*, 83, *145n.5, 180n.10*

Reichmann, Theodor, 111, *111n.24*
Richter, Hans, 92, *92n.7, 110n.21*, 116
Richter, 'Jean Paul', 37, *37n.19*, 157
Titan, 157, *157n.3*, 234
Ritter, William, *183n.21*
Roller, Alfred, 20, *20n.3, 155n.16*

Rosé, Arnold, *20n.1*, *99n.3*, *117n.1*,
132, *132n.8*, 135, 145, 155, 178
Rosé, Eduard, *117n.1*
Rosé, Justine (*née* Mahler), 20, *20n.1*,
40n.1, 42–3, 47, 57, 60, *67n.33*,
83, 96, *117n.1*, 132–3, *132n.8*,
133n.10, 135, 145, 167
Rott Hans, *47n.1*, 116, *116n.30*, 146,
146n.3
Rottenberg, Dr Ludwig, 139, *139n.3*
Rubinstein, Anton, 174, *174n.16*
Rückert, Friedrich, 173–4, *173n.12*

Saga Society, the, *23n.4*
Schanzer, Marie, *see* Bülow, Marie
von
Scheffel, J. V. von, *180n.8*
Schiller, Friedrich, *113n.25*
Schillings, Max von, *58n.12*
Schindler, Alma Maria, *see* Mahler-
Werfel, Alma Maria
'Schnützelputz-Häusel'(**M.**'s summer-
house at Steinbach), 55,
55nn.3&4, 56–7, *132n.6*, *148n.5*
Schoder, Marie, *see* Gutheil-Schoder,
Marie
Schönaich, Gustav, 119–20, *119n.8*
Schoenberg, Arnold, *144n.13*
Schopenhauer, Arthur: *Die Welt als
Wille und Vorstellung*, *36n.15*,
67n.15, *67n.34*, *136n.1*
Schraml, Richard, *57n.11*
Schubert, Franz, 147, 169, 226
Moments Musicaux, 128
Schuch, Ernst von, 80, *80n.2*
Schumann, Robert, 123, 169, 179
Frauen-Liebe und -Leben, 169
Symphony No.1, 122
Schwerin, 51
Sedlmaier, Sophie, 99, *99n.2*
Shakespeare, William, 30
Smetana, Bedřich, 101, 180
Dalibor, 101–2, *101n.6*, 180

Soldat-Röger String Quartet, the, 10,
42n.3, *143n.10*, 186
Spiegler, Nina (Nanna) and Albert,
71n.41, 110, *110n.22*
Stägemann, Max, 159, *159n.13*, 233
Stefan, Paul, 9, *21n.5*
Steinbach am Attersee, 15, 29, 40,
40n.1, 43, 52–3, 55–7, *55nn,1,2&4*,
58n.13, *66nn.28&29*, 75, *75n.8*,
96, *132n.6*, 148, *148n.5*, 154
Stoll, August, 163, *163n.20*
Strauss, Johann, 19, 128
Strauss, Richard, 37–8, *42n.5*, 136,
136n.2, *141n.5*, *144n.13*, 184–5,
184nn.24&26
Aus Italien, 136, *136n.2*
Sulzer, Joseph, *125n.16*, *143n.12*

Tchaikovsky, Piotr Ilyich, 166,
166n.27
Eugene Onegin, *166n.2*
Overture '1812', 122
The Queen of Spades, *166n.2*
Symphony No.6 ('Pathétique'),
166, *166nn.26&27*
Theuer (**M.**'s architect), 133–4, 147
Toblach (Dobbiaco), 96, *96n.2*

Ursula, St, 152, *152n.10*
Unterach (am Attersee), 15, 58,
58n.13, 65, *74n.3*

Verdi, Giuseppe, 138, 179
Aida, 175
Vienna, *passim*
the Burgtheater, 134
Lueger as Mayor of, 122, *122n.13*
M.'s circle in, *71n.41*, *109n.17*,
110n.22, *119n.8*, *166n.26*, *184n.23*
M.'s desire to return to, prior to
1897, 51, *74n.2*, 80
M.'s student life in, 81–2, *174n.16*
M.'s professional life in, 20, 80, 96,
98–101, 107, 121–2, *166n.27*

M.'s works published in, 109
performance of Symphony No.1
  in, *158n.5*, 231
the Prater, 93, *93n.9*
Ringtheater fire in, 181, *181n.14*
Vienna Conservatory, the, 9, 20, 23,
  23nn.1&2, 24, 43, *57n.8*, 81, 90,
  101, 163, *163n.20*
Vienna Court Opera (Hofoper), 20,
  20n.3, 51, 80, 92–4, *92n.7*, 98–
  109, *107nn.13&14*, 110–11, 114–
  16, *115n.27*, 117, *117n.3*, 119–20,
  120n.9, 127, *133n.12*, 134, 137–8,
  155n.16, 157, 162–4, *163n.20*,
  172n.9, 175, *175nn.1&3*, *183n.22*
  M.'s appointment as Director of,
    96, 103, *105n.11*
  M.'s début at, 89–92
  M.s initial appointment at, 80,
    80nn.1&2
Vienna Philharmonic Orchestra,
  20n.1, *23n.2*, 118–19, *118n.4*,
  120–3, 125–7, 136, 142–3, *145n.1*,
  161, 177–8, 185
Voltaire, 227

Wagner, Cosima, *114n.26*, 119
Wagner, Richard, 30, 38, 50, *53n.2*,
  66, 75, 91–2, 95, 98, 100, *107n.13*,
  111–12, 116, 119, *119n.7*, 123,
  130n.2, 138, 140, 141, 143, 147,
  164, 180–1, 229
  The Flying Dutchman, 92, 93, 107–8
  Lohengrin,   89–90, 91–2, 182,
    182n.20
  Die Meistersinger, 23, *75n.6*, *78n.1*,
    92, 116, 137–8, *163n.21*
  Parsifal, *108n.16*, *111n.24*

Der Ring des Nibelungen, 27, *34n.13*,
  61n.19, 98–101, 116, 117, 119–20,
  120n.9, 157; *Das Rheingold*, 98–9,
  117, *117n.2*; *Die Walküre*, 94,
  94n.13, 99–100; *Siegfried*, 100–1;
  Götterdämmerung,   101, *101n.5*,
  119–20, *120n.9*
Siegfried Idyll, *78n.2*
Tristan und Isolde, 116
Walter, Bruno, *43n.6*, *67n.34*, 75,
  75n.8, *155n.16*, *163n.20*, *166n.26*,
  175, *175nn.1&3*, 179, 185
Weber, Carl Maria F. E. von, 61,
  138, 153, 176–7, *177n.5*, 180–1,
  180n.10, 230
  Euryanthe, 180, *180n.10*
  Der Freischütz, 91–2, 92–3, *180n.10*
  Oberon, *153n.12*, 180, *180n.10*
  see also Mahler, Gustav, works:
    Drei Pintos, Die
Weber, Baron Karl von, and family,
  33, *33n.10*, 53, 159, 170–1,
  170n.5, 176, 230
Weingartner, (Paul) Felix, *165n.24*,
  183n.22, *184n.24*
Weyregg, 15, 55, *55n.2*, 69
Wilhelm I, Emperor, 159, *159n.10*
Wilt, Marie, 94, *94n.12*
Winkelmann, Hermann,   108–9,
  108n.16
Wlassack, Eduard, 105, *105n.11*, 117
Wolff, Hermann, 51, *51n.7*
Wondra, Hubert, 155, *155n.1*
Wörther See, 16, 133, *133nn.11&13*,
  134n.15, 145, 167–8, 171–2,
  172n.9

Zichy, Count Géza, 115–16, *115n.28*